W9-AKX-230

ALSO BY JOSEPH KASTNER

A Species of Eternity (1977)

This is a Borzoi Book
Published in New York
by Alfred A. Knopf

A World of Watchers

A World of Watchers

JOSEPH KASTNER

With illustrations from the work of
LOUIS AGASSIZ FUERTES

Alfred A. Knopf   New York
19 🐕 *86*

THIS IS A BORZOI BOOK
PUBLISHED BY ALFRED A. KNOPF, INC.

Copyright © 1986 by Joseph Kastner

All rights reserved under International and Pan-American Copyright Conventions. Published in the United States by Alfred A. Knopf, Inc., New York, and simultaneously in Canada by Random House of Canada Limited, Toronto. Distributed by Random House, Inc., New York.

Grateful acknowledgment is made to the following for permission to reprint previously published material:

The Commonwealth of Massachusetts, Department of Food and Agriculture: excerpts from *Birds of Massachusetts and Other New England States*, by Edward Howe Forbush. Copyright 1925, 1927, 1929 by The Commonwealth of Massachusetts. Copyright renewed 1952 and 1955 by The Commonwealth of Massachusetts. Permission granted by The Commonwealth of Massachusetts and Houghton Mifflin Company.

Harvard University Press: excerpts from *October Farm and Concord River* by William Brewster. Reprinted by permission.

Houghton Mifflin Company: excerpts from *A Field Guide to the Birds* by Roger Tory Peterson. Copyright 1934, 1939, 1947 by Roger Tory Peterson. Copyright renewed by Roger Tory Peterson. Reprinted by permission of Houghton Mifflin Company.

Library of Congress Cataloging-in-Publication Data

Kastner, Joseph.
A world of watchers.

Bibliography: p.
Includes index.
1. Bird watching—History. I. Title.
QL677.5.K37   1986   598'.07'234   86–45275
ISBN 0-394-52869-7

Manufactured in the United States of America
FIRST EDITION

for Joel
Jonathan
Karen
Marianna
Matthew
and Paul

Contents

Illustrations   *ix*
Prologue   *3*

1. The Forerunners: Indians and Early Bird Watchers   *6*
2. The Recruiter: Spencer Fullerton Baird
    and His Army Missionaries   *17*
3. The Model Watcher: William Brewster
    and the Nuttall Ornithological Club   *30*
4. The Great Sparrow War:
    A Nationwide Bird Watch   *39*
5. The Prodigious Troublemaker:
    Elliott Coues and His Key   *48*
6. Men of Standing: The Linnaean Society
    and Two Roosevelts   *60*
7. The Protectors: The Audubon Society
    and the Conservation Movement   *70*
8. The Good Fellows: The Delaware Valley Ornithological
    Club, Witmer Stone and Charles Pennock   *85*
9. The Collectors: The Cooper Ornithological Society, the
    Shooting Controversy and Joseph Grinnell   *97*
10. A Pastime for Chums: The Egg Hunters   *113*
11. A Friend of Bird and Birder: Edward Howe Forbush and
    the Birds of Massachusetts   *120*
12. The Independent Midwest: The Wilson Ornithological
    Society, Thomas Roberts and Althea Sherman   *132*

13. The Scientist and Her Singer:
     Margaret Nice and the Song Sparrow   *145*
14. The Imbuers: Elizabeth Dickens
     and the Woman Writers   *156*
15. The Great Connector: John Burroughs, the Poets, a
     White House Watcher and Henry Ford   *169*
16. Revolution in the Bronx:
     Chester Reed, Frank Chapman, Ludlow Griscom and
     the Bronx County Bird Club   *185*
17. The Guide: Roger Tory Peterson
     and His Historic Book   *195*
18. Listers and Savers: Bird Watchers by the Millions   *207*

     Epilogue: Henry Thoreau and Gilbert White   *217*

     Acknowledgments   *223*
     Bibliography   *225*
     Index   *231*

An All-purpose Artist: Louis Agassiz Fuertes, a portfolio, follows page 84

Illustrations

Black and White

The illustrations opening each chapter are from Louis Agassiz Fuertes' field sketches, printed courtesy of the American Museum of Natural History.

Eastern Screech-Owl   iii, 3, 217
Northern Mockingbird   6
Hooded Merganser   17
Ashy Storm-Petrel   30
Greater Roadrunner   39, 145
Scaled Quail   48
Northern Goshawk   60
Golden Eagle   70
Gambel's Quail   85
Magnificent Frigatebird   97
Great Blue Heron   113
Pomarine Jaeger   120
Cooper's Hawk   132
Fulvous Whistling-Duck   156
Virginia Rail   169
Gyrfalcon   185
Barred Owl   195
Anhinga   207

Color (following page 84)

Rufous Hummingbird (courtesy American Museum of
  Natural History)

Red-breasted Merganser (Courtesy American Museum of
  Natural History)

House Sparrow (Courtesy American Museum of Natural
  History)

Chestnut-sided Warbler (Courtesy Louis Agassiz Fuertes
  Papers, Department of Manuscripts and University
  Archives, Cornell University Libraries)

Slate-colored Junco (Courtesy Louis Agassiz Fuertes Papers,
  Department of Manuscripts and University Archives,
  Cornell University Libraries)

Pergerine Falcon with Green-winged Teal (Courtesy
  Academy of Natural Sciences of Philadelphia)

Pileated Woodpecker (Courtesy American Museum of
  Natural History)

Burrowing Owl (Courtesy Academy of Natural Sciences of
  Philadelphia)

Wild Turkey (Courtesy American Museum of Natural
  History)

Gyrfalcon (Courtesy Charles B. Ferguson)

A World of Watchers

Prologue

A bird is singing in my brain . . .
LOWELL

Again and again in the unorganized chronicles of American bird watching, there is a fleeting episode in which the watcher is overtaken by a kind of surprised enchantment that leaves a seal on his mind and perhaps his soul. Some bird watchers have set down images of this magic which haunt their dutiful notes on sightings and ranges and rump spots.

There is, for example, the New England doctor who saw and shot a swan and, sitting in his boat, heard what he had always thought was a myth—the song of a dying swan. "Most plaintive and musical," he called it, "like the soft running of the notes in an octave." And the U.S. Army captain, deep in hostile Indian country, who stepped from the mess hall for an after-dinner smoke and saw that the frontier orioles had paused in their hunting for insects to watch, fascinated, the smoke curling up from his cigar. And the scarlet tanager that "flamed through the green foliage like a vision . . . the fiery trail of a meteor" and determined the future of a pioneering ornithologist. Or the moments, years apart, when two boys, one of whom was to become the world's most famous industrialist and the other was to become the world's most famous living natu-

3

ralist, looked into a bird's eyes and never again could put birds out
of their heads.

For years, bird watching was mostly a one-man affair, though
birders throughout the country kept in touch with one another and
exchanged experiences through natural history societies. The age of
organized bird watching began a little over a century ago when a
group of young Brahmins in Boston formed an ornithological club.
As similar groups were formed in other cities, bird watching remained
largely a patrician pleasure. It was impelled into its present-day, far
less exclusive popularity half a century later by a group of young men
who did their birding in that most plebeian of habitats, the Bronx.

Along the way, the bird watchers, more than any other group in
the natural sciences, led America into its present conservationist state
of mind. They also expressed, more sharply than most groups, the
American ambivalence about using and misusing nature. Many of
America's earliest conservation regulations were concerned with
birds and it was the study, only a few decades ago, of the effects of
pesticides on bird eggs that dramatized for a careless world the ines-
capable inter-dependencies in the environment. The struggle over
how to deal with nature—whether to exercise man's biblically sanctioned right to use it however he wished or whether to preserve it for
nature's sake and his own—went on ceaselessly within the birding
community.

This book does not differentiate between two constantly used
terms: "bird watchers" and "birders." The distinction is often subjective. Birders, in one aspect, show a special interest in adding to the
number of species they have seen. Bird watchers share this interest
but may concern themselves more with habits of birds. Both categories meet a standard definition: "observing birds in their natural habitat . . . often with binoculars."

Nor is this book directly concerned with ornithological science,
except as it affects bird watching. It is about the people who watch
birds: what they saw and learned and felt; how they served themselves
and the creatures they studied; how they banded together in frater-
nal interest and fought each other in brotherly disagreement; how
they grew into by far the largest of all nature groups—and why they
watch. In no field science is it harder to draw a clean line between the amateur and the professional than it is in ornithology, and
everyone is included here: the enlightened amateur, the literate
semi-professional, the bird-walking professional.

There seems to be a subspecies of bird watchers taken up with classifying their pursuit: whether what they do is an art or a discipline, a game or a study, either, as one observer put it, is "the most scientific of sports or the most sporting of sciences." It is not the custom today to suggest that bird watchers watch birds out of love. The term "bird-lover" seems to embarrass some of them. But it is hard, on reading what they have felt, not to believe that watching birds generally involves a kind of love. Certainly not if we remember Mary Elizabeth Byrd, a dedicated bird watcher of Florida, who, to understand birds better, read straight through forty years of the proceedings of a foremost ornithological society (it took her two years) and, having reached an understanding, decided to give herself, quite literally, to the creatures she so cared about. She set down instructions in her will on what was to be done with her ashes. "My body I bequeath to the plankton of the sea," she said, "to feed the little fishes—in turn to feed the birds."

1

The Forerunners

The first known bird watchers in America were, of course, the Indians but there is no straightforward way to study their watching because none of them left written records. Still, there is plenty of evidence that the Indians were superb observers. A highly respected ornithologist named Henry Weatherbee Henshaw, who went out birding with some Apaches in 1872, confessed they "put me fairly to shame" at spotting birds—they felt white men were blind.

The best clues to how well Indians watched birds come from the names they gave them. The Malecite Indians of New Brunswick called the spotted sandpiper *nan a-mik-tcus,* or "rocks its rump," the name taken from *nama missuk,* or rocking chair. Leach's storm-petrel was *men-he bi-meh-sit,* or "skims the water," a domestic derivation from *men he bimet,* a skimmer squaws used to remove scum from boiling soup. The spruce grouse was *ses-e-ga-ti g-hes,* or "bird that picks at the buds of evergreens and weeps," a reference to both its eating habits and the reddened skin around its eyes.

Songs were echoed in many names. *Kwsi a-wis* is the pine siskin's note and *hwip-o-lis* mimicked the whip-poor-will. Migration time gave the ovenbird the name *sag-is-b' gnuk-es,* "bird that comes when buds

open." The nighthawk was *pik-teis-kwes,* an onomatopoeic name that
an ethnologist describes as an "indelicate though graphic allusion to
the booming noise heard at the end of its downward plunge."

Other Indians gave plain descriptive names. To the Pomos the
hairy woodpecker was *xale voko buko,* or "tree digger," and the cedar
waxwing was *xunu tsuts,* or "forehead sticking up," which is what the
waxwing's crest does. The Chippewas had a wry name for the house
wren: *o-du-na-mis-sug-ud-da-we-shi,* or "making big noise for its size."
To the eastern Cherokees the red-tailed hawk was *uwes' la' oski,* or
"lovesick," for its lonely whistle. Snipe and some plovers were *qule'
diskon' zhe,* or "bill dragging on the ground"; and the mockingbird,
admired for its intelligence, was *tsusko digis ski,* or "head eating," from
the Cherokees' belief that eating a brain makes any creature smart.
Warblers so puzzled the Cherokees that they left many species without names, apparently because they could not tell one from the other
—a touch of nature that makes them kin to modern bird watchers who,
looking the birds up in their field guides, find them lumped together
in the category "confusing" warblers.

Though they had great curiosity about nature and understood it
well, the Indians satisfied their curiosity more by being descriptive
than by being analytic and studying the relationships in nature. Since
there are no written records, scientists are somewhat awkward in
trying to place Indians as natural historians. One indigenous American who did leave a bird record was Garcilaso de la Vega, son of an
Inca princess and a Castilian nobleman. Writing about his homeland
years after he had gone to live in Spain, he described the condor with
its enormous wingspread, the multitudes of pelicans and a small
brown bird that the conquistadores insisted on calling a nightingale
because it resembled the European bird despite the fact that it sang
so badly that the Indians considered its song an ill omen.

For all their skill as observers, the Indians do not qualify, in modern terms, as birders. Watchers today may ascribe their interest in
birds to a myriad of different things, from loving freedom to liking
fresh air to seeing in birds some proof of a Creator's universal plan.
But what establishes a modern birder as serious is the life list, a
written record of all the birds he or she has ever seen. This is the
birder's common denominator, the be-all—and, sometimes, the end-
all—of birding. The Indians, so far as anyone seems to know, did not
keep lists. The white man, as soon as he came to America, did.

Thomas Hariot, in his *A Briefe and True Report of the New Found Land
of Virginia,* in 1591, said he had seen "four score and six" kinds of

birds but specified only a few of them. Most, including a stately sand-hill crane and a delicately detailed flamingo, can be identified through drawings made for the report by John White, the first known bird artist of the Western world, who was briefly governor of Virginia and grandfather of Virginia Dare, the first English child born in America.

Captain John Smith, busy setting up the colony at Jamestown, still found time to make the first detailed list for the colonies: the "eagle . . . the greatest devourer, hawkes of diverse sorts, partridges, wild turkies, woosels or blackbirds with red shoulders" along with "some other strange kinds unknown by name." Like all birders, he excused a short list, complaining of Virginia's birds that in summer "very few are seen."

The French explorers also took time out from colonizing to describe odd American birds. Champlain wrote of one with an "acquiline" beak—the black skimmer—and took home to his king a couple of red-winged songbirds, probably cardinals. Armand Louis de Lahontan, in his list of some fifty birds, remarked on the "comical stupidity" of the grouse, whose courtship drumming ritual made them easy targets for hunters. Nicolas Denys, while governor of Acadia (Nova Scotia), wrote a *Description and Natural History of the Coasts of North America,* which was concerned chiefly with ways to exploit the New World's resources. Pausing in his chase after profits, he paid attention to the local birds. The beauty of the hummingbird, whose throat "when it is seen in a certain light emits a fire brighter than the ruby," attracted him. But generally he made more mundane comments. The brant was good to eat when "roasted or boiled but not salted," while young herons are better than old—they are always fat, the old are always thin. There is a touching memorial to Denys in the dialect of local Malecite Indians, whose name for the veery interprets the bird's lovely song as *Ta-ne li-ain Ni-ko-la Den'-i, Den'-i,* or "Where are you going, Nicolas Denys?"

William Wood, after spending a few years in Massachusetts, published *New England's Prospect* in 1634, setting his list to rhyme:

> *The harmonious Thrush, Swift Pigeon, Turtle-dove*
> *Who to her mate doth ever constant prove:*
> *The Turky-Pheasant, Heathcocke, Partridge rare,*
> *The carrion-tearing Crow, and hurtful Stare [blackbird]*
> *The long-lived Raven, th' ominous Screech Owle,*
> *Who tells as old wives say, disasters foule . . .*

Wood had a sharp birding eye and a better ear than his rhymes indicate, adding nice touches such as "bellowing bitterne" and "tatling Oldwives," as he called the garrulous oldsquaw ducks.

The best birder in the colonies, in the judgment of Elsa Guerdon Allen, the authority on early American ornithologists, was John Clayton, a clergyman who spent several years in Virginia and in 1688 described forty-five birds, ten more than Wood had rhymed. He was the first to mention the mockingbird, though he noted two varieties, a gray and a red, the latter probably the brown thrasher, a mimicking cousin to the mocker. His list included a night raven, which was probably the whip-poor-will, and a "didaper," a felicitous name for the grebe.

Other early names had their own charm. John Lawson, in his 1709 *A New Voyage to Carolina,* listed black flusterers, swaddle-bills and tutcock—gulls, scaup and snipe. His catalog of fifty-six land birds and fifty-three water fowl was impressively long but rudimentary: "Woodpeckers, five sorts; blackbirds, two sorts. . . ." As many settlers did, he gave English names to American birds—bullfinch for purple finch, nightingale for mockingbird—a habit which has made a mess of American popular nomenclature, confusing the American robin, for example, with its distant English kin, robin redbreast. But one statement should endear Lawson to American birders. "Birds in America," he said flatly, are "more beautiful than in Europe."

Mark Catesby spent several years in the colonies between 1712 and 1726 gathering specimens for English naturalists and drawing them with considerable skill and an innocent beauty. In his *Natural History of Carolina, Florida and the Bahama Islands,* he recorded a quarter of the birds that live in the eastern United States, an achievement that gives him a claim to be called—along with several other naturalists— the "Father of American Ornithology."

One of the better lists was compiled during the Revolution by an English soldier, Sir Charles Blagden, a forerunner of the American military men who, decades later, contributed significantly to ornithology. A man of wit and good connections, Sir Charles was a friend of the great explorer Joseph Banks; of the famous English chemist Henry Cavendish (who left him sixty thousand pounds in his will); of the famous French chemist Claude Berthollet (in whose house he died); and of Samuel Johnson, who found him "a delightful fellow." Filling in the dull days aboard a British warship by counting and collecting American birds, he noted that robins were so tame that it was easy to shoot them, that southerly winds brought "prodigious

flocks" of brant, that the once-tame upland plover had already grown
shy and wary because of over-shooting, that the Indian name for the
green heron was "fly up the creek." On coastal patrol from the Caroli-
nas to Rhode Island, Blagden studied seventy-nine birds, and while
anchored at Newport he made a sighting that would puff up any
birder: of a black skimmer, a bird that was not recorded again in
Rhode Island for 150 years.

All these observations were made not merely to count the kinds
of birds but to enlarge knowledge and to organize it, which was a
major task of scholars and scientists in the age of the Enlightenment.
As explorers and settlers sent in descriptions and specimens of New
World marvels that the Old World had not known about, the classifiers and the namers tried to make some order of them. The earlier
American collectors and observers automatically sent their findings
and samples to Europe for scientific processing. Towards the end of
the eighteenth century, a pair of postrevolutionary Philadelphians set
out to do this at home by dealing with the characteristics and group-
ings of America's birds. Dr. Benjamin Smith Barton, physician and
teacher, made an orderly catalog of some two hundred birds and put
into the vocabulary terms birders still use today—"resident species,"
"accidentals," "visitants." His more important contribution was for-
warding the work of William Bartram, son of John Bartram, the finest
field botanist in the colonies. Poet, artist, traveler and guide to a
whole generation of American naturalists, William Bartram put together *Catalogue of Birds of North America.* It not only listed 215 species
but also noted migration dates, nesting habits and songs, much in the
manner of modern life histories, and reflected Bartram's interest in
studying live birds in the field rather than, as was general European
custom, of dead specimens in the study.

What was, in turn, particularly important about Bartram was his
influence on Scottish poet and schoolteacher Alexander Wilson, who,
with Bartram's tutoring and encouragement, wrote and painted the
first true American ornithology. Wilson's life-long involvement with
American birds began the day he landed in America in 1794 and shot
the first bird he came upon—a red-headed woodpecker, the most
beautiful bird he had ever seen, he said, immediately regretting that
he had killed it. Teaching himself, with Bartram's help, to know
American birds and to draw and paint them, he created in his *American
Ornithology* a masterwork of art and natural science which for decades
was the basis for all bird study in America.

Already in the young republic there were bird watchers everywhere, making notes and lists, eager to share their findings with other watchers and proud to contribute to Wilson's books. They worked so assiduously that, he remarked, "scarcely a wren or a tit could reach the Canadian border before I had received intelligence of it." Mordecai Churchman of Easton, Pennsylvania, who was busy enough as cashier of the bank and undertaker for several towns, still had time to write Wilson about the habits of the local chimney swifts which raised their broods in the chimney of the courthouse and made a local judge's mansion their evening rendezvous. Watching from his living quarters above the bank, Churchman was not able to tell Wilson about the swallows' fall migration because, he wrote, "I was not so fortunate as to be present at the general assembly when they concluded to take their departure."

Bishop James Madison, first president of William and Mary College, gave Wilson his own observations on rails and buntings and supplemented them with reports on seabirds that he had extracted from voyagers from Europe who came by to visit him. Useful information about rails had been given him "by Mr. Skipworth, our consul in Europe," who reported that several "came on board" many miles out at sea. The notorious General James Wilkinson, who once plotted to set up his own Louisiana empire, shared his knowledge of game birds with Wilson, while John L. Gardiner, the princely proprietor of Gardiner's Island off Long Island, informed him on the behavior of eagles, and a "young lady" in Middletown, Connecticut, sent Wilson drawings and notes on the bay-breasted warbler. An eclectic scientist of New York, Samuel Latham Mitchill, wrote at length on the already endangered heath hen, "Mr. Coffer of Fairfax County, Virginia" provided interesting details on the diets of hummingbirds, and another Virginian, President Thomas Jefferson, sent Wilson some misleading data on the wood thrush. The president, who commented on seventy-seven birds in his *Notes on Virginia,* was also responsible for one of the finest bird lists ever compiled by an American. It was brought back at the president's explicit instructions from the Louisiana Territory expedition by Meriwether Lewis, an extraordinary naturalist who described scores of birds new to American natural history and gave Wilson access to his findings and to his specimens.

Wilson's *Ornithology* was the first bird guide Americans had but it was not of much use in the field. It came in nine large volumes and some five hundred sets in all were printed. It was the standard reference work for birders for decades until John James Audubon came along to eclipse Wilson as an artist if not as a reliable watcher.

Son of a French sea captain, born in Santo Domingo in 1785 and brought up in France, Audubon emigrated to America in 1803 to take up a career as a businessman. He was a prospering merchant in Henderson, Kentucky, until, in 1819, some unfortunate ventures forced him into bankruptcy and—fortunately for American art and ornithology—into doing for a living what he had always done for his pleasure: study and paint America's birds. Unable to find support in the United States he went to England, where he found patrons to subscribe to his masterpiece, *The Birds of America.* Like Wilson's *Ornithology,* on which Audubon drew for some of his information (and for a few of his drawings), *Birds of America* was too big and expensive to be of any use as a birder's field guide. In the 1840s, a small edition of *Birds* was published and this, along with his *Ornithological Biography,* became the work that generations of birders turned to.

Meanwhile, the nearest thing to a modern bird guide had been written by Thomas Nuttall, a Yorkshireman who had come to America and made himself the finest and farthest traveled field naturalist of his day. His *Manual of the Ornithology of the United States and Canada,* published in the early 1830s, was small, inexpensive, filled with useful information and clear woodcut drawings, and had a success even the best selling of today's field guides might envy, going into dozens of editions right up into the early 1900s.

Towards the middle of the century, bird watchers began to profit from the publication of local ornithologies. The earliest of these was *A Report on the Ornithology of Massachusetts,* prepared by William B. O. Peabody in 1839. A few years later Jacob Post Giraud published his *Birds of Long Island.* A businessman, Giraud came briskly to his point. Most natural history books, he pointed out, are too expensive. His book, which cost two dollars, would be within the reach of gunners, whom he apparently considered his main audience. With it, he said, they could "become more thoroughly acquainted with birds frequenting Long Island," where 286 of roughly 500 known species of American birds could be seen.

Giraud's text was concise and helpful and his watching instructions were strict. Birds change with the seasons, he said, therefore pay attention "to the bills, tarsi and feet." Keep an eye on plumage, habits, nests and eggs. "The place to study ornithology is in the open air," he declared, "from nature, the best of all preceptors. The poetry of ornithology is entirely lost on closet ornithologists" (those who stick to their laboratories). Making what was then a novel suggestion, he proposed that bird distribution be studied regionally, by state or by county. "Pursuing this plan," he wrote, bird watchers "would be able to obtain such species of birds as visit their section and also have an opportunity of studying their habits which affords greater pleasure than labeling a dried skin received from a distance." In this way, he said, "many interesting facts would be acquired relative to the migrations and habits of many species. It is highly probable," he added, putting out bait for ambitious birders, "that new species would be discovered even in those sections supposed to be thoroughly explored."

A man who, according to a biographer, was "reliable, firm in his friendships and very decided in his opinions" (as a young farmer in New Jersey, he grew two corn crops in one season just to prove it could be done), Giraud prospered by supplying provisions to ships in New York harbor and could afford to take time out for his birding. When he was in his late forties, he gave up his business, his Long Island home and his habit of fraternizing with other naturalists, and became a recluse in Poughkeepsie, New York. From time to time, he came out to give lectures on birds to the students at Vassar and he left the college his collection of bird skins, perhaps the finest of its day. He also left a classic birding admonition. "Those who pass through life without stopping to admire the beauty, organization, melody or habits of birds," he said sternly, "rob themselves of a very great share of the pleasures of existence."

Thomas Brewer, like Giraud, was a part-time but wholehearted birder. A Boston physician, he gave up medicine to become editorial writer for the *Boston Atlas,* the most influential Whig paper of the day, and then went into book publishing. No matter how he made his living, he always watched and studied birds, becoming the country's leading authority on oology (study of birds' eggs and nests). An indefatigable contributor to Audubon, who referred to him repeatedly as "the accomplished ornithologist, Dr. Brewer," he sent Audubon "a very interesting item . . . the surprising ingenuity" by which the yellow poll warbler (yellow warbler) outwits the cowbird, which always lays its eggs in other birds' nests. When it does this to a yellow poll, Brewer wrote, the warbler simply builds a second story over the eggs and lays another clutch there, thus never incubating the intruder's egg. In one instance, he went on, after a cowbird's egg "had been thus concealed, a second was laid, which was similarly treated thus giving rise to a three-storied nest."

"As mark of estimation in which I hold him," Audubon named a new "bimaculated" duck after Dr. Brewer. It turned out to be not a new species but a hybrid between a mallard and a gadwall and the name did not stick. Later Audubon found one that did: Brewer's blackbird, which has the reputation of being a bully that attacks smaller birds. The doctor was also unfortunate in another namesake, Brewer's sparrow, which is probably the drabbest member of that numerous group. An important link between an era of American birding that was passing and one that was emerging, Dr. Brewer came to look on himself as a grand old man of American ornithology. But he wound up, in the eyes of a younger generation, more as a cantankerous old fogy.

By 1850, after Thomas Nuttall had left America for his native England and Audubon could no longer paint, there were only two men who were considered practicing professional ornithologists in the United States. One was George Newbold Lawrence, of Albany, New York, who was concerned with systematics and contributed more to his specialty than the skills of birding, although he did leave some Manhattan watching records—of passenger pigeons migrating past the present site of Grant's Tomb and of a flight of meadowlarks speeding down Broadway past Fortieth Street.

The other working professional was the brusque, wry-spoken, self-centered curator at the Academy of Natural Sciences in Philadelphia, John Cassin. The first first-class American-born ornithologist, Cassin found himself at the center of American ornithology when the academy acquired the world's largest collection of bird skins, put together by the French nobleman Victor Massena, duke of Rivoli (after whom Cassin later named the Massena partridge [Montezuma quail], giving him a place in nomenclature beside his beautiful young wife, after whom Anna's hummingbird was named).

Cassin was almost paranoid about the collection, refusing to allow anyone else to handle the skins, working so hard at studying, sorting, systematizing and describing them that he got arsenic poisoning from the chemical used to preserve them. Begrudging the time he had to take to attend to his printing business, he left his collection only to serve in the Union army. Captured by the Confederates, he was sent to the notorious Libby Prison but survived to return to his birds after the war and publish *Illustrations of the Birds of California, Texas, Oregon, British and Russian America . . . 1853 to 1855,* the first full work on western birds. The only American well versed in both American and European ornithology, and the only one scientifically respected abroad at that time, Cassin was still unabashedly patriotic in his birding. Challenging Thomas Bewick, the famous English artist and nature popularizer who had boasted of the European jay's ability to mimic dogs and pigs, Cassin rejoined that the jay has not the "taste or talent" for accurate imitation "shown in such an eminent degree by the famous songster of this country, the mockingbird."

As other ornithologists did later, Cassin relied on the birding observations of army officers stationed in or exploring the West. A prized contributor was Colonel George A. McCall, later inspector general of the army, "the accuracy of whose knowledge of the birds of western America is unrivaled," Cassin declared. The accurate colonel also had his poetic side. Once, he wrote, he "halted to rest my jaded mules in the toilsome march across a desert where for hundreds of miles the whole crust seemed to have been reduced to ashes." In this "vast plain of desolation," he went on, he first heard the *"kaa-wale, kaa-wale"* of the Gambel's partridge (quail) "as he strove to cheer his mate whilst occupied in the tedious task of incubation." Touched by something "extremely plaintive in this simple love song," McCall listened and then, in the interests of science, shot a pair of the birds, unpoetically reporting that he found mesquite leaves and wild gooseberries in their crops.

Another time, up before daybreak, the colonel was riding across the plain "half asleep and numb with cold" when a covey of blue partridge (scaled quail) wakened him to "see heavenly dawn," the sun sparkling "on a whole country white with frost." Turning, he saw a "wonderful illusion, cruel mockery . . . a broad lake of bright water with noble trees growing on either hand." He was able to persuade himself that it was a mirage only because he knew "he had just ridden over that counterfeit lake." The meat of the partridge, he added, getting back to business, had "plump muscle and delicate flavor."

The colonel, who seemed to do much of his bird watching on horseback, paused once to listen to a curve-billed thrasher's "dulcet notes flowing with exquisite fullness." The bird, he wrote approvingly, was "as retired and simple in his manners as he is gay and brilliant in his song" and he could not then think of "molesting him whose vesper chaunt had just enlivened that wild, secluded vale." But, he went on, "I cannot acknowledge even now, without a tweak of contrition and self-reproach" that he shot one later—"a sacrilegious act." He hung it up in a tree and something ate it. "A just reward," he said penitently.

Captain J. P. McCown sent Cassin a description of the Texas cardinal (*Pyrrhuloxia*) and also testimony to the unsophistication of frontier birds. When he stepped out on the porch of the mess hall at the Ringold Barracks each evening for his after-dinner cigar, the hooded orioles would "desist for a moment in their incessant hunting for spiders" and "watch the smoke with great curiosity."

Cassin represented a change in the way naturalists conducted themselves and their work. Natural history in America had been dominated by adventurous men like Bartram and Wilson, Audubon and Nuttall, who went out alone on long and often perilous trips to see and shoot, paint and record nature. With Cassin and others this romantic era ended and natural history took on its modern, more institutionalized aspect, governed by closet naturalists who rarely went into the field themselves, using reports sent in by others as material for their own work. Cassin delivered a little sermon to naturalists too tempted by the lures of the field. "Betake thyself not to the wilderness," he said, for "longer than forty days." This instruction, as time went on, tended to separate the birders from the ornithologists but there were, happily for the arts of bird watching, a great many naturalists who paid no attention to crusty John Cassin's precept.

2

The Recruiter

The man who most neatly joins the old era of American birding, which ended with Audubon, to the modern age, and who also set those ages most clearly apart was Spencer Fullerton Baird, who gave his name to several birds (Baird's junco, Baird's sandpiper, Baird's sparrow) as well as to a period (the Bairdian Era of Ornithology) and to a tradition (the Bairdian School of Ornithology).

The Bairdian period began, one might say, in 1858, when Baird, with the assistance of Cassin and Lawrence, published *Catalogue of North American Birds,* a work listing, locating and briefly describing all the known and verified birds of the continent north of Mexico. It was the most complete, reliable and orderly roster ever put together in America, an indispensable reference for birders and a basis for all the guides and check lists that bird watchers use today.

Baird himself was, in his work, the most complete, reliable and orderly American natural scientist of his time—though, in his quiet way, a free spirit. He seems to have inherited this spirit, along with his first name, from his grandmother, Lydia Spencer Biddle, of Philadelphia. After her husband had lost his money in land speculations promoted by the revolutionary patriot Robert Morris, Lydia Biddle put her mind and will into several business ventures and prospered (with the help of her son-in-law, Charles Penrose, an influential political figure, whose son, Boies Penrose, decades later became a famous Republican politician and president-maker). Mrs. Biddle's business helped provide for her family though her eccentricities somewhat embarrassed them, especially her archaic manner of dressing. But she brushed off the complaints that what she wore was outlandishly out of style. "When I was young," she said, "anything Miss Spencer wore *was* the fashion!"

Her grandson had his own eccentricities, which turned out eventually to be highly practical. He was apparently born with the urge to make lists. As a boy in Carlisle, Pennsylvania, he listed the money he got and spent, the books he lent and borrowed, the ages of the members of his family (he had not been able, he admitted with the scrupulousness that marked him later as a scientist, to obtain the ages of two aunts), and of "songs that I sing" (although the family did not remember his singing, only whistling).

Despite the family doctor's warning that he was afflicted with heart palpitations, he insisted on going on excessively long walks. He went twenty miles to Harrisburg on foot to return some library books and then back home the same day. Starting one morning, he walked sixty miles across the mountainous country and was ready for another ten miles at 11 p.m., when he had to stop for lodgings. At the end of 1842, adding up all his walks for the year, he came out with twenty-one hundred pedestrian miles. He also walked tirelessly after birds, watching them, shooting them, then dissecting them, preparing their skins, classifying them and recording them.

While a student at Dickinson College, from which he graduated in 1839 when he was sixteen, he had two encounters that determined his career. Lent a copy of Wilson's *Ornithology,* he cut all his classes for a day to study it. On a trip to Philadelphia a short time later, he saw Audubon's epic *The Birds of America,* only recently completed, and he promptly, made himself known to Audubon in a letter describing a flycatcher he had seen and could not find in any work on birds, including Audubon's. The artist responded promptly, saying he thought it was a new species, which he named the yellow-bellied flycatcher. Would Baird please get some specimens for him? he asked. Baird's style and description, he added approvingly, showed that "an old head may be found from time to time on young shoulders."

The next year, Baird went to New York for a half-hearted try at studying medicine. It was an extraordinary place and time for a young birder and he paid at least as much attention to birds as to anatomy and pharmacology. Up at Minnie's Landing, the Audubon home on the Hudson, the artist gave him some drawing lessons on condition that he tell no one what he was doing. Downtown, Baird kept the company of the best-known naturalists in the city at the taxidermy shop run by John G. Bell, who prepared skins for Audubon and almost everybody else and made his shop an informal information exchange for naturalists, a forum for their arguments and a working laboratory where Baird could see and study an ever-changing collection of birds and animals. Bell was so impressed by young Baird that he invited Giraud and Lawrence to hear him explain wing markings on birds. Giraud took the young man to see his fine bird collection and generously gave him some spare skins. So did Audubon, who also gave him introductions to important birders.

Baird quickly became a familiar figure in natural history circles, already showing his aptitude for helping other scientists and being helped by them, for gaining not only their respect but their warm friendship. Few other men in the often testy community of birders engendered so much affection and so little enmity. Audubon invited him to come along on his last great jaunt, a trip up the Missouri River to "undertake," wrote the artist, "besides acting toward me as a friend to prepare skins of birds or quadrupeds." Baird could keep half the birds for himself and a fourth of the quadrupeds, excepting new or rare species.

Baird's family, worried about his heart palpitations, persuaded him to decline the invitation. Though Audubon regretted this, he still felt warmly towards his young friend, and on his return gave him a few dozen bird skins he had brought back. In 1844, counting his collection, Baird found he owned 1,568 skins and he kept diligently adding to them. In a single day, May 5, 1846, he noted in his journal, he "shot 41 birds, stuffed 33." Next day it was "20 shot, 16 stuffed," and the following day, 26 shot and 22 stuffed.

Medicine had long since been forgotten by Baird and in 1845, when he was twenty-two, he took a job as honorary, i.e., unpaid, professor at Dickinson College and curator of its natural history collections. The next year the college added money to honor and gave him four hundred dollars' annual salary to teach natural history and mathematics ("I consider $400 very small," grumbled Audubon when Baird wrote to tell him the good news). Having taught himself mathematics, chemistry, German, Spanish and Italian, Baird within a year was also teaching chemistry and his pay was raised to a thousand dollars a year.

Such eminent naturalists as Louis Agassiz, the charismatic teacher at Harvard, and Asa Gray, the most eminent American botanist, came to call on the young professor. In 1847, when the fledgling Smithsonian Institution was looking for an assistant director, the natural history community joined to help Baird get the job. Audubon wrote a glowing "testimony to your knowledge and high character and zeal" and John Cassin suggested that Baird write his own letter which he would then sign. Baird's influential uncle, Charles Penrose, did his part and Baird himself offered, as an inducement, to bring along his large collection of birds, beasts and minerals.

All kinds of obstacles kept him from going. For one thing, the Smithsonian was short of money. Most of its endowment had been spent putting up an unsuitable building, which was, in addition, so poorly constructed that repairs kept draining away its reserves. The Smithsonian's secretary, as the director was called, was Joseph Henry, a brilliant physicist whose experiments in electromagnetics had helped make possible the invention of the telegraph and the electric motor. Though he thought well of Baird, who had done research for him, Henry was suspicious of political or any kind of pressure and, possibly, of Baird's tendency to amass collections—a place full of specimens was not Henry's idea of what his institution should be. Henry would not give Baird the appointment but neither did he appoint anyone else. Finally in 1850, yielding to necessity and Baird's acknowledged qualifications, he took him on as assistant secretary. Baird showed up at the Smithsonian with four thousand bird skins, several thousand eggs and nests, five hundred jars and kegs of reptiles and fish, innumerable boxes of insects—all of which Henry would gladly have thrown out.

As assistant secretary, Baird set out to remake natural history in America, notably ornithology. This he accomplished partly with his own publications. His *Birds of North America,* a revision of his *Catalogue,* has been called "the most important single step ever taken in American ornithology." In its thousand pages Baird systematized, correlated and correctly named North America's birds, thereby giving American birders the first coherent reference for their watching. In building up for the Smithsonian a collection of specimens that ornithologists could readily consult, he abetted and guided the work of fellow scientists.

Henry had known how knowledgeable his new assistant secretary was as a naturalist but he could hardly have guessed what a treasure he had gained as an administrator. Though his own special field was birds, Baird was one of the finest American generalists in natural sciences, well grounded in mammalogy, mineralogy, meteorology, geology. He knew the needs of a museum on both the inside and the outside. From his own collecting and filing, he had worked out problems of arranging and storing specimens. At the Smithsonian, he had cabinets built to uniform specifications with interchangeable trays and drawers. He designed a new wing for the institution so that the standard cabinets would fit into any space, including the awkward spots between windows and in alcoves. In an inspired move that would occur only to a man who never ignored the obvious, he standardized the size and shape of Smithsonian publications so that they would all pack neatly.

From his field work, Baird knew exactly what his specimen collectors needed, so he sent them apparatus, papers, books, advice, encouragement, instructions, questions and time-saving tricks. They could spare themselves the tedious work of cleaning the flesh from fish skeletons, he knew, by putting the carcass in a tub of water with a lot of tadpoles, which would do the work gently and thoroughly, eating off the flesh and leaving the bones clean and intact. "No bride ever devoted more thought and attention to her trousseau," Baird's daughter once recalled, "than did my father in fitting out each of these explorers and he watched the progress of each missionary with anxious personal interest."

His "missionaries" were of all kinds and he found them everywhere, enlisting anyone with interest and knowledge. Susan Fenimore Cooper, daughter of the famous author, was asked to help get fish specimens from the New York lakes near her home, especially the Otsego bass. She not only did so but also delivered a paean to the local salmon trout as "very rich and delicate" and superior to those of other areas.

Baird knew Miss Cooper as one of the better bird watchers of her day. Though she spent much of her time as her father's copyist and secretary, she managed to write on her own a novel under the ornithological pseudonym of Anabel Penfeather and a nature journal entitled *Rural Hours* which, first published in 1859, was so popular that it was reprinted some forty years later. Taking a census of birds as she walked down a village street, Miss Cooper determined that maples with their forked twigs were favorite abodes, while sumacs were shunned. Watching loons dive after a fisherman's line, she had the depth measured and found that the bird would go down ninety-five feet to steal a fish. She expressed her approval of orioles, which "in spite of their fanciful costumes" were "just as well behaved as the robins . . . bearing an excellent character . . . industrious and skillful" and at nest weaving "most diligent."

An extraordinary group of missionaries came to Baird through his wife, a helpmate of many virtues. "Mrs. Baird," he wrote a friend, "is first rate, not the least fear of snakes, salamanders and such other zoological interestings." She was most obliging. During Baird's courtship she suffered her suitor to come calling with whatever book he was currently studying, waking him up to send him home after he had fallen asleep over it. Out on a walk once, when he saw a fish he wanted and bemoaned his lack of a net, she sacrificed her bonnet for his science. She also, said Baird, "reads my letters, crossing i's and dotting t's, sticking in here a period and there a comma and converting my figure 7s into f's." To all these helpful qualities she added a most important relationship: her father, Sylvester Churchill, was the army's inspector general. This gave Baird special access to a unique group of far-traveling naturalists, the officers of the U.S. Army.

It may seem strange today to think of employing the military in the pursuit of natural history. But the explanation is simple. In the 1850s, the War Department was assigned to map possible routes for transcontinental railroads. It sent out several expeditions to study and chart the territories to be covered—the historic Pacific Railroad surveys, which went looking for routes across the northern, central and southern parts of the West. Following the tradition that Thomas Jefferson had begun with Lewis and Clark, the army encouraged members of the expeditions to make natural history studies and collect specimens. Through his father-in-law, Baird set out to recruit naturalists from the ranks. "I had a long talk with General [Winfield] Scott," he wrote. "Promises everything. Our new secretary, Jefferson Davis, will no doubt do whatever is needeful." The new secretary of war already had an interest in natural history, stimulated when he was a student at Transylvania College by a brilliant and eccentric teacher named Samuel Constantine Rafinesque. Davis gave Baird what he said he needed: help in getting suitable officers assigned to useful birding spots—although, Baird noted, he "kicked up" a "terrible fuss" over Baird's willingness to give away duplicate specimens, which Davis considered his department's property.

Working with Davis, Baird found many military men to serve as correspondents. Captain George B. McClellan, later the commander of the Union armies, sent him specimens from the Texas border. "I must confess to a little astonishment at the amount and value of the collection," Baird wrote the captain. "I am so accustomed to have promises made with little or no result that although feeling assured that you would keep yours, I was entirely unprepared for what you have done."

He must have been more astonished at the results he got from one cadre, the army's medical officers, whose tours of duty took them, in the last half of the century, far into what was still an unexplored and perilous western wilderness. A versatile group, they not only ministered medically to the troops, but took up guns when necessary to fight the Indians and also collected flora and fauna for that interesting and demanding man back at the Smithsonian who, often as not, was responsible for their being out where they were in the first place.

They took willingly to Baird's work. As men of science they understood the need for precise observation, careful checking and clear reporting. Because of their profession, they were at home in anatomy, taxonomy and nomenclature, which is the basis for ornithological reporting, and they could dissect and preserve specimens. As men of intellect and education, stuck at the uncultured edges of civilization, they were pleased to have a way to stretch their minds and satisfy their scientific curiosity.

Through his many sources, especially his father-in-law, Baird learned which army doctors might serve him best, arranged assignments which would be satisfying both to them and to him, provided them with material for collecting and permission to do it and soon had them contributing to the Smithsonian and to general knowledge. Several of them became bulwarks of American ornithology. In fact, a whole volume about them exists, *Ornithologists of the United States Army Medical Corps,* which is basic to ornithological history. And the names in modern bird guides bear memorials to them: Hammond's flycatcher, after William Alexander Hammond, who sent Baird birds from Kansas and the Dakotas; Coues' flycatcher (greater pewee), after the most controversial bird watcher of his time; and even a warbler named *Verivorma virginiae,* after a bird-watching officer's wife.

This last was William Wallace Anderson, whose observations at his post in Burgwyn, New Mexico, led Baird to call the area "the greatest center of rare birds in the U.S." He sent in reports on the white-tailed ptarmigan, engraved a copper plate of a *Vireo solitarius,* and not only honored his wife by making her namesake to a warbler but also, after her piano was dreadfully broken during the long mule-train trek west, rebuilt the whole instrument and tuned it himself. His association with the Smithsonian broke off when he joined the Confederate army and became its second-ranking medical officer. After the war he was in touch with Baird again and sent him specimens.

The Civil War divided Baird's contributors. One of his notes states that he received "from Drs. Foard and Crawford" specimens of several Texas birds. Dr. Andrew Jackson Foard went over to the Confederate side and distinguished himself as chief medical officer for the armies of Generals Bragg and Beauregard and of General Johnston on his retreat through Georgia. Dr. Samuel Wylie Crawford, loyal to the Union, was assigned to Fort Sumter, and there saved an enemy's life by pumping out the stomach of a Confederate officer who, very thirsty, picked up a tumbler and drank a lethal dose of medicine while waiting for Major Anderson to sign the articles of surrender. Dr. Crawford went on to heroic service as an officer of the line at Gettysburg, where he took up the flag at Little Round Top after the color bearer had been shot. Like so many other bird watchers he became, after the war, an early supporter of conservation.

Baird had kept his eye on James Graham Cooper, whose father, William, had been one of New York City's leading naturalists. When young Cooper graduated from medical school Baird persuaded him to sign up as surgeon in the army and got him assigned to the survey that explored the northwestern forty-seventh parallel route, a project commanded by Baird's excellent correspondent, Captain McClellan. Working with a fellow surgeon, George Suckley, Cooper made many contributions to the historic reports on the expeditions and later wrote *Ornithology of California,* which Baird himself edited. Cooper was a minutely observant biographer. Ravens, he reported, liked to feed on weakened and straggling cattle they would follow across the plains but "when nothing better is to be had, they eat lizards, snakes and bird's eggs." Lewis' woodpecker, he reported, disdains "to toil for its food like its laborious relatives." It "rarely ever raps on trees," willing to settle for grasshoppers and berries. As will be seen later in this book, Dr. Cooper went on to become the mentor of California's birders.

William Alexander Hammond, who as surgeon general of the army remade the whole obsolete medical corps and as a pioneering neurologist and psychiatrist opened the country's first sanatorium for nervous diseases, was a useful birder for Baird, sending specimens from Fort Riley, Kansas. He later benefited by having on his hospital staff a young Hungarian patriot named János Xántus, who had fled his country to escape service in the Austrian army and wound up voluntarily in the U.S. Army. A self-taught ornithologist, Xántus was encouraged by Hammond to collect birds and become a wonderful source for Baird. He was, said Baird, "the most accomplished and successful explorer in the field of natural history I have ever known or heard of," and his collections were "much larger and more complete than any made in America during the same period of time by any collector." Between 1855 and 1861 he shipped to the Smithsonian more than one hundred twenty boxes of specimens totaling some ten thousand items. In his *Birds of North America,* Baird lists about a hundred birds sent him by Xántus.

Xántus immortalized his general by suggesting the name *hammondii* for a new flycatcher he found and his own name was given to half a dozen species, including a hummingbird and a murrelet. A completely dependable naturalist, Xántus was an utterly unreliable autobiographer. He claimed without any basis in fact that he came of a noble Hungarian family, had traveled to America as assistant to the Prince of Württemberg, had stayed to teach three languages at the University of Louisiana and to serve as a captain in the U.S. Navy. None of this was true but Xántus was unregenerate about promoting himself. With Baird's help, he was appointed consul in a Mexican town, did some basic studies of Mexican birds but was fired for exceeding his authority. Making his way back to Hungary he impressed naturalists there with stories of his American achievements and was appointed director of the Budapest Zoological Gardens, where he served with distinction.

One of Baird's most formidable correspondents was a captious German immigrant named Charles Emil Bendire, who began his army life as a noncommissioned officer in the medical corps and wound up a major. Thrown out of a theological seminary in Germany for what his biographers uninformatively call "peccadilloes," he came to America, joined the dragoons, became a surgeon's assistant and, learning on the job, was made a medical officer. Twice during his long career he was decorated for bravery; first at the battle of Trevilian Station in Virginia in 1864 and later at Canyon Creek, Montana, for "gallant services" against the Indians. After that battle he rashly walked in on the fierce chief Cochise and argued him into a truce.

Baird found Bendire to be a bumptious man, sensitive to nonexistent slights, jealous of other birders, and miserly about his superb collection of birds' eggs. With what a friend called his "suavity, sagacity and tactfulness," Baird made himself persona grata to the suspicious Bendire. "He smoothed Bendire's ruffled plumes effectually," the friend noted, and added: "Few persons whom Baird ever got

hold of escaped him afterward, chiefly for the reason that few desired
to get away from what he would and could do for them."

A painstaking watcher, Bendire was both scrupulous and vivid in
his reporting. When the whip-poor-will was courting, he noted, the
female would grunt *"gaw gaw gaw,* undoubtedly a note of approval or
endearment" and her "whole body seemed to be in a violent trem-
ble." The male "sidled up and touched her bill with his," which made
her move "slightly to one side . . . first one would move away followed
by the other and then it was reversed . . . equally bold and coy at the
same time . . . the female as timid and bashful as many young maidens
when receiving the declarations of their would-be lovers."

Bendire was, at heart, an oologist, fascinated by eggs and nests,
and his judgments on birds were biased by their nesting habits. The
great horned owls got low marks from him: they are poor nest builders, often using old hawk and heron nests instead of building their
own and, moreover, making scanty repairs. What's more, they are not
sensible about laying their eggs, sometimes starting so early in February that the eggs freeze. The owls did, however, have the saving grace
of being good providers for their young. In one nest were the bodies
of a muskrat, a mouse, a rabbit, a woodcock, two eels, four bullheads,
four ruffed grouse, and eleven rats with their heads eaten and their
bodies untouched.

A deep passion for eggs bursts out in Bendire's description of
those of a chuck-will's-widow:

> the shell fine grained . . . the ground color of such a subtle tint
> that it is almost impossible to describe it accurately; it varies
> from a rich cream with a faint pinkish suffusion to a pale cream
> . . . a pure white, blotched, marbled and spotted with different
> shades of brown, tawny, fawn and Isobel-color underlaid and
> mixed with lighter shades of ecru drab, lavender, pearl gray
> and pale heliotrope purple . . . endless variations in the style
> of markings.

Bendire himself had many helpful birding friends in the army and
their reports to him show how much of a solace and stimulus birding
must have been to them on their generally boring duty. The Goss
brothers, Captain Benjamin F. and Colonel Nathaniel S., who later
wrote *The Birds of Kansas,* between them kept track of western birds
from turkey vultures in southern California to Swainson's hawks in
North Dakota to Mississippi kites in Kansas. The kites were observed

"with sticks in their bills, flying aimlessly about as if undecided where to place them." Captain P. M. Thorne of the Twenty-second Infantry stationed at Fort Duncan, Texas, found the bobwhite there "so unsophisticated that a covey would not even squat when my dog pointed at them; they would move on slowly, chattering to each other, evidently talking the matter over." Captain William L. Carpenter of the Ninth Infantry confessed to a dereliction of birding duty when out with a butterfly net one day near his post he came upon a sage grouse and stood for five minutes just admiring its beauty—he was so touched by it that he went off without collecting the bird. The captain explained that he had to divide his loyalties between the major and the company cook. He had shot a wild turkey, he told Bendire, but "not this time for the Smithsonian, as the men clamored loudly for roast turkey without arsenic." There was no clamoring when he brought back sage grouse. The highly aromatic sagebrush on which they fed "renders it so objectionable for the table" that they were eaten only when nothing else was around.

When Bendire retired from the army in 1883, Baird persuaded him to become honorary curator of the oology department at the Smithsonian and to bring all his eight thousand eggs with him. A few years later, Bendire published *Life Histories of North American Birds, with Special Reference to Their Breeding Habits and Eggs,* which has a high place among American bird books of the nineteenth century.

From his office at the Smithsonian Baird marveled at what he had wrought. "The string of scientific expeditions which I have succeeded in starting," he wrote in 1857, "is perfectly preposterous," and he went on to catalog them: to the North Pacific and Bering Strait to South America and the Paraná and Amazon rivers, to Oregon, Greenland, Mexico, Salt Lake City, laying off the expenses of his collectors mostly on the army or navy. Though they dumped an enormous work load on him, Baird never lost touch with his most remote correspondents, writing as many as three thousand letters a year in his own hand. When he finally acquired a secretary, he increased his output by dictating rapidly without ever asking her to stop and read back what he had said.

The letters, which enrich William Healey Dall's biography of Baird, were a mixture of concern, instruction, encouragement, and sharp-edged pleasantries. "If you will write the heavy artillery," he replied to one correspondent's overlong letters, "I will pepper you with musketry." He had to put up with a good deal of oddness, notably from an accomplished artist whose belief in phonetic spelling forced Baird to decode such messages as: "Daer Sur, I delivert thos drawing there ur 17 in number wisch I workt very hard an averich 11 haur par day. With respaegt yours, John H. Richard."

Baird's letters were often followed up by boxes of equipment. To Robert Kennicott, birding for him up north on the Mackenzie River, he sent egg drills, books, a blowpipe, a horse pistol, instructions for packing eggs ("moss is not good," Baird told him, after a shipment had arrived with many eggs broken. "Cotton or paper twisted around the big eggs, like globular sugar plums, is best"), a burning glass, arsenic, glass eyes for birds, ribbons and jewelry, five thousand steel needles, sheets, India rubber pillowcases, handkerchiefs, a good gun and fifty cigars.

Meanwhile Baird was making his own monumental additions to the literature of American ornithology, collaborating with Thomas Brewer and Robert Ridgway on the five-volume *A History of North American Birds.* The huge collections he had amassed at the Smithsonian and the reports that accompanied them made possible the most complete study done up to that time of the continent's birds. This work, largely written by Brewer, refined the life history, a form of bird biography which included all relevant data about species: appearance, habits, songs, habitat, nests, eggs. Through all his work, Baird conceived a distinctive American approach to ornithology. European ornithologists in writing on birds would emphasize their own conclusions, skimping on the evidence that led to them. Baird generally laid out his evidence in full, giving others the chance to come to their own conclusions. What he began in American ornithology was carried on by his disciples—notably Ridgway, Joel Asaph Allen, Elliott Coues—in the Bairdian School of American ornithology, an approach characterized, one historian has said, by its "peculiar exactness, conciseness, careful analysis."

In 1878, when Secretary Henry died, Baird was unanimously chosen to succeed him. It was, actually, mostly a change of title. For years, Baird had been running the Smithsonian. Fighting off political job seekers, he kept corruption out of his unwieldy domain and gained an enviable reputation in Congress. Once grudging about support, it willingly voted Baird funds to establish the National Museum (of Natural History) to house the Smithsonian's overflowing collections. One senator, conferring an ultimate accolade, said that Baird "gets two dollars worth for every dollar we give him." Fellow scientists appreciated not only Baird's wisdom and support but also his tact. He avoided as much as possible all social functions and meetings because the close air of auditoriums made him drowsy and he worried about falling asleep during a colleague's lecture. When he was elected secretary he was so pained by the shower of congratulations that he left Washington until the fussing was over.

By that time his interest had shifted. The generation he had raised and guided was, while enormously expanding the science of ornithology, also spawning the first generation of organized bird watchers. Now, transferring his attention to fish, he founded the oceanographic center at Woods Hole, Massachusetts. The last years of his life—he died in 1887—were spent in semi-retirement. He had handled authority wisely at the Smithsonian. As Henry's assistant secretary he had served loyally while still keeping his independent and differing views. As secretary, he chose his successors and gracefully handed responsibility over to them. He shared a philosophy of power with his friend John Cassin, who expounded it in a letter to Baird. As to ambition, Cassin wrote, "one man aspires to universal empire— nearly succeeds—another is perfectly satisfied with balancing a straw on his nose—success better than universal empire—I have somewhat tried the universal empire business—hereafter my attention shall be directed greatly to perpendicularity of a straw rightly placed, as above signified."

Perhaps what enabled Baird to work under great strains without seeming himself to strain, and to deal unselfishly with self-seeking politicians and self-centered scientists, was the clear quality of his mind and an almost childlike temperament that he kept throughout his life. Amid everything else, he found time to help bring up a daughter, Lucy, to whom he was a fond if sometimes impossible father. Before she could get to the latest copy of *St. Nicholas* magazine when it came every month, her father would make off with it. He became so absorbed in *Little Lord Fauntleroy* when it was being serialized in the magazine that, on meeting the author, Frances Hodgson Burnett, he coaxed her into revealing, before the final installment appeared in the magazine, how Fauntleroy eventually fared with his curmudgeon grandfather. When he made up bedtime stories for Lucy and got his heroes and heroines safely past ogres and witches and ravenous beasts, Baird would finally come to "and they lived happily ever after." At which point, though his desperate daughter implored him to stop there, he would go on with "until one day in going by a soap boiler's they unfortunately fell into a vat and were made into soap."

3

The Model Watcher

Spencer Baird had organized the science of ornithology and, as a by-product, the disciplines of birding. The arts of bird watching, in America, were formally organized in the autumn of 1871, when, as a history of the Nuttall Ornithological Club put it, "two young ornithologists of Cambridge formed the plan of meeting weekly to read Audubon and compare views and notes respecting various ornithological questions." After a few weeks of reading and comparing notes, William Brewster and Henry Henshaw were joined by "kindred spirits," friends of Brewster and mostly, like him, members of established Boston families. Their meetings, held at Brewster's home on Brattle Street, led to the formation in 1873 of the Nuttall Ornithological Club, the first American organization devoted to studying and watching birds. When the club got around to defining what was expected of a member, it called for "good moral character, genuine interest in bird study, a reputation for accuracy, and qualities of heart and mind that make a man clubbable."

There were other very specific membership requirements. A Resident Member had to live within the Cambridge city limits. If he moved beyond them, he had to resign. Birders in outlying areas, such as New York and Washington, were welcomed as Corresponding Members, and they, in turn, welcomed the chance to join. Within three years there were ninety-six of them, outnumbering the twenty-three residents. The club, however, was governed by the Cambridge members, and they were pretty much governed by William Brewster, who became its permanent president—except for one early period when, for reasons the club's records do not make clear, he peremptorily resigned the office. He was reelected the following year. Becoming more and more expert in his science, he was appointed first curator of birds at the Harvard Museum of Comparative Zoology, and in that role he became a focal point of American ornithology. But the duties of a scientist in studying and classifying never distracted him from the pleasures of watching.

He was the model watcher, patient of eye and precise of ear, eager to report some bird that no one else had ever reported but skeptical of his claim until he had proof, taking delight in the new, yet never, even after decades of watching, untouched by the familiar. In two books drawn from his journals, *Concord River* and *October Farm,* Brewster conjures up, as well as anyone ever has, the charms of bird watching. He listens as a woodcock rises—"its wings whistle steadily," then the bird "floats evenly downward like a dusky ball of thistledown" with "a succession of soft and exceedingly liquid notes." The most immediate of watchers, he stands at a dove's nest looking into the unblinking eyes of the setting bird. They stare at each other for three minutes, during which time Brewster blinks his eyes thirty-six time and the dove does not blink even once. Back at the nest three days later, he observes the downy young opening their eyes. Persistent, as birders must be, he is back again in a few weeks to watch the wary fledglings fly off "with a clapping noise."

Some kind of avian empathy permits him to come up close to birds. At a vireo's nest, where a female is sitting on four eggs, he strokes the bird's back without arousing a protest. She flies off, however, when he touches her head. He caresses a woodcock in her nest, strokes a screech-owl roosting in a clump of oak sprouts and has a conversation with a great horned owl "in the best owl language that I could command"—not good enough, apparently, for the owl simply flies back and forth, puzzled. Another time, conversing with a long-eared owl, he squeaks like a mouse and the owl, hearing the sound of its prey but finding the source in this unmouselike creature, hovers bewildered, two feet above his upturned face.

He pries into the manners and morals of his subjects. Orioles are fastidious eaters, pecking at cherries on the trees, savoring and slowly tasting them, not pulling them off. Robins are greedy, gobbling the cherries whole—but "not without some difficulty," Brewster adds, pleased that bad habits do not pay off. With dispassionate distaste, he watches blue jays out on an egging raid flying from tree to tree until they have taken all the eggs in the area, ignoring the smaller parent birds who chase frantically after them. Troubled, he sees a downy woodpecker pecking at a female's head "inspired by the lust of killing and not by sexual ardor" and, despite "her cries, piteous and incessant, finishing the foul deed" and flying off to feed on a lump of suet.

He misses nothing. A male red-winged blackbird creeps up a hillside towards a female, songless, with wings quivering. Raptly watching a fox sparrow scratch seed from under the snow, he calculates that it jumps one to three inches forward, then jumps backward, flinging snow, and leaves six or eight inches behind until the seed is uncovered. And how exact he is: a veery giving "the finest most copious music," sings "every evening in the large red oak sitting on the same branch on the same twig always facing towards the northwest."

The domestic habits of birds absorb him. A redstart building its nest uses milkweed bark fiber one day, cocoon fiber the next and winds up with a lining of horse hair, dry grass, birch bark, grapevine and mullein. The female rose-breasted grosbeak builds the nest by herself while the male sits by, singing "gloriously." A male flicker, when his female is killed, takes the family chores all on himself, dutifully pumping insects into the bills of his young. Sticking his head up a chimney to watch swifts nesting, Brewster notes that the male shares the nest-sitting duty with the female and that its nighttime twittering is "infinitely more tender and musical" than the daytime song, adding, less sentimentally, that the birds frequently void their excrement at night.

He does his watching on foot, in his canoe, or from his carriage. Starting out in his buggy from Cambridge at ten o'clock one May morning behind his horse, Charlie, he finds the whole bird world flinging itself at him. Least flycatchers and yellow warblers mingle in an apple orchard while yellowthroats sing in an ash and a yellow-rumped warbler sings in the scrub oaks. He sees thrashers and a towhee, purple martins, black-and-white creepers (warblers). There are black-throated green warblers at Walden Pond, a white-throated sparrow on the roadside, four Carolina (mourning) doves at South Lincoln walking at the edge of a rainwater pool. He arrives at his farm in Concord at one o'clock in a state of sated contentment.

On a midsummer morning he floats down the Concord River in

his canoe through "a wildflower garden of exceeding beauty," white water lilies, purple pickerelweed, creamy white buttonbushes, hearing unseen singers. He moves over to the drowsy resident of a muskrat pond and, by scratching its back, puts it to sleep. Paddling to his landing, he watches a kingfisher chase and pummel a robin, for no reason he can think of except perhaps as "chastisement."

He birds from dawn into dark, keeping his door open on a September night to hear the migrating thrushes and warblers as they pass over. Listening critically to bird songs, he decides that the measured cadence of Bachman's finch (sparrow) and of the hermit thrush are "almost equally spiritual in quality." His ears are well tuned and his descriptions are delicate—a female bluebird sits on a rock in Holden's pasture with two males dancing and fluttering about her, "warbling in a deliciously soft undertone." Even-handed in his judgments he gives crows the benefit of musical doubt by insisting that he hears in their gurgles, whistles and clucks some "rich notes." Although he finds the catbird's song "singularly unmusical, rasping stuttering very trying to my ears," it is "perhaps not similarly displeasing to those of his mate."

Sometimes, but rarely, he interferes with nature. Seeing two ovenbirds hovering around a black snake, trying to keep it from finding their nest, he moves in to shoot the snake and the birds fly off. When he sees a sharp-shinned hawk eating a blue jay alive, tearing into the "raw living flesh" as the jay cried "piteously," Brewster goes after his gun but comes back too late. The hawk has flown off after having exulted with "savage joy" in the "agony of its victim."

The clichés of bird lore do not blind him to realities, for example, on the sureness of hawks as hunters. A falcon, diving after a pigeon, misses with its claws and clumsily hits the bird with its breast—not the accepted image of the fiercely graceful predator. Hawks, he concludes, have little perseverance. They often give up if they miss their first strike. Nor does he spare himself his own errors. Having disparaged blue jays by stating that their skill in imitating other bird calls had been grossly overrated—they get the form of the call, not the tone, he had said—he has to reconsider. Puzzled several times at hearing the call of a red-shouldered hawk when there was no hawk anywhere around, he finally realizes from the constant presence of jays that they were doing the calling, mimicking the hawk so well both in form and tone that even Brewster's ear was fooled. "I am forced to withdraw," he says, ever the gentleman-scientist.

And he never tires of learning something new. After having

watched birds for three or four decades, he is still delighted to discover that juncos in early April go off to roost for the night at 5:35
p.m., when the sun is still well above the horizon, while fox sparrows
wait until twilight to retire.

Brewster, who was born in 1851, started out with a gunner's interest in birds, as so many birders did, shooting birds for sport, then for
his collection of bird skins. With his best friend, Daniel Chester
French, who later became famous as a sculptor (*The Minute Man* at
Concord and the Lincoln Memorial in Washington are his works), he
went out collecting nests and eggs—"a too common habit of boys at
that time," Brewster remarked contritely some years later. Brewster's
father had a copy of Audubon's *Ornithological Biography,* which the two
boys read diligently, and French's father had some skills in taxidermy
which he taught the two boys. Cambridge was a wonderful place for
birding in those days. In Fresh Pond, Back Bay and Brickyard Swamp
they could see woodcock, snipe and solitary sandpipers. One fall,
northern (red-necked) phalaropes by the thousands lit on the Charles
River—the son of the drawbridge tender at Craigie Bridge used to
keep an eye out for them for local birders. On July 6, 1870, in his
backyard, Brewster shot a passenger pigeon that was raiding the cur-
rant bushes. Looking out his window, he watched a beleaguered whip-
poor-will huddling in an apple tree, beset by a host of misguided
robins which took it for an owl.

Ill health kept Brewster from attending Harvard but he was well
tutored at home and had plenty of time for birds. In late spring he
would go up to Lake Umbagog in Maine and, enduring hosts of
midges and mosquitoes, would come back with rare skins and eggs.
In winter he went to Florida to see birds which have since become part
of birding mythology—Carolina parakeets and ivory-billed woodpeckers. Wealthy enough to make his pastime a full-time occupation
and eventually a profession, Brewster became the leader of Boston's
birders, his tall, loose-jointed figure presiding Jove-like—with what
his friend French called "a transparent goodness in his face"—over
the meetings of the Nuttall Club as they flowed along on the stream
of his words and comments. He came to preside also over all collections both at the Museum of Comparative Zoology and in his own
private museum at the back of his home.

His garden was a haven for birds and, inevitably, a favorite hunting
place for the neighborhood cats. After many experiments to frustrate
the cats, Brewster finally succeeded by putting up a wire fence on top
of which he spread a heavy large-meshed fish net hooked to flexible

garden stakes. A cat, climbing up the fence, would step on the net and the stakes would bend down, leaving the cat bouncing helplessly while Brewster, from his window, enjoyed its plight. The fence could not keep out a predatory screech-owl but that was a lesser menace and Brewster finally welcomed it as one of his more faithful tenants.

Like the bird lady in almost every community who takes in maimed or orphaned birds, Brewster took in ailing birders. One of them was a young Cambridge neighbor, Henry Davis Minot, who published an ambitious book, *The Land-Birds and Game-Birds of New England,* at the age of sixteen. It filled a real need for a regional guide, sold out its first edition and was cherished by readers for its fresh and loving approach. Years later, after Minot's early death, Brewster undertook to edit another edition, as a kind of memorial, and in the process showed how amiable a friend and strict a scientist he could be. Other ornithologists had attacked Minot for his methods and for making claims he later had to give up. Brewster, as editor, praised Minot for having "a clear head, a fine heart and a well-defined purpose," then balanced this praise by saying that Minot made "statements of more than doubtful scientific accuracy," a most chivalric way of defining error. In footnotes to Minot's text, Brewster corrected what he gently called the author's "marked naivete." When Minot stated that the long-billed marsh wren was never heard to sing, Brewster drops in an asterisked demurrer that it is "really a conspicuous and persistent" singer. When Minot accuses the loggerhead shrike of cruelty and "murder in the first degree" for its habit of impaling its prey on some sharp object, Brewster says that he sees no more cruelty in this than in man's hanging up poultry in a butcher shop.

Brewster's friendly hand was extended, while he was at the museum, to an aging Indian birder named Simon Pokagon, chief of the Pottawattamie tribe of Michigan, who asked Brewster if he would be interested in an article he had written on the bluebird. His rate, he informed Brewster, was one cent a word. Son of the chief who had sold the federal government the tribal lands on which Chicago was built, Pokagon was educated at Jesuit schools and Oberlin and spent much of his life trying to get the government to pay his tribe for the land it had bought (not until 1896 did the Supreme Court finally order the government to make good on its contract).

As the most eminent birder of his race, Pokagon wrote for ornithological journals as well as for *Harper's, The Review of Reviews* and *The Chatauquan.* One subject was "Kegon Penay-segant Win-ge-see," the osprey. To study it, Pokagon set up his wigwam beside a water lily lake, trimmed his clothes with sprays of flowers and, while waiting, listened to the "wild vespers of unnumbered whip-poor-wills" as the "feathered warblers of the wild opened the matinees of love and gratitude." A "clean industrious bird," he called the osprey, "living almost entirely on fresh fish which it obtains through its own skill and labors," a far better bird than the admired eagle which steals the osprey's catch and, when it cannot do this, is content to feed on "putrid meat."

The chief had clearly studied the white man's way of writing about nature and adopted it with panache. He has been cited as a reliable authority on the passenger pigeon. When the birds nested and mated, Pokagon wrote, they created "the greatest tumult. I tried to understand their strange language and why they all chatted in concert . . . uttering to their mates those strange bell-like wooing notes which I had mistaken for the ringing of bells in the distance."

Distracted from birds by his tribal duties, the chief visited Lincoln in the White House trying to get the payments owed his people. He smoked a peace pipe at the battlefront with General Grant, who gave Pokagon a cigar and thanked him for having furnished Indian soldiers to the Union army but could do nothing about money. Pokagon was still trying thirty years later at the Chicago world's fair, where he was the hero of Chicago Day, ringing the new replica of the Liberty Bell, and, as a historian of the event wrote, addressing "the assembled thousands on behalf of his people. At the close of his address, a grand rush was made by the eager crowd for the old man, with whom he shook hands until his arms gave out."

After Brewster had bought his article for $6.25, Pokagon offered him two copies of "The Redman's Greeting," printed on birch bark, for one dollar with a photograph of the chief (usually twenty-five cents) thrown in free. Brewster's kindly correspondence ended soon after with a letter from Pokagon's son saying that his father had suddenly died, just as his autobiographical work, *Queen of the Woods*, was being published. Would Mr. Brewster like to purchase a copy?

In 1891 Brewster bought three hundred acres of land in Concord on a spot that Thoreau had loved and called it "October Farm," the title of one of his posthumously published journals. All the birders of his and later generations came to watch birds with him and his ever-present dog, Timmie. When he had fallen very ill in 1918, Brewster heard that Timmie, too old to know where he was, had been run over in the middle of a road and killed. He dreamed, Brewster wrote in his journal, that he himself had crossed the Styx and found Timmie waiting there to greet him. Not too long after, he followed Timmie, having left instructions that his grave be marked: "For lo, the Winter is passed, the rain is over and gone, the time of the singing of the birds is come."

Meanwhile the Nuttall Club had served a significant purpose for American birding. In 1876 it began publishing a bulletin, and ornithologists and bird watchers everywhere were delighted to have a place to print their findings. Although natural history societies in several cities published journals that were, in good part, concerned with birds, the Nuttall *Bulletin* was the first publication devoted entirely to them. Its contributors and editors—Spencer Fullerton Baird was one—set new standards for both observing and writing about birds, demanding accuracy and thoroughness and making tough judgments on the often haphazard, unverified reporting that plagued much ornithological writing. When it published local lists, which were to become a prime source for the developing science, the *Bulletin* invited experts to evaluate them. After one *Bulletin* reviewer complained that a "List of Birds of Central New York" had given no dates, localities or authorities for its facts, the author confessed that he had no grounds for some thirty of his entries and had taken another twenty from an already published book.

This hard-eyed approach also brought a kind of testiness that continued to pervade birding discussions. James G. Cooper sharply corrected Brewster on the nesting habits of California purple finches and Dr. Thomas Brewer corrected an Elliott Coues correction of a Brewer statement on the northern shrike. For all his seniority among birders, Brewer found himself in rough company at the *Bulletin*. When a reviewer found fault with his *Birds of New England* for not being exact enough, Brewer flared up at what he called "insinuations both gratuitous and unjust." The reviewer, a respected birder named H. A. Purdie, responded mildly that his efforts to correct errors were "not very graciously received." This did not soften Brewer. "When I ask for bread," he retorted, "he gives me a stone. I ask for facts and he gives me only opinions. Here all controversy on my part ends."

The editors unbent somewhat for the granddaughter of America's most famous birder, Maria Audubon, who wrote about an albino robin that fed on her lawn. One morning she found it "in deadly combat with a mole" which had it "firmly by the wing." Miss Audubon went out, freed the bird and chased the mole away. She could imagine no reason for the fight: "we knew that the mole had not climbed a tree and we had never heard of a robin eating a mole." But next morning

on the lawn "lay the mole and the robin, beautiful in death, to use
poetic license for they really looked very unpleasant . . . the robin very
much ruffled as to plumage and bloody about the throat and under
the right wing; the mole with the glossy coat all the wrong way and
severely pecked about the head and throat. There was no life in
either."

After several years, it became evident that the club was simply a
local manifestation of a rapidly spreading interest in birding, which
the club itself had helped create and enhance. Its corresponding
members were making the club an embryonic national society, particularly by their work as contributors to and editors of the *Bulletin.* In
1883 Brewster and others proposed to form an American Ornithologists' Union with a wide membership. They invited an interested
group and Brewster drew up an agenda assuming that he would
automatically become president. But when the founding group met,
Elliott Coues was chosen as temporary chairman, Eugene Bicknell of
New York as secretary. The copy of Brewster's original agenda, now
in the Union's archives, has a little note in Brewster's hand: "Exit
W.B."

He did not exit and the disappointment did not diminish his interest in the American Ornithologists' Union or his influence on it. He
continued, meanwhile, as perpetual president of the Nuttall Club—
and "The Nutt" continues an active life today. The AOU quickly
became the national organization for American ornithology. The Nuttall Club generously gave the Union all rights to its *Bulletin,* its list of
subscribers, its good will and even its knowing editor, Joel Asaph
Allen. Since the tie that would bind the AOU membership together
would be its journal, there was considerable and often contentious
discussion over what to call it. By tradition, birding journals have been
named after birds—*Ibis* in England, *Alauda* (lark) in France, *Emu* in
Australia. Largely at Coues' insistence—he was a most insistent man
—the AOU chose *Auk* as the title. This was greeted derisively by many
members who, as the editors reported it, complained that "Auk is an
awkward name" and that "the auk is already defunct and that The Auk
is likely to follow suit."

The name remained and AOU went about its business, which was
to advance science, protect birds, collect material, acquire a library,
be a central point for American ornithology. It accomplished all these
aims with a good deal of sense and vision—and argument. In fact, it
had barely fledged when it flew into its first big controversy.

4

The Great Sparrow War

At the first meeting of the American Ornithologists' Union in 1883, the agenda included discussions of nomenclature, bird migration, bird anatomy and "the eligibility or ineligibility of the European house sparrow in America," i.e., should the house sparrow be granted the right to be called an American bird?

To today's birders, this seems an odd question because the house, or English, sparrow (*Passer domesticus*) is the most ubiquitous bird in the country, ever-present everywhere—city and seashore, farm and desert, plain and mountain. When the question was posed, however, it was an avian upstart, a recent immigrant whose brash takeover of the habitats of native birds had angrily divided the ornithological community. In Boston, it started what has been known as the Great English Sparrow War and later on, throughout the country, it brought on the most concentrated bird watching America had ever known.

It seems too unassuming a bird to be a *casus belli.* It is small, drab, a poor singer, not at all choosy about where it lives. Tolerant of humankind, it has had an easy time making itself at home everywhere in the world except in the nomenclature of ornithology. For one thing, though it has been commonly called English sparrow, it is not English. It originated, probably, in the Middle East and had to come across a continent to settle in England, and get its vernacular name. For another thing, for a long while it was considered to be not a sparrow but a weaver finch, which further orphaned it for a weaver finch is not, taxonomically, a true finch (and, moreover, is more correctly called a weaver bird). It was only a few years ago that the English sparrow was given its own family. Separated from the weaver bird family, it was put into the Passeridae. It is not unusual for birds to be shunted from one classification to another, but the house sparrow is a persistent bird and is likely to stay where it is. It has to share its name, in America, with a great many other birds called sparrows which are themselves taxonomic interlopers. The song sparrow, tree sparrow, etc., are not sparrows or Passeridae but Fringillidae related to cardinals and buntings.

This long rejection by the classifiers perhaps reflects the more general opinion of *Passer domesticus,* which is considered such a pariah that it is one of only a handful of songbirds not protected by federal conservation laws. Anthropomorphic birders have ventured the opinion that just because it is such a taxonomic outcast, *Passer domesticus* has decided to take over the world in which it seems so unwelcome. Some twenty thousand years ago it had broken out of its home in the Middle East, pushed its way in all directions, and by 1800 was well established everywhere in Europe and parts of Asia. Today it flies clear around the globe and is seen on every continent except for Antarctica.

In 1853, it was "successfully" introduced into America—ornithologists used to put those quotation marks around "successfully" to dissociate themselves from any implication that they thought the introduction was a good thing. An earlier attempt to colonize the birds in the U.S. had failed, but this time they made themselves at home in the Green-Wood Cemetery in Brooklyn. They had been brought in because they had the reputation of being busy breeders and voracious eaters of insects and it was hoped they would end a plague of cankerworms and spanworms that were eating the leaves of American trees. They lived up to their reputation as breeders but not as insect eaters, turning out to be largely vegetarian, for though they did eat some destructive insects, they preferred the undigested grain found in horse droppings.

Nevertheless every American city seemed to feel it had to have English sparrows. It was a sign of progress, someone observed, like installing illuminating gas. Soon they had been introduced—or had introduced themselves—into cities from Portland, Maine, to Galveston, Texas. Within a couple of decades, however, the English sparrows were being looked on as a nuisance and even a menace. While they did eat cankerworms and spanworms, they also usurped the nesting places of insect-eating native birds and this brought on an epidemic of tussock moths. Sparrows not only disdained the moths but drove away the birds that normally ate them.

The sparrows were the tough new kids on the block. Belligerent, greedy and prolific, they soon outnumbered the original inhabitants, taking over their nesting cavities and chasing bluebirds and martins from parks and backyards. People began to object to what someone called "their prompt and confident manner of taking possession of new territory, their rank hoodlumism." After a while, the sparrows' spread was followed like some kind of black plague. By the early 1870s, they were in every state east of the Mississippi and someone calculated that in Illinois there was one sparrow for every three human beings. In 1875, one was reported in Utah and another in San Francisco. They were tracked to Tucson and Tombstone. A California postman saw a single one at the Santa Fe depot in Buena Vista and ten years later reported six large colonies of them along his rural route. They became a cause of local conflicts, enemies trapping them by day and supporters sneaking up in the dark to set them free.

Nowhere did they engender so much bitterness as in Boston, where the arguments over the abrasive birds were aggravated by a number of abrasive birders. Charles Pickering, at the Boston Society of Natural History in 1867, was first to call the alarm over the persecution of native birds by these intruders. A scholarly man, he went back into history and found that when cuneiform writing was invented by the Sumerians about 3000 B.C. "the sparrow was selected for the hieroglyphic character meaning 'enemy.' " In the early 1800s, a French naturalist had stated that "sparrows are impudent parasites" and in England the controversy reached into the peerage, bringing from Lord Lilford the considered conclusion that the sparrows did "decidedly more harm than good." But when an opinion was solicited from the duke of Wellington's gardener, he replied that though they were destructive of the duke's green peas, he felt that on the whole they were "of very great advantage to gardeners."

The Boston partisans denounced both the birds and each other. Elliott Coues attacked the sparrow as "a nuisance without a redeeming quality." Thomas Brewer, who led the defense, responded by suggesting that Coues was a liar. Henry Ward Beecher, the great Unitarian preacher, came into the fight by accusing Coues of "treason" for having "incited a riot" against the sparrow, and Henry Bergh, founder of the American Society for the Prevention of Cruelty to Animals, called Coues a murderer.

At a meeting of the Nuttall Club, Theodore Roosevelt, at that time a student of natural history at Harvard, reported that in Egypt, where he had spent some time with his family, he had seen farmers shooting the sparrows that were feeding in the grain fields. He himself had observed the sparrows, in and around New York, assaulting song sparrows and snowbirds (juncos), driving purple martins from their homes and once actually mobbing and killing a yellow-bellied woodpecker (sapsucker). Farmers in the Hudson valley, he added, shot them for eating the buds on their fruit trees. Dr. Brewer led a counterattack, sneering at Roosevelt for his youth. A letter apparently written by Brewer referred to Roosevelt as "sophomoric" (literally true since Roosevelt was in his second year at college) and accused him of drawing "upon a vivid imagination for his facts. He tells the world when he was in Egypt—at what age he does not tell . . ." Actually Roosevelt was only twelve when he was in Egypt but was already an accomplished field naturalist.

In the end, the war was a standoff. Though the opponents of the sparrow came out best in the debates, the defenders had their way in the field. When several shrikes, attracted to the Boston Commons by the easy supply of birds, began to decimate the sparrow population, the misguided mayor went to the rescue by sending a park employee out to shoot the shrikes. Some years later, the American Society of Bird Restorers, declaring that the sparrow had evicted native birds from the Commons and the Public Gardens, demanded that their "avian ghettos" be destroyed. This time the mayor sent squads of men who pulled down four thousand nests, broke thousands of eggs and blocked five thousand nesting holes. But when the Humane Society protested, the mayor called off his men.

More significantly for American birding, the sparrow wars set off the first exercise in national bird watching and got thousands of Americans to pay thoughtful attention to their birds. The U.S. Department of Agriculture was assigned to discover whether the bird was a bane or a benefit to American farmers. In a pioneering effort of both organized birding and economic ornithology, Walter B. Barrows of the department sent out a questionnaire in 1886 to five thousand people around the country asking a set of detailed questions about the sparrow. By then the sparrows were a matter of such concern and passion to Americans that he received an amazing thirty-three hundred answers. The results of this epic bird watch were published in 1889.

From 1855 to 1870, Barrows reported, there was no animus towards the sparrow in America except from "intelligent naturalists" and from some European immigrants who warned that the bird had been a pest back home. In some parts of Germany, for example, farmers were required by law to shoot them and meet a quota of carcasses every year. Too busy for bird shooting, many farmers hired professional hunters and let these mercenaries meet the quotas. Still, Barrows noted, sparrows were welcomed by many immigrants to America for whom their chirpings were pleasant reminders of the homeland. The birds were imported, however, to eat insects, not to promote nostalgia. In the 1860s and 1870s, he reported, there was "a veritable sparrow boom," which pushed prices so high that people joined together in groups to import them. City councils everywhere bought the sparrows as pest killers and the investment seemed justified since they multiplied so rapidly. Soon it was not necessary to pay for them. The sparrows would fly into railroad grain cars and ride along, eating as they went. Shooed out by the trainmen, they would take up residence wherever they landed, finding their way to grain fields, feed stores and to city streets with horse droppings.

By the late 1880s, the enthusiasm for the bird had largely passed. P. Vanburgh of New Lexington, Kentucky, indignantly filling out his questionnaire, reported that sparrows pecked holes in the fruit on his apple trees. David C. Voorhees of Blawenberg, New Jersey, complained that the bird "attacks and devours grapes greedily," and they stripped H. C. Huff's farm in Meriden, Connecticut, of a hundred sunflowers in two days. They broke Charles Clapp's grape vines in Albion, Indiana, and injured peach blossoms in Albany, Georgia. George T. Welch of Passaic, New Jersey, accused them of "ingratitude": after he had fed them all winter and spring, they tore the petals from his crocuses "in pure wantonness." They are "hardy, prolific, aggressive . . . possessed of more than ordinary cunning," reported John F. T. Edwards of Ironton, Missouri, and J. B. Stokton in Toronto, Kansas, said that "all summer long there seemed to be newly hatched birds in the nest." Colonel C. J. Seldon of Memphis, Tennessee, ruefully recalled that three pairs had been introduced into the city in 1871 and fifteen years later "they infest city and suburb."

The enormity of their reported crimes against man and nature was appalling. They were accused of robbery, murder, civic disorder, criminal neglect, even arson. They were said to molest bluebirds, usurp the nesting boxes of purple martins, steal eggs from wrens and swallows, take worms away from robins. In Washington, D.C., their droppings made park benches unsittable and their nests clogged building drains. In Albany, New York, J. A. Lintner saw the woodbine on buildings at the corner of Broadway and Spencer streets alive with sparrows while the nearby maples were crawling with unmolested caterpillars. In Pottsville, Pennsylvania, sparrows lined their nests with cotton waste, and sparks from iron mills, landing in the nests, started numerous fires.

Barrows did find, among the replies to his questionnaires, a few good words for *Passer domesticus.* Judge John C. Ferris of Nashville, Tennessee, called them "a blessing to any community that raises vegetables." Arthur Thatcher of Jerseyville, Illinois, credited them with saving his strawberries by picking white millers off the leaves, and F. T. Jenks of Barrington, Rhode Island, was grateful to them for eating up an infestation of aphids and rescuing his peas. Robert B. Roosevelt of New York City, differing with his nephew Theodore, said that while robins took his cherries, sparrows have taken "never a single one." A Roosevelt neighbor, Eugene Schiefflin, encouraged the sparrows to feed with his chickens in his Twenty-ninth Street backyard, cherishing them for eating "the measuring worm from which a sensitive lady shrinks in disgust." Mary Kouwenhoven of Brooklyn praised the sparrows for their bravery in standing up to an unkind world where people hate them, boys stone them and cats eat them. The birds, she went on, wear "plain sensible clothes and Mrs. Sparrow's husband is always good to her."

Still, all in all, Barrows' watchers damned *Passer domesticus.* Among those who raised fruits and vegetables, for example, 422 were against the sparrow and 279 were for it, and even many of the latter had reservations. Answering Barrows' carefully considered questions about their attitudes towards birds, 79 admitted that they generally disliked all birds, while 837 specifically disliked English sparrows.

The report accelerated a movement to get rid of the sparrows. Eight states removed them from their lists of protected birds and local protective ordinances were ignored. In Indianapolis, T. W. Hill trapped forty thousand sparrows but said they were still superabundant. The council of the town of Oregon, Missouri, provided free gunpowder to sparrow shooters. In Stoughton, Wisconsin, hoses were turned on their nests. In Painted Post, New York, A. J. Wood fed them strychnine, and in Providence, Rhode Island, Eli Blake did his bit by taking 995 eggs from the ivy on St. Stephen's Church. In

Albany, New York, a game dealer served both the public good and his own pocketbook by selling sparrows at twenty-five cents a pair as "reed birds," or bobolinks, which were considered delicacies: "They make excellent pot pies," he advertised, "and are much superior to quail." He sold seventeen hundred pairs in one week. The Department of Agriculture recommended their use as food because of "their nutritious value and as a means of reducing their numbers."

The state of Ohio offered a bounty for the birds—ten cents a dozen—but gave up after a while when someone calculated how much the scheme was likely to cost. Some forty million birds might be killed the first year, it was estimated, at the modest cost of only $400,000. But success would boost the bill. As the projected decrease in population made killing less easy, hunters would want more pay per bird and the state might face a total bill of some $11,000,000 with the prospect that, even if most of Ohio's sparrows were exterminated, new generations would keep flying in over the border. Bermuda, a territory much easier to defend, had tried the bounty system and, after spending £800, had given it up as a lost cause. In fact, no place seems to have succeeded in getting rid of the birds unless one counts May Island off the coast of Scotland, where the one local pair died after the resident horse left for the winter, and the island of Lundy in Bristol Channel, where the sparrows left after all the human inhabitants did. Natural disasters were no help. In the great New York blizzard of 1888 thousands of sparrows froze to death, with only a temporary effect. After the San Francisco earthquake and fire of 1906 they were observed "rebuilding as assiduously as ever."

If insults could kill, the bird would long since have been exterminated. Few birds have achieved such a bad name among birders. William Leon Dawson, a respected California birder, declared that "without question the most deplorable event in the history of ornithology was the introduction of the English sparrow." One bird watcher, after counting a pair copulating fourteen times in succession with five-second pauses between sexual acts, accused them of being immorally oversexed, obsessed by "furor amatorius, the male suffering from satyriasis and the female from nymphomania." Bird journals, dedicated to loving all feathered creatures, fulminated that the sparrow's "introduction was an overwhelming catastrophe . . . as if some foul odor had forever defiled the fragrance of our fields and woods."

In all the hullabaloo, there were a few who kept birding's faith: that if man ever has trouble with a bird it is man's fault, not the bird's. The

English sparrow simply did what any normal bird would do: tried to establish itself in a new habitat. Since it has, among other assets, a bigger brain per body-ounce than most birds, the sparrow is more efficient at adapting and establishing itself. Introducing an alien species is always a risky matter. The European starling, innocently brought into the United States from England because, like the sparrow, it was supposed to destroy insects, has become as big a pest. Asian birds, like the crested mynah, brought into Hawaii, have almost completely driven out a number of native species. Some introductions have been benign. The pheasant, for example, introduced from China via Hungary, has become an agreeable resident. So has the elegant mute swan. European goldfinches were brought in to Long Island and survived for decades until the 1950s, when a bulldozer tore up their last habitat.

The established populations of the English sparrow in the United States, meanwhile, have been stabilized, not by insult or mortal injury but by the coming of the automobile. The easy pickings from horse droppings have vanished, the city feed and grain stores have gone and the sparrow population explosions have ceased. Its dominance in eastern cities has been challenged by an immigrant from the American West, the house finch, which has settled and spread in the East and proved aggressive enough to drive sparrows from some of their urban strongholds. It is a prettier bird than *Passer domesticus,* has a sweeter song and gets along better with most other birds.

The wars against the sparrow have moved to far-off places. New Zealand, which first welcomed them, later set bounties on them, with the usual lack of success. In the 1950s, China launched its own sparrow war. Children, students and soldiers beat gongs and fired guns day and night without stop to allow the sparrows no rest. After three days the birds fell down from exhaustion and were disposed of—though not altogether exterminated, of course.

Back at the American Ornithologists' Union, the Council in 1889 decided that *Passer domesticus* was an ineligible species and would not appear as a North American species on the official lists. But, as might be expected, the sparrow survived this excommunication, pushing its way in as an "introduced" species but not establishing itself in the AOU's official *Check-list of North American Birds* until 1931, eligible at long last.

The feuds stirred up in the Great English Sparrow War lasted for decades. Elliott Coues would not let even Thomas Brewer's ghost rest. Long after the old birder had died, Coues was still writing that Brewer had "made a fool of himself" over the birds. "The harm he did," Coues went on, "was incalculable and his name deserves to be stigmatized as long as there is a sparrow left in the United States to shriek *Brewer! Brewer! Brewer!*"

5

The Prodigious Troublemaker

In attacking Dr. Brewer so relentlessly, Elliott Coues, the most prodigious of all American ornithologists, was turning against a man whom he had once listened to respectfully as a counsellor and called a "kind friend." But Coues' life was full of inexplicable switches, of unneeded wrangles, of infidelities to his wife and friends and colleagues, and even to science. He was, as a member of the army medical corps, one of Baird's best military birders. In the dedication of one of his major works, he called Baird "Nestor of American Ornithologists" and named his son and also a sandpiper after him. Yet when Baird refused, wisely, to give Coues a post he had asked for, Coues slandered his mentor, accusing him of being afraid to have any rival around him. Coues collaborated happily and brilliantly with other ornithologists, yet called them "liars" and "cads" when they occasionally measured their praise of him. The most demanding of scientists, he insisted on hard proof of all observations. Yet, with the same assurance he displayed in describing the birds he saw, he described the ghosts that came to call on him when he took his afternoon naps.

In the course of his life, he managed to turn against almost everything he cared for. But not birds—not since that day in his childhood when the sight of a red bird marked him for life. "The first bird that ever arrested my attention," he once recalled, "was a scarlet tanager which flamed through the green foliage like a vision. The fiery trail of a meteor could not have left a more indelible impression. I verily believe the sight of that tanager determined to some extent the particular bent of my mind for ornithology."

The bent of his mind was also determined by the characters of his parents: the sensitivity of his observant mother, who wrote lovingly about nature and once took a census of the orioles nesting on their street in Portsmouth, New Hampshire (there were seventeen); and the boldness and perversity of his father, a shipowner who, though he named one of his fleet the *Isaac Newton,* spent years trying to refute Newton's laws of gravity. This hereditary mix produced in Elliott Coues a man of superb perceptions, exacting procedures and intemperate conclusions.

Like Spencer Baird, he showed his ornithological promise when very young and Baird himself recognized it. The two met after the Coues family had moved to Washington in 1854. Baird invited young Elliott to watch him prepare bird skins, gave him some of the Smithsonian's leftover specimens and in 1860, when Coues was only seventeen, paid his expenses for a birding trip to Labrador. Coues repaid Baird by bringing back 185 bird skins and nine sets of eggs and by writing several useful papers on his trip. Four years later, having studied medicine and entered the army medical corps, Coues joined the ranks of Baird's soldier-scientists. At Fort Whipple, Arizona, Lieutenant Coues collected birds busily and complained endlessly: that the Apaches made the place unsafe for birding excursions; that he had to shoot at Indians instead of at birds; that he had to take part in what he called "the massacre" of one tribe. But he made profitable field trips on a mule he named Jenny Lind, for its musical bray, and by the time he returned East he had shipped dozens of boxes, trunks and crates of specimens, including 250 species of birds, to Baird, and brought with him material for a book on the birds of Arizona. Having written three thousand pages, he destroyed the manuscript after a friend made some disparaging remarks about it. This was just as well because it cleared the way for his first significant work, *Key to North American Birds,* one of the handful of books that have led birding into new grounds.

The purpose of his *Key,* Coues wrote in a letter to Baird, was to enable "anyone without the slightest knowledge of ornithology to identify any specimen in a few seconds. It is, so far as I know, unique in our science. I have made my wife test it and without knowing a tarsus from a tail, hardly, she has in every instance given the scientific name of the specimen." The *Key* did this by noting general characteristics of a bird which would lead the user to more specific characteristics and thence to exact identification. He gave an example of what someone like Mrs. Coues would go through. "We have in hand," he wrote, "a little black and white spotted bird which we often see climbing about our fruit trees boring holes in the bark . . ." and went on to give clues to the bird's identity: toes (four, two being jointed), the tail (twelve stiff feathers), the back (no transverse color bars or white streak), length (less than seven inches), the upper mandible (ridged). One clue led to another until the genus *Picus* was suggested. Turning to the *Picus* section of the *Key,* Mrs. Coues would proceed through white-headed woodpecker, red-cockaded woodpecker, Texas woodpecker, hairy woodpecker (very close but too long) and finally to the answer. "It is a downy woodpecker, *Picus pubescens*!," the *Key* exclaims.

Of course, Mrs. Coues would have had to know that the mandible is part of a bird's beak and would have needed a bird specimen before her to examine it closely—and the actual procedure was far more laborious than this synopsis makes it sound. And it might have been, moreover, that Coues found the downy woodpecker too difficult an example because in the next edition of the *Key* he discarded *Picus pubescens* and substituted *Turdus migratorius,* the familiar robin and the nearest thing to an identification set-up he could have found.

Still, nothing quite like the *Key* had ever been produced before. Previous bird books, like Wilson's or Audubon's, were loosely organized sequences of descriptions. Identifications were usually made by ploughing haphazardly through the pages and illustrations until a likely candidate showed itself. Baird's ground-breaking *Birds of North America* was of great use but largely for those who knew or were willing to learn their way around taxonomy and nomenclature. The *Key* was a shortcut for the relatively unsophisticated. Published in 1872, it was praised by ornithologists and quickly sold out its two thousand copies.

Coues at this time was at Fort McHenry in Baltimore, where he spent more time on ornithology than on medical duties, writing scores of papers and in 1874 publishing his *Field Ornithology, Comprising a Manual of Instruction for Procuring, Preparing and Preserving Birds, and a Check List of North American Birds.* The manual was a how-to guide for birders, which after poetically answering the question Where will you go to look for birds? ("some come about your doorstep unasked . . . others spring up before you like the flowers that enticed Proserpine . . . their music answers the sighs of the tree tops") submits a prosy list of "Implements for Collecting: The double barrelled shotgun is your main reliance. Get the best one you can afford for your particular purpose which is the destruction of small birds with the least possible damage to their plumage. Begin by shooting every bird you can"—coupling this sad destruction, however, with the closest observations upon habits. Pierce the bird's brain with a knife to kill it quickly. Record, label and measure carefully and promptly, noting sex, age and contents of stomach. Don't neglect the plainer females, just to get the showier males. Fifty birds shot is a good day's work. "I am satisfied," he said, "to average a dozen a day." Don't be queasy about taking eggs: "Robbing birds' nests is cruel but not nearly so cruel as shooting." Birders reading this today, appalled by such seemingly callous instruction, should remember that, in those days, identifying birds exactly meant having specimens not in the eye's memory or on a film, but in the hand to study and prove that this was what the bird watcher really saw.

The "Check List" that made up most of Coues' volume is of more lasting importance. Largely concerned with classifying and naming, it brought Baird's work up to date and untangled many confusions. It set a precedent by giving prominence to subspecies of birds, a matter many ornithologists studiously avoided as unnecessary and even undesirable—"feather splitting," they called it. Coues' "Check List" was an indispensable tool and became the basis for the subsequent check lists, issued periodically by the American Ornithologists' Union, which is the final authority on American birds.

Coues' next assignment, again promoted by Baird, was as naturalist on a commission settling the exact course of the forty-ninth parallel boundary between the United States and Canada. Here he augmented his scientific reputation by his observations on the reason northwestern birds were paler in plumage than others in the country—the low annual rainfall made the countryside dry and drab and the birds' protective coloration adapted them to the environment. He also enhanced his reputation for being ornery by his disputes with the expedition's commander, Major Marcus Reno, who achieved military notoriety later by his actions at the battle of Little Big Horn. Reno and Coues disagreed over Coues' duties—Coues haughtily insisted that he was there as a naturalist, not as a doctor to treat soldiers, and challenged the major to a duel. It never took place, of course. Coues did ingratiate himself with other officers of the expedition by donating some of his day's scientific collection to the company mess. "I always thought," he said, speaking of the green-winged teal, "that it looked better" at the table "than it did in my collecting chest."

Posted to Washington, Coues completed his *Birds of the Northwest* in 1874 and *Birds of the Colorado Valley* in 1878. Based in good part on the work of other naturalists attached to army expeditions, they were enhanced by Coues' learning and by his gift for both close observation and evocative description. The song of the canyon wren, he wrote,

> a curious little animated music-box, is perfectly simple. It is merely a succession of single whistling notes, each separate and distinct, beginning as high in the scale as the bird can reach, and regularly descending the gamut as long as the bird's breath holds out, or until it reaches the lowest note the bird is capable of striking. These notes are loud, clear, and of a peculiarly resonant quality; they are uttered with startling emphasis.

The black-and-white warbler has a "queer screeping song," he wrote, coining a word and a nice piece of birding onomatopoeia. The prairie warbler sounds "like the plaints of a mouse with a toothache."

His first entry in *Birds of the Northwest* regretted that he had not seen a single Missouri skylark (now called Sprague's pipit), though Audubon had reported them as abundant. In a postscript, added after the book was ready to be printed, Coues was the exultant watcher. "Since I penned the foregoing last year," he wrote, "my wishes have been satisfied in the most satisfactory manner." He had seen flocks of skylarks and their "wonderful soaring action, their inimitable matchless song," delighted him. "Lost to view in the blue ether," he rhapsodized, it "sends back to earth a song of gladness to cheer the weary, give hope to the disheartened and turn the most indifferent, for the moment at least, from sordid thoughts. No other bird music heard in our land compares to the wonderful strains of this songster," though, he added, getting back to earth himself, they cease "when the inspiration of the love season is over."

Although both the *Northwest* and *Colorado* books consisted basically of life histories, they went beyond that to include treatises on synonymy (i.e., all the names a bird has ever been given), and a bibliography. This latter was, in effect, Coues' entrance into a field in which he was to distinguish himself. It testified to the willingness of this free-wheeling scientist to take on the driest and most tedious of scientific chores. He had read just about everything anybody ever wrote about American birds and his lists of references are awesome. Over the years, he established ornithological bibliography as a necessary study, undertaking a mammoth "Universal Bibliography of Ornithology" that went back to Aristotle. For all his erudition, efficiency and ambition he found the task too much for him and he quit after completing three installments relating to American birds and a fourth dealing with British publications. This last so impressed English scientists that several dozen of them, including Darwin, Wallace and Huxley, petitioned the U.S. War Department to give Coues a leave of absence to go to Europe and complete his "Universal Bibliography." "It takes a sort of inspired idiot to be a good bibliographer," Coues said, and when he tried to get others to take over the work he could not finish, he found no one inspired or idiotic enough to do it. Among the thousands of titles he listed, incidentally, were more than two hundred by Coues himself.

Not content with science, Coues ventured into poetry, rather awkwardly. "Have you listened to the carol of the bluebird in the spring?" he wrote. "Has her gush of molten melody been not poured forth in vain?" He was more genuinely poetic when he was not trying to be and from time to time struck upon some astonishing images: "The song of the birds is the closest approach, in animate nature, to the ringing of the hydrogen bells in the physics of light."

A busy and contented time in Washington was ended by Coues' misbehavior. After years as a pampered member of the medical corps, given assignments he liked and plenty of time for his own work, he was brusquely assigned in 1880 to his old post as assistant surgeon in Fort Whipple, Arizona. He stormed at the army and furiously blamed his wife, who, in fact, was almost certainly the cause. Or, more correctly, Coues himself was. Self-centered and volatile in his private life, he had made a hasty early marriage and equally hasty divorce, yet continued for years to arrange hotel trysts with his discarded but still willing ex-wife. His second wife put up with his derelictions—affairs with several women, including the wife of a prominent senator. When her patience ran out, she took what Coues looked on as a terrible revenge, persuading the army to exile him from Washington. With "devilish malignity and ingenuity," he railed, she had done her best to "thwart, hamper and degrade . . . an unjustly, cruelly and terribly wronged man."

The army, obviously irritated by his scandalous behavior, would not listen to Coues' pleas. Whimpering that he had been guilty only "of a disregard of conventionalities," Coues wrote Baird: "For God's sake, Professor, help me out of this ditch where I have been left to lie after being butchered in as foul a plot as was ever gotten up to destroy an innocent if unwary man." After several months in limbo, he managed to separate himself from the army and, shortly, from his wife.

This was 1881. Without the steady income from the army, Coues had to take any work he could get. He had finished editing *New England Bird Life,* a successful book written, on the face of it, by Winfrid A. Stearns but actually mostly by Coues (William Brewster slyly congratulated Stearns on "his choice of an editor"). He wrote about a hundred articles on natural history for an American supplement to the *Encyclopaedia Britannica* and spent eight years as zoological editor for *The Century Dictionary,* contributing some forty thousand definitions. The dictionary was a landmark in American lexicography and Coues' work was of the highest order, as he himself was the first to say. "The greatest issued since Johnson," he said of the dictionary, and of his own work in it, "by far the most important and enduring thus far."

All the while, he was revising his two seminal works, the *Check List of North American Birds* and his *Key to North American Birds.* The *Check List* revision was extensive because of new knowledge and because Coues, who was as close to being ornithologically omniscient as any man ever was, took on the knotty problems of etymology, orthography and orthoepy, that is, of derivation, spelling and pronunciation. Greek and Latin names of birds, he wrote, had in the past been "transferred to ornithology in a wholly arbitrary manner." The species *trochilus* referred in ancient work to the Egyptian plover but modern ornithology has made it a genus of hummingbirds. Little or no reason went into the change, he declared, only "the will of the namer." Any reader trying to "discover erudition, propriety and pertinence in every technical name of a bird will have his patience sorely tried in discovering what lack of learning, point and taste many words imply."

As for orthoepy, he remarked that most names were pronounced with "glaring improprieties" and he proposed to see them "adorned with the charm of scholarly elegance." Correct pronunciation of Greek and Latin is a lost art, he went on, defining the differences between the various methods. He himself came out for what he called the Roman method (for example, *c* pronounced as *k*) and he built his own interpretations on what he felt was the classical approach. This might "succeed in preventing those barbarisms and vulgarisms which constantly come from the lips of some persons of great accomplishment in the science of ornithology."

His etymology went exhaustively into the derivation of bird names, drawing on his own vast well of arcane knowledge. Taking up the European redwing, or *Turdus iliacus*, he says: "*iliacus* relating to the ilia or haunches" or to Troy; "application obvious in neither case." It might be, he surmises, that the name really derives from a thrush that Aristotle called by this name. The pygmy nuthatch draws him off into mythology to point out that the original pygmies "were a race of African dwarfs at war with the cranes." In the case of *Icteria virens*, the yellow-breasted chat, *icterus* means jaundice and the name comes from the fact that a sufferer was supposedly cured by seeing this yellow bird. *Salpinctes obsoletus* (rock wren) comes from *salpinx*, a trumpet, for its loud, ringing call, and *obsoletus* is used in the sense of effaced, the bird being dull in color and self-effacing. Lapsing from good taste, he remarks that *Cardinalis virginiana*, or Virginia cardinal, is "euphemistically" named for Elizabeth I.

His new, improved *Key* had an impact far beyond the scientific. A modern work for birders, it served them as guide, instructor, encourager. "The most outstanding publication of his entire life," it is called by his authoritative biographers Paul Russell Cutright and Michael J. Brodhead. Whole generations found in it the clues they needed and it remained for half a century a work of highest use. Decades after its publication, Ernest Thompson Seton, the famous nature writer, called the *Key* a "blessing . . . the first successful effort to take exact bird knowledge from the museum and give it to the multitude . . . those who love to hold our birds not as skins but as loving friends." And as late as the 1930s, Frank Chapman, whose own guide had become a standard reference work, wrote "there has never been a bird manual comparable to Coues' 'Key' . . . inexhaustible store of information . . . technicalities made attractive and intelligible even to a novice."

Though his colleagues were impressed by Coues' etymological tour de force—a thing "never done in this country before," remarked one admirer—some made scholarly corrections. One declared that Coues was "open to criticism in numerous particulars" and had been guilty of "reductio ad absurdum." In an expectedly caustic response Coues waved this off as "Ornithophilologicalities . . . a ventilation of very little learning on very small provocation," which gave him a feeling of "mixed amusement and consternation," of being "sent down to the foot of the class for missing our lesson and kept in after school to learn it.''

Such exaggerated reactions made it hard for co-workers to keep their balance with Coues. A compelling man, he was charming in company, helpful to his fellows, admiring of other people's work, possessed of ''a vividness, a fire that made his presence felt even when he was silent,'' a contemporary wrote. ''When he arose to speak, the air was charged with possibilities. Every word in the dictionary seemed to be at his command and one had the comfortable assurance that he would choose the right one.'' The rare quality of being both intuitive and systematic made him a first-rate scientist. A scathing wit made him a feared enemy or, for that matter, a feared friend. Although he worked effectively with others in forming the American Ornithologists' Union—he, Brewster and Joel Asaph Allen had sent out the original call for its organization—and in establishing the foundations of modern American ornithology, he went out of his way to differ with the other AOU members. Their ''present attitude,'' he wrote, ''is unfriendly . . . through petty jealousies to which my nature is such a stranger.'' In a marvelous piece of righteous self-deception, he went on: ''I am not a man to give any sign of the hurt excepting a contemptuous indifference . . . a haughty unconcern.'' Whereupon, he called the eminent Robert Ridgway ''a cad'' and accused the honorable C. Hart Merriam of ''cowardice and dishonesty.'' When Baird, asked by Coues to support him in a comprehensive work on American mammals, refused to trust such a huge job to such a troublemaker, Coues turned ungratefully on the ''Nestor of American Ornithologists.'' Baird, he wrote a friend, has a ''settled policy never to have one of his peers or betters about him'' and his ''establishment is simply a hatching house of henchmen who make an honest living by doing what they are told to do.'' Inexcusably, he hinted that dark plots were being hatched at the Smithsonian, although Baird might be ignorant of the unsavory doings, thus making the secretary out to be either corrupt or stupid.

After a while, the ornithological community stopped being surprised at such abandonment of fact or friendship. But it was nonplussed and embarrassed when Coues gave up the demanding rigors of science for the murky areas of mysticism. Members of the Philosophical Society of Washington could hardly believe their ears when, in 1882, he gave a lecture on what he called ''Biogen,'' which he defined as ''soul-stuff,'' not ''ordinary matter'' but the substance of a ''spiritual body.'' He enlarged on this later, declaring that at death the soul obeyed the Darwinian laws of evolution, changing into something higher than the material and living "henceforth in a world of light and life teeming with veritable spiritual existences"—not "supernatural," as it was termed, but "natural."

His spiritualist thinking was reinforced when he met and was intellectually overcome by Mme Helena Blavatsky, an extraordinary woman who gained a great reputation as a medium and who became the founder of Theosophy, a religious system derived mostly from Eastern beliefs. "The greatest woman of this age who is born to redeem her times," Coues called her. He edged himself into the presidency of the Theosophical Society of America and launched an enthusiastic study of spiritualism. "Can Ghosts Be Investigated?" he asked in a published letter, and his answer was that of course they could be. He himself had smelled, seen, heard and touched ghosts, had examined pieces of their nails and hair, and had frequently talked with them. Going on to support mental telepathy, he became the hero of a growing army of believers in the occult.

But, as always, Coues' ambitions brought him trouble. In 1889 he was thrown out of the Theosophical Society, possibly because, in a badly managed power play, he had tried to take over. Turning on Mme Blavatsky, he told the *New York Sun* that she was immoral, corrupt and promiscuous and had used him to give credence to her "claptrap," to support "the fraudulent schemes of a pack of scoundrely vulgarians." Mme Blavatsky promptly sued the *Sun* for libel and, unable to back up his assertions, Coues left the newspaper helpless in its own defense. It abjectly apologized and completely disowned Coues.

Coues also fomented controversy in a more useful cause, women's rights. Though he was a womanizer—until, in 1887, he married a woman of talent and taste and some wealth who brought him happiness and a relief from financial pressures—he had a high regard for women as intellectuals. The greatest scientists, he said, were "men who possessed those peculiarly feminine powers of creative imagination and those intuitions which enabled them to divine truths they had afterward to support and defend with their slower masculine logic." Attacking organized religion for denying women their rights, he managed to offend churches not just with his criticisms but with his language, referring to the Church of England as "that emasculate bastard of the scarlet woman of Rome."

Carrying out his preachings, Coues supported the careers of several women who had great influence on bird watching—Olive Thorne

Miller, Florence Merriam Bailey and Mabel Osgood Wright (who was
his collaborator on several popular birding books). He helped Maria
Audubon edit and publish the journals of her grandfather. Turning
his talents to editing, he resurrected the long-neglected journals of
the Lewis and Clark expedition, restoring much of the material that
was thrown out in the early editions, annotating the text to explain the
zoological and botanical discoveries that made the expedition probably the greatest of all American natural history explorations. He went
on to enhance the reputations of other figures of the past, bringing
out editions of the travels of General Zebulon Montgomery Pike and
the journals of western trappers and hunters. And in a gesture to the
future, he was responsible for establishing the career of the finest
American bird artist since Audubon, Louis Agassiz Fuertes. When still
a student at Cornell, Fuertes showed his bird drawings to Coues, who
commissioned him to illustrate his book *Citizen Bird* and thereby introduced him to the ornithological world.

In his later years, Coues seemed to mellow, mocking his own ego.
"I left Camp Omniscience years ago," he wrote in 1893, "and since
then haven't known more about everything than some other people."
For all his intellectual deviation, he kept his standing as an ornithologist, serving as president of the AOU for three years and agilely
straddling science and quasi-science at the Chicago world's fair by
presiding over both the World Congress on Ornithology and a Psy-
chical Science Congress.

He lived comfortably with the supernatural. "Every afternoon," he
wrote, "I lie down for a brief rest before dinner. Occasionally though
perfectly awake, there comes upon me the peculiar sensation of the
ghost chill. I find my own consciousness projected objectively so that
my conscious self stands out in the room and views my body lying on
the lounge. My conscious self finds itself surrounded by phantoms,
most of them . . . persons who appear to be strangers while others
resemble acquaintances who have long been dead. They seem to walk
about and converse, though not audibly. After a few brief moments,
the spectacle vanishes and I feel myself on the sofa again. It is obvious
if ghosts exist at all, that they must be made of something."

After his death, he announced, he would communicate with his
friends from the beyond. This brought, in 1899, a wry obituary from
the *Maine Ornithological Journal:*

He will be missed especially by those who were so unfortunate
as to displease the Dr. and receive a vigorous shower of sar-

casm from his ever-ready vocabulary of stinging words. The Dr. was a firm believer in ghosts and it remains to be seen if he was as positive or correct in his belief in spirits as he was in matters pertaining to Ornithology. He promised some of his intimate friends before his death to appear to them after his demise. . . . Now they are waiting with no little interest to see if he will keep his agreement.

6

Men of Standing

One of the conveniences of birding is that it can be a solitary occupation. No company is needed. But one of its charms is that company is welcome, adding both to the pleasures of birding and to its productivity. Just one extra pair of eyes and set of experiences geometrically increases the chances of spotting and identifying—and, of course, getting other birders to believe that the bird claimed is the bird seen. Even the most single-minded bird watchers enjoy company. Audubon went out for a couple of bird walks with Alexander Wilson in Kentucky (they spotted sandhill cranes and passenger pigeons) and with Thomas Nuttall (they bagged an olive-sided flycatcher). Spencer Baird went out birding with Thomas Brewer (they collected eggs).

It was not, however, until the Nuttall Ornithological Club set an example that birders began to coalesce into societies dedicated basically to the study of birds. Within a couple of decades after that first gathering in Cambridge men in other cities did something about their urge to get together and talk about birds. The Linnaean Society was founded in New York, the Delaware Valley Ornithological Club in Philadelphia, the embryonic Wilson Club in Massachusetts and in the Midwest, the Audubon Society in New York (briefly) and in Massachusetts (permanently), the Cooper Ornithological Club in California. The American Ornithologists' Union had sprung from the Nuttall Club.

In the beginning and for a long time afterward membership in most of the groups was restricted pretty much to the upper sections of society—to professional and business men with the means and leisure to pursue what was to most of them a serious avocation and to a few a science. The organizers of the Linnaean Society were men of standing in the city and in its early years the roster was studded with names like Vanderbilt, Belmont, several Roosevelts. The men who actually founded the society had high standing in the birding community as well. The founders got together in 1878—on March 7, its precise records state, "at 7 ½ p.m. to take steps toward the formation of a local society of Natural History" but mostly to talk about birds. And what do men who get together to talk about birds talk about?

At the first meeting, Eugene Pintard Bicknell talked about "The Animal and Vegetable Life of the Past Winter." The warm weather had been a mixed blessing to birders, he said. There were fewer of the birds which usually come south with the cold but "an extraordinary abundance" of fall residents which stayed on. At subsequent meetings, members heard monologues and dialogues on the range of juncos, the breeding of crossbills, the secretive habits of woodpeckers. S. D. Osborne's observations on "Peculiar Spotting of Eggs" brought some arguments or, as the meeting's records deftly put it, "excited much remark." The question of the English sparrow brought only mild discussion and the conclusion that the cankerworm had decreased not because of the sparrow, which had been imported to fight against it, but because a parasite had been killing off the worm. The recording secretary made an error in noting the reading of a "List of the Summer Birds of the Adirondacks by Robert Roosevelt Jr. and H. D. Minot." In the minutes, a marginal note in red ink makes a correction: "Robert" is changed to "Theodore." It was an understandable error. Robert Roosevelt, uncle of Theodore, was a well-known nature writer and Theodore only a fledgling naturalist. The society made some amends by electing Theodore, who was away from the city at Harvard, as a corresponding member.

William Dutcher, an insurance man who was to become the first effective head of the Audubon Society, asked his fellow members a question: "Is not the fish crow (*Corvus ossifragus* Wilson) a winter as well as a summer resident at the northern end of its range?" and answered yes. Clinton Hart Merriam, the distinguished zoologist who was elected first president of the society, lent an orotund air to a meeting with his remarks on the Adirondacks. "Its stern Achaean shores were washed by the waves of countless ages, he intoned, "before the undermost strata of the Lower Silurian were deposited upon them entombing many of the Trilobites, Brachiopods and other curious inhabitants of that vast ocean, [leaving] torn pages of fragmentary chapters that constitute but a half told story to excite our imagination and regret."

Then, skipping over the aeons and into present bird business, he spoke about "woodpeckers in the burnt over woods . . . mourning warblers in the brambles . . . the clear mellow whistle of the Peabody bird [white-throated sparrow], the sadder note of the wood pee-wee," giving a homely aside by noting that robins were noisy while eating mountain ash berries but quiet near their nests. Another time, Dr. Merriam told the ghoulish story of a short-tailed shrew and a mouse which were put together in a box: the half-blind shrew could not find the mouse or keep up with its dartings; but it persevered, got the mouse by the ear, nibbled at it, climbed up on its back, finished the ear and went through the skull into the brain, all in fifteen minutes.

Bicknell was one of the most faithful talkers, although his style was not very conversational. In February 1884, speaking of Catskill Mountains summer birds, he remarked that "knowledge is virtually reducible to a recognition of the law of latitudinal equivalent in altitude obtaining in the distribution of terrestrial life qualified by observations scanty and sporadic." Departing from this style and, as naturalists tend to do, from his subject, he complained of the "excessive stupidity" of porcupines: he had grown out of patience with several of them which kept gnawing into his cabin even after their fellows had been shot dead.

The talk often turned to natural disasters. Frank Chapman, a younger member, described the mockingbird's use as a seismograph. During the "memorable South Carolina earthquake" of 1887 the mocker heralded its approach by "peculiar twitterings before the rumble became audible." In the blizzard of 1888 fifty bluebirds took refuge in Paul Babcock's chicken coop while thousands of less prudent birds died. The winter of 1889 was a very good one for "myrtle" (yellow-rumped) warblers in Englewood, New Jersey, because there were lots of bayberries.

When attendance grew sporadic—the June meeting failed to attract a quorum—the society took prompt measures. By a vote of thirteen to two they ordered that a fine of twenty-five cents be levied on anyone missing a meeting, though the twenty-five cents would be remitted "upon receipt of a written valid excuse." If anyone scheduled to read a paper did not show up, the fine was one dollar, no excuses accepted. Absentees could keep in touch with each other through the society's "Proceedings" and "Transactions" and the AOU's *Auk,* though not always amiably. Dr. Charles Conrad Abbott, an old-line birder who welcomed fellow bird watchers to his estate on the Delaware River, was shocked at the inhospitality that greeted his writings. Reviewing a catalog of New Jersey birds, Frank Chapman found "unpardonable errors" and scolded the doctor for having shown "lamentable ignorance of the subject and lack of original investigation." A. A. Allen, reviewing another of Dr. Abbott's books, *A Naturalist's Ramble About Home,* called it "popular and pleasant," then added cryptically that "New Jersey birds, as Dr. Abbott describes them, seem to have a way of their own." Abbott says that bank swallows are the earliest to come and leave but, Allen pointed out, others reported the reverse. Abbott's statement that young owls are still too young to fly in October, Allen said tactfully, "contradicts general belief."

All birders are thin-skinned about criticism. Mention to one that a new species he had proudly added to his life list on a trip to Cape Cod has never been seen outside Alaska and he will take it as an insult more to his integrity than to his eyesight and perhaps stay pointedly away from you on the next bird club walk. Dr. Abbott carried his sensitivity to an extreme. Grudgingly admitting missteps, not errors, he dismissed almost all other birders from his company and lived out his days as an ornithological loner.

Linnaean meetings were above all a place to exchange gossip about local birds. Clinton G. Abbott, no relation to the peevish doctor, reported that fifty goldfinches were wintering on the Columbia University campus. Warblers were plentiful out at Pocantico Hills in the spring of 1891 but 231 birds were killed colliding with the Fire Island lighthouse on a foggy autumn day, 115 of them migrating yellowthroats. Frank Chapman counted four thousand English sparrows bathing in a little pool in Central Park and Dr. William C. Braislin, who made Brooklyn his birding bailiwick, caught a savannah sparrow in Flatbush, then went over to Manhattan and saw thirty-four crossbills. The Carolina wren was slowly moving north and had extended its range up along the Hudson from Manhattan to Piermont. The tufted titmouse, also edging its way north, had been seen on Staten Island but was still timid about crossing the Hudson. A cap-

tive mockingbird had escaped its cage in 1893 and was nesting a
bare hundred feet from the Natural History Museum, where the Linnaean Society met, an exciting event since mockers were very rare in
the North at that time. A few weeks later, the mocker was reported
missing from Manhattan but the next February Frank Johnson reported one wandering at Blithewood, Long Island.

The membership by 1890 had grown to sixty-nine and for the first
time a woman was included in what had been an all-male society.
Mrs. F. E. B. Latham was the pioneer and over the next few years was
joined by other women, including Florence Merriam, Olive Thorne
Miller and Mabel Osgood Wright, all of whom wrote bird books that
were in a few years to delight, inform and convert generations of
children. Women seemed to have been passive members, rarely giving papers. In 1900, Grace Beach, breaking the tradition of female
silence at meetings, announced that she had identified sixty-one species at Dingmans Ferry, Pennsylvania, during the first week of May,
an enviable list for either sex. Mrs. E. G. Foster did some literary bird
watching, scouting the birds mentioned in Tennyson's poems. There
were sixty-three species, she said, and she was able to identify fifty-one
of them.

The society represented the new collective era of ornithology and
bird watching but it had a reminder of an older time in its honorary
member, Daniel Giraud Elliot. Elliot had been born in 1835, and
when he began birding, a bird watcher had very few places to turn to.
"My cousin, Jacob Giraud," he said, "had just entered the close of his
career. Audubon with decayed mental facilities had entered upon the
last year of his life. In Boston neither Allen nor Brewster had appeared. . . . In all the length and breadth of the land there was not
a periodical devoted to the ways of birds."

Elliot himself was devoted to them and expressed his feelings
gracefully in his *The Wildfowl of North America* and *The Shorebirds of North
America.* He was the one who heard the swan song noted in the Prologue of this book.

> I had killed many swan and never heard aught from them at any
> time save the familiar notes. But once when shooting in Cur-
> rituk Sound, a number of swan passed over us at a considerable
> height. We fired at them and one splendid bird was mortally
> hurt. On receiving his wound the wings became fixed and he
> commenced at once his song which was continued until the
> water was reached, nearly half a mile away. I am perfectly

familiar with every note a swan is accustomed to utter but never before nor since have I heard any like those sung by this stricken bird. Most plaintive in character and musical in tone, it sounded at times like the soft running of the notes in an octave, and as the sound was borne to us, mellowed by the distance, we stood astonished and could only exclaim: "We have heard the song of the dying swan."

They recovered the bird, Elliott went on, "and the skin, made into a screen, adorns the drawing room of my friend."

There was, of course, much more to the Linnaean meetings than reminiscence or reports on sightings. The study of the Malecite Indian bird names, cited in a preceding chapter, originally appeared in the *Proceedings*, which grew into a significant repository for ornithological findings. Setting a pattern for its future, the society became a breeding place for watchers and workers—William Dutcher as a leader of the early conservationists and Frank Chapman as a guide to several generations of birders.

In the March 1904 minutes, an interesting address was listed: "Theodore Roosevelt, White House, Washington, D.C." The president, who liked to remark, "Once an ornithologist always an ornithologist," had been a continuing member of the society, though he had made no contribution to its records since that early Adirondacks paper a quarter-century before. A dedicated and expert birder, he was the best ever to occupy the White House, better even than Thomas Jefferson, who was an accomplished naturalist, or than his cousin Franklin, who was a member of the American Ornithologists' Union.

When he was thirteen years old, Roosevelt studied taxidermy at John Bell's famous shop on Broadway at Worth Street—a "promising taxidermist," Bell called him. Young Theodore entered Harvard with the intention of becoming, he said, "a scientific man of the Audubon or Wilson, or Baird or Coues type." Though he took honors in his natural science courses, filled his room with stuffed birds and became a member of the Nuttall Club, he grew dissatisfied with the way Harvard taught natural history—too much laboratory, not enough field study—and he gave up on ornithology as a profession. He remained a birder, and according to Paul Cutright, author of *Theodore Roosevelt, the Naturalist,* was "one of the best field naturalists we have ever had in the United States." His Adirondacks list, produced with his classmate Henry D. Minot, who was Brewster's friend, relied more on bird song than on sighting for his identifications—Roosevelt was near-sighted but extraordinarily sharp-eared. Years later, when he took a famous bird walk in England with Lord Grey, the foreign minister of England (now best remembered for his remark, as war broke out in 1914: "The lamps are going out all over Europe; we shall not see them lit again in our lifetime"), he astonished the Englishman by listening to unfamiliar songs just once and identifying them correctly whenever he heard them again.

While at the White House, the president birded constantly and his letters to his children were filled with bird news. "Mother and I were waked up by the loud singing of a cardinal in a magnolia tree just outside our window," he noted one spring. There were more purple finches coming steadily to the White House grounds than ever before, which pleased him, but he fretted over the difficulties of identifying warblers, especially female. "People looking into the White House grounds and seeing me stare into a tree," Roosevelt once remarked, "no doubt thought me insane," and his wife added, "And as I was always with him, they no doubt thought I was the nurse in charge." The president's sister, Corinne, recalled going for a morning walk with the president and picking up a feather from the ground. He commented: "Very early for a fox sparrow."

When Mrs. Lucy W. Maynard, compiling *Birds of Washington and Vicinity*, asked the president what birds he had seen at the White House, he sat down and in his own hand listed fifty-seven, adding another three dozen he had seen in Rock Creek Park and other parts of the capital. Later, remembering some omissions, he sent Mrs. Maynard a supplementary list and corrected his listing of "bush sparrow." He meant tree sparrow, he said, but noted, quite correctly, that this is a misnomer: the bird is more often seen in a bush than a tree.

Down at Pine Knot, Maryland, which served as a kind of Camp David of its time, Roosevelt in 1907 made a controversial sighting: he said he saw several passenger pigeons, a bird declared extinct in the wild and not verifiably seen since 1898. Arguments still go on today over whether Roosevelt was the last man known to have seen this vanished bird. He could well have been for he was always very cautious about his claims. When he spotted a saw-whet owl at the White House he called in an ornithologist before reporting it—"so that the bird sharps won't elect me to the Ananias Club," he explained.

In the roster of associate members of the American Ornithologists' Union for 1897, halfway down through the *R*'s, just before "Roosevelt. Theodore, Oyster Bay, Queens Co., N.Y." comes "Roosevelt, Franklin D., Hyde Park, New York."

So far as is known, Theodore Roosevelt never went birding with his fellow member and young cousin, Franklin. They could have made, ornithologically at least, a fine symbiotic pair, Theodore sharp of hearing and Franklin sharp of sight. People used to complain to Eleanor Roosevelt that they had been snubbed by her husband, who had gone by them on a street without any notice. She could not explain this, she would reply. "When Franklin had passed people and didn't recognize them," she observed, "he always said he was short sighted. That," she went on, "has always seemed strange to me. For as long as I have known him, Franklin could always point to a bird and tell me what it was."

Like his cousin, Franklin was already watching birds when he was very young. At a German spa with his family when he was seven years old, he met the earl of Liverpool, a devoted birder, who identified the local birds and invited him for a bird walk in England. Though rather shy at that age, Franklin said he "would go anywhere to see those birds" and took the earl up on his offer. Franklin was encouraged in his interest. His grandfather gave him a membership in the American Museum of Natural History, headquarters of the Linnaean Society, as a reward for writing an essay on birds. His father, on Franklin's eleventh birthday, gave him a shotgun on condition that he not shoot any bird during the nesting season. His mother, Sarah, noted that day in her diary: "Franklin went out at 7:45 a.m. with his gun and shot his first crow." He asked that it be mounted and it was. As he kept on collecting birds, he studied taxidermy so he could prepare his own specimens. He "didn't know what he was letting himself in for," Sarah wrote, and "sometimes turned rather green." When the arsenic-dust preservative he had to use made him really ill, the job was turned over to professionals. One day, Sarah recalled, Franklin came in looking for his gun. Why? she asked. A winter wren was sitting on a branch outside and he wanted it. Would it wait for him to come back with his gun? Oh, yes, said Franklin. A few minutes later he came in with the obliging bird.

After a few years he had three hundred specimens, many of them set up in the entry at Hyde Park, where a visitor, politely asking about them, could hear an accounting of Franklin's ornithological feats from his doting mother. The birds were very precious to Franklin and when he was away at school, he would caution his mother to keep an eye on them, especially when young cousins came to visit. "I hope you will seal up my birds before the babies come to stay with you or else I should be afraid of the consequences," he wrote, and nagged about the housemaids who, after dusting the bird cases, always put the birds back in the wrong order. In a letter from Groton in 1889, he wrote: "I had a most delightful experience yesterday." With William Brewster's nephew, he had visited Brewster's museum in Cambridge: "a little place in his yard . . . where he had the finest private collection of American birds in the world."

At Hyde Park he kept a careful record of "Birds shot and stuffed or skinned by F. D. Roosevelt." On February 16, 1896, when he was fourteen, he noted: "Saw 5 pine grosbeaks, one downy woodpecker, chickadees, nuthatch." Another entry: "Below o all day. Saw about 50 pine grosbeaks." In 1896, he was put up for membership in the American Ornithologists' Union. "I am to send about 1 dozen grosbeaks to Museum for local collections," he wrote, proud at having thus entered the ranks of semi-professional collectors. But he had trouble filling the order. Three days later he had seen twenty-five of the birds but had not been able to get a clear shot at any of them.

Like Theodore, who after he had left the U.S. presidency took over the presidency of the Long Island Bird Club, Franklin was a bird watcher all his days. In May 1942, he organized an expedition, inviting Ludlow Griscom, the finest field ornithologist of the time, to come along. The little trip, made in the troubled early months of the war, is one of the most touching episodes in American birding. Up at dawn on a damp, cloudy morning, the president sat wrapped in blankets in an open car from which his Scottie, Fala, who had expectantly jumped in, was evicted. The party stopped at a pond to listen to a whip-poor-will, a catbird and some early-rising sparrows. The president, talking in half whispers, had trouble at first remembering the songs, but as he listened, memory came back, and he began to identify them. Rain cut the excursion short but the president, going back into his other world, must have been content when he signed the party's listing sheet. The party had spotted 108 species, including eighteen different warblers, including a waterthrush and an ovenbird, a cuckoo, nine species of sparrows and an eagle.

Roosevelt's birding is recalled at Hyde Park now by several dozen of his birds that still stand in their glass case—in proper order, it is hoped—and by a green-backed heron, looking as if it had just escaped the case, perching on a cornice nearby. His bird records are cited in the definitive regional work *The Birds of Dutchess County,* written from Maunsel Crosby's notes by Ludlow Griscom.

Roosevelt was responsible for leading Crosby and Griscom to one of the most accomplished birders in the country. Crosby, who owned a large estate called Grasmere, where he held open house for birders, knew just about every bird and watcher in Dutchess County but he had never heard of Arthur Bloomfield until Roosevelt mentioned him. Bloomfield lived virtually next door to Roosevelt on the estate of Colonel Archibald Rogers. The Rogerses' sons were Franklin's boyhood friends and he was constantly over there, going down frequently to the bottom of the garden to see Bloomfield's bird collection. Few other birders visited there because, though he was more knowing about local birds than almost anyone else around, Bloomfield was Colonel Rogers' butler.

Being in service, he was never invited to share his knowledge or join any of the very active local birding groups. So the colonel's butler became a closet ornithologist and a superb one. His employer gave him a little house on the grounds for his specimens and took him on hunting trips where Bloomfield could gather more of them. Following Roosevelt's suggestion, Crosby and Griscom went to see Bloomfield in 1923 and found him "a man of humble means, and limited resources . . . alone and unaided, devoid alike of companionship and instruction," whose only reference was "an antiquated edition of Coues Key." He gave his visitors a "courteous and hospitable" reception and showed them his hundreds of specimens, ten of which Crosby himself had never known to be recorded in Dutchess County.

His specimens were impeccably kept and labeled, his identifications impressively accurate, his notes and diaries full of invaluable data on bird comings and goings. He had records of a saw-whet owl shot in Hyde Park in 1891; a short-eared owl shot in 1909; a horned lark, an irregular visitant, in 1892; and a rare northern pileated woodpecker in 1891. An "eagerly sought" (Griscom's words) Cape May warbler was shot in 1907 and a Bicknell's thrush, a rare transient, in 1923. "In many ways," Griscom wrote, this was "the most important work done in this period" in the area. The colonel's butler got a special gratification from that visit. Mr. Crosby and Mr. Griscom, Bloomfield told his distinguished visitors, were the first people he ever had a chance to talk to who knew as much about birds as he himself did.

7

The Protectors

The Audubon Society's namesake, were he still alive, might have hesitated at endorsing the motto the society long held—"A bird in the bush is worth two in the hand"—and the society's members today wince at some of the entries in John James Audubon's journals, such as: "I call birds few when I shoot less than 100 per day." But the first group to make bird protection a main purpose, and the first to become widely popular, came quite legitimately by its name. John James Audubon was the one figure known to all bird watchers of the time. His work was guide, good reading and useful reference for birders. And his widow was the teacher of the man who formed the first Audubon Society.

When Audubon died in 1851, Lucy Audubon set up a school for children who lived near the estate Audubon had built in upper Manhattan. One of her pupils was George Bird Grinnell, whose family had bought land from Mrs. Audubon, and as might be expected, he grew up to be a bird watcher and, in time, a founder of the American Ornithologists' Union. As editor of *Forest and Stream,* an outdoors magazine, he worried about the extirpation of wild birds and in 1886 called for the formation of a society to protect them. In honor of the artist, he proposed calling it the Audubon Society.

A deluge of enthusiastic answers came and, to "foster the zeal of the thousands" who enrolled—in one year, almost forty thousand—he started *Audubon* magazine. Its first issue contained one of the earliest studies on the usefulness of hawks, which were then considered an unmitigated menace to farmers, in keeping down rats and other vermin. Another article drew an ominous parallel between what could happen to birds and what had happened already to the quagga, a species of zebra which had been exterminated because there was such great demand from bootmakers for its hide. (But later, when a too ardent conservationist wanted to protect the English sparrow, the magazine let its position be stated by one reader, General F. E. Skinner, who put it bluntly: "Kill the English sparrow.")

Taking up what was to become a most successful crusade, the magazine attacked the current fashion for adorning women's hats with bird plumes. In an article sardonically headlined "Birds are worn more than ever," the poet Celia Thaxter wrote that the woman who wears them carries "a charnel house of beaks and claws and bones upon her fatuous head." But when a birdless bonnet is worn, "the face beneath, no matter how plain it may be, seems to possess a gentle charm."

The response to Grinnell's proposal was not only much more than he expected but far more than he could handle and he had to give up the Audubon Society and the magazine after a couple of years. His idea came to life again in 1896, when a group of women in Boston formed the Massachusetts Audubon Society to fight the slaughter of birds for millinery. This was the first bird-watching society in which women had a major role, but still, in looking for a president, the organizers chose a man, the eminent William Brewster. Within two years there were similar Audubon societies in fifteen states, and in 1901 a confederation was formed, the National Association of Audubon Societies for the Protection of Wild Birds and Animals (today the National Audubon Society). Two leading members of the Linnaean Society were recruited to lead it. William Dutcher, a prosperous insurance agent, was chosen president and he set out to create a wide base for the Audubon societies by building local chapters and finding dedicated men to work as wardens to protect birds. Frank M. Chapman, author of a *Handbook of Birds of Eastern North America,* the best bird

guide of its time, arranged to have his new magazine, *Bird-Lore,* serve
as Audubon's official organ.

The Audubon Society made a point of appealing to average rather
than expert birders and found them everywhere. In Wyoming the
organizers, having hopefully sent out a thousand pledge cards, had to
dispatch an emergency order for another thousand. In Oklahoma,
Miss Alma Carson, secretary of the state's society, reported that "one
can enter scarcely a farmhouse or schoolhouse or assembly of country
folk" without hearing talk of "our birds." In Pennsylvania, *Bird-Lore*
reported, "bands of merry boy scouts" signed the Audubon pledge
to protect birds while appreciative Missouri farmers reported that
there were ten times as many birds around, partly because boys had
stopped thoughtlessly killing them now that the Audubon Society was
teaching them not to. Success brought some attempts to sabotage and
to take advantage of the Audubon's success. From the Midwest came
stories of impostors who went around warning people not to sign
membership applications because they would be turned into promis-
sory notes which the signer would have to pay. The society also
tracked down reports of a "prepossessing little widow" who swindled
people into joining Audubon and kept the dues herself.

Young and old, the societies preached, should love birds and,
loving them, must keep them from harm. In fostering the first large
conservation movement in America, birders finally took on a role that
had been waiting for them for a long time. The belief that nature must
be preserved had been associated with birds ever since the settlers
first came to America. Back in Bermuda in 1616, when the colony was
only a few years old, officials issued the new world's first conservation
edict: a proclamation forbidding "the spoyle and havock" of the
cahow, a native seabird which had been killed for food during a
famine. In 1621, the edict was made stronger but despite this the bird
disappeared. For three centuries it was considered extinct until, in
this century, a few were spotted and their nests found on rocky off-
shore islets where they still live, though precariously.

By the early 1700s, with colonists already worrying about the
noticeable decline in wild ducks, turkeys and seabirds, New York and
Massachusetts had passed laws giving some protection to game birds.
Through the nineteenth century, state by state, songbirds came under
the protection of the law: robins in Massachusetts in 1818; insect-
eating birds in Connecticut in 1850; nests and eggs of non-game birds
in Vermont in 1851; "small and harmless birds . . . small owls" in
Massachusetts in 1851. Ohio, however, rejected a law protecting pas-

senger pigeons because "no ordinary destruction can lessen their myriads." In 1842, a Supreme Court decision written by Chief Justice Taney (historically known for the *Dred Scott* decision) had ruled that river bottoms were public lands, not private, and that states had jurisdiction over them, thus giving an important extension to protective laws.

There had been no bird societies to speak up for the birds but some individuals did. Alexander Wilson, appalled at the greedy shooting of robins for the markets, concocted a hoax which he told about in his *Ornithology*. Some "humane person," he wrote, referring anonymously to himself,

> took advantage of a circumstance common to these birds in winter to stop the general slaughter. The fruit called poke-berries is a favorite repast with the robin after they are mellowed by the frost. The juice is of a beautiful crimson and they are eaten in such quantities by these birds that their whole stomachs are strongly tinted with the same red colour. A paragraph appeared in the public papers . . . intimating that they had become unwholesome and even dangerous food and that several persons had suffered by eating of them. The strange appearance of the bowels of the birds seemed to corroborate this account. The demand . . . ceased almost instantly; and motives of self preservation produced at once what all the pleadings of humanity could not effect.

The Nuttall Club and the American Ornithologists' Union were concerned with protecting birds and the AOU drew up a model bird-protection law which called for restrictions on shooting songbirds and collecting their eggs. New Jersey and New York were the first states to pass laws based on it and by 1910 all but a dozen or so states had followed. While it may have been compassion for birds that impelled the crusaders, legislators were moved more by arguments that birds were "friends of the farmer," eating up destructive insects that damaged crops. The economic ornithologist who studied the role of birds in agriculture became a person of importance in the bird world and his cold-cash testimony was listened to with respect. The new profession gathered statistics by the acre, dissected birds by the flock, and, laboriously counting the contents of their stomachs, found irrefutable evidence that birds' usefulness in eating insects outweighed whatever damage they did to crops.

Most birding groups that had been forming were more or less local and were interested primarily in watching and studying birds. The Audubon federation was different: it had a national character and, as its prime purpose, the protection of birds. And in its campaigns to save birds, it helped coalesce the conservation movement. Its philosophy and example—and just as important, its members—broke the way for the powerful environmental movements of today.

In their early days, the Audubon societies fought most effectively and vociferously against the collecting of bird feathers for women's dress and its success in this crusade gave it a prestige that enhanced all its other activities. The plumed hat, fan and wrap, decorated with feathers of ostrich or egret or even small songbirds, was the essential fashion at the end of the nineteenth century. The monstrous killing of birds for milliners and dressmakers went beyond belief or counting: five million birds a year at the least, possibly three or four times that number. In Florida, herons were killed by the tens of thousands for the few dozen usable feathers that could be plucked from them. Describing a heron rookery in a southern swamp littered with corpses, T. Gilbert Pearson wrote of "plumes stripped from their backs . . . flies swarming up with hideous buzzings . . . young orphan birds clamoring piteously for food which their parents could never again bring them."

Birders railed at all those responsible for the trade, both the sellers and the buyers. All a hunter's "sordid mind can grasp," cried one naturalist, "is a pair of pretty wings and a lady's fan." Women who wore the plumes were assailed with epithets: "Murderers! Killers of baby birds!" Members of the General Federation of Women's Clubs pledged not to wear "any such badge of cruelty." Frank Chapman reported that on a couple of afternoon bird walks down Fifth Avenue, he had counted what he called "hat birds": forty species, including warblers, owls and woodpeckers, as good a list as he might have gotten on a more orthodox bird walk. (In England, the crusading duchess of Portland prevailed on Queen Victoria to abolish the use of egret plumes on officers' headdresses. On Sundays, at church, the duchess would make notes on which ladies wore plumes and later send them instructive notes of protest.) The propaganda helped. In 1901, *Bird-Lore* hailed the news that "velvet flowers of exquisite colors and workmanship have taken the place of any but ostrich feathers with people of refinement. . . . Fewer grebe muffs and capes are seen." It went on, reflecting the upper-class snobbishness of Audubon's leaders, to say that tern feathers are only for the "real loidy what haunts cheaper shops lunching on either beer or soda."

Lobbying everywhere, the society and its allies persuaded state legislatures to prohibit the sale of bird feathers. In New York, the milliners hired a bright young lawyer and politician, Alfred E. Smith, to defend them but even his skills could not defeat a strong anti-feather bill. Opposing him in this legislation was the man who, two decades later, was to fight him for the Democratic nomination for president, State Senator Franklin D. Roosevelt. Feather merchants were pushed into desperate actions. In a single month, three New York feather factories burned up and one insurance company, checking back, found that there had been five such fires in 1908, eleven in 1909 and twelve in 1911. It cancelled all its feather-factory contracts.

There was, as there is so often among birders, some dissent. Dr. F. W. Langdon of Cincinnati defended the milliners. Most birds used in the trade, he argued, are gulls, terns and herons, whose "song" is "a mere squeak or squawk, anything but musical to human ears. Except for their feathers, they are not in any degree beneficial to humans." Enough "undesirable" birds like shrikes, jays and crows are killed for millinery, he said, to make up for the few songbirds that are shot. And even if all those killed were songbirds, he wound up, it would have little effect on the country's three-billion-bird population.

State laws were not strictly or uniformly enforced and the conservationists kept after the federal government to do something. In 1900 Congress passed the Lacey Act forbidding interstate trade in any bird protected by a state. Zealous members of Audubon societies became self-appointed enforcers. When Louise Stephenson, an active birder in Arkansas, learned that a dealer named Caraway of Alma, Arkansas, had actually advertised that he would sell bird skins "for millinery purposes in large quantities at reasonable prices," she took him right into court. The accused man wrote a plaintive letter to Mrs. Stephenson:

> I have to inform you that through your information, I was indicted by the grand jury for exporting wild birds from this state for which I will have to pay a heavy fine, costs etc. It may have been your duty to have reported me to the court but to be plain and honest with you, I did not even know there was a law. I am a lawful abiding citizen, born and reared in this state, a Democrat and a southern man—if you had kindly written me beforehand explaining that there was a law against shipping birds I, of course, would have ceased doing so at

once. It is hard for me to pay out the money besides the unpleasant notoriety I get. I don't believe I would have treated
a person like you have me for I believe in that old adage: Do
unto others as you would have them do unto you.

Neither Mr. Caraway's injured innocence nor his appeal to the Golden
Rule moved the birders. It served him right, they replied.

Not that the birders themselves were always straightforward. During their campaigns someone started the story that collectors in Canada were raiding the breeding grounds of geese and ducks and ship-
ping freight cars full of eggs to American lollipop makers, who needed
the albumen to give their products the proper sticky consistency.
Congress was ready to appropriate five thousand dollars to investigate this oological outrage when *Forest and Stream,* staunchly conservationist though it was, investigated the story and pronounced it a fake.
Still, the great lollipop hoax did call attention to the cause of conservation, and some birders felt that, since it helped bring about the
protective Egg Act of 1902, the means may have been justified.

The national laws, however, merely reinforced the actions that
states had taken without going further. The Audubon Society and its
allies, a mixed group that included sportsmen and ammunition makers, felt there should be more. They urged Congress to invoke the
federal government's power over interstate commerce and put all
migratory and insectivorous birds under "the custody and protection
of the government of the United States." State's rights congressmen
held up passage of the bill but the Migratory Bird Act of 1913 was
finally passed by a familiar legislative device, tacked on unobtrusively
as a rider to an agriculture appropriations bill. President Taft signed
without reading it and when told later what he had done he said he
would have vetoed it as unconstitutional.

As a matter of fact, in the first test case to come up—involving a
wealthy South Dakota banker who was fined $250 for shooting—two
federal judges did declare it unconstitutional. While the Supreme
Court was considering an appeal, Senator George P. McLean of Connecticut successfully maneuvered a Migratory Bird Protection Treaty
with Canada through the Senate in 1916. The treaty became the law
of the land and in this roundabout way the purposes of the protectionists were achieved. The Supreme Court, when the issue finally came
before it, ruled that the treaty was valid and that states did not have
exclusive jurisdiction over wild birds. Wild birds, declared Justice
Oliver Wendell Holmes, himself an avowed protectionist, are "not in

the possession of anyone, and possession is the beginning of owner-ship."

Yet, Audubon members discovered, this did not altogether end their anti-plumage war because milliners could still legally get plumes from abroad. In London feathers were sold literally by the ton—in 1908, for example, dealers sold 6,800 tons of bird of paradise feath-ers, 8,902 tons of kingfisher feathers and 15,000 tons of sooty tern feathers. In Venezuela, largest exporter of plumes, hunters killed more than a million birds a year. When the Audubon alliance set out to close this loophole, a Senate committee held up their proposal, largely because of Senator James A. Reed of Missouri, noted and rather feared for his intimidating wit and immovable stands. Speaking for the Democratic leadership, Reed wondered

> why there should be any sympathy or sentiment about a long-legged, long-beaked, long-necked bird that lives in a swamp and eats tadpoles and fish and crawfish . . . Why worry our-selves into frenzy because one lady adorns her hat with one of its feathers which appears to be the only use it has? Let human-ity utilize this bird for the only purpose that the Lord made it for, namely . . . so we could get aigrettes for bonnets of our beautiful ladies.

"What a distorted mind and heart!" spluttered *Bird-Lore,* and the Audubon Society, through its extensive school network, enlisted an army of fledglings. Children, under the direction of their teachers, wrote their congressmen on behalf of birds. "Some superintendants and principals looked upon the zealousness of their teachers with discouraging indifference," wrote *Bird-Lore*'s editor, until they learned that congressmen were taking their underage constituents very seriously, replying that they would do their best for the birds. Senators were so persuaded that they deserted their party leaders and voted for the provision.

Trying to ease the withdrawal pains, the Audubon Society allowed its name to be used commercially on a new hat on which embroidery replaced egrets, herons, etc. The Audubon hat, it proclaimed, is one "wherein beauty is achieved without robbing the feathered kingdom of its plumage." The hats cost five to fifteen dollars but did not seem to have many takers.

The fight against plumes and plume hunters drew the Audubon Society into a literal life-and-death war. In several states its game wardens had constant skirmishes with poachers. In a gun battle in South Carolina, Warden Jake Ward and his deputies drove off three poachers, Jackson Mitchum, Jake Jordan and Luther Miller, who were shooting egrets in a preserve. In Alligator Bay, Florida, three Whitman brothers were arrested after a gun battle with wardens who confiscated eight illegal egrets. L. P. Reeves, whom *Bird-Lore* called "a young and prosperous farmer," was shot from ambush and killed by two "notorious fish pirates" of Branchville—"a nest of criminals"—after he had warned them against shooting birds. In Placida, Florida, Warden Columbus G. McLoad disappeared; his hat, with two axe gashes in it, was found in his sunken boat. Guy Bradley, a warden of Flamingo, Florida, described as "a fearless righteous man who had hunted plumes in his younger days," caught two hunters with some newly killed egrets. When he tried to arrest them, they shot him and left his corpse drifting in his boat until it was found by some boys who wondered what the vultures were circling over. Bradley's murder became a national scandal and his martyrdom brought new support for bird protection.

More peaceably, but just as fiercely, Audubon members and officers were fighting to get local bird-protection laws passed, then fighting just as hard to enforce them—and to keep them from being repealed or weakened. They were constantly reminded, in reading *Bird-Lore,* how endless and wearying a battle it was. In Michigan, Audubon members helped defeat a bill that would have legalized the shooting of meadowlarks, and paid bounties for kingfishers and great blue herons, which were accused of endangering fish, and for "chicken" (red-tailed) hawks, accused of killing poultry. But Ohio, because of farmers' pressures, set a bounty on hawks. In New Jersey, a proposal to remove flickers and mourning doves from the list of protected birds was defeated and in Oregon the varied thrush was saved from a similar threat. Connecticut protectionists lost their fight to prohibit snipe shooting in the spring, although supporters of other anti-protectionist bird bills were, in the evangelical language of *Bird-Lore,* "defeated and demoralized."

In Massachusetts and New Hampshire laws "inimical to bird protection" were beaten and in Oregon intense pressure on the governor, again with schoolchildren joining in, got him to veto a bill that would have permitted farmers to shoot any birds they thought were hurting their crops. But Colorado stubbornly persisted in paying bounties for sparrow hawks (American kestrels) even after hearing evidence that they ate hordes of grasshoppers that periodically plagued farmers. In Florida, Audubon successfully opposed a law that would have destroyed buzzards because they spread hog cholera, a dubious accusation. In Alaska, under a bounty system that paid fifty cents to one dollar per bird, more than forty thousand eagles were shot before protectionists were able to stop the slaughter. California, pushed by plume hunters, exempted sea and bay birds from protective laws but Alabama through the efforts of a few dedicated bird lovers passed strong conservation laws.

The year 1909 was a bad one for the birds. Illinois removed protection from hawks, New Mexico from roadrunners, Utah from blackbirds, great blue herons, bitterns, magpies and kingfishers. These losses were hardly offset by laws in Montana and Nebraska protecting doves. A majority of people in New England were reported to be in favor of conservation but in Rhode Island, the Audubon Society's representative charged, "secret and powerful influences" defeated a bill setting up the office of state ornithologist. The state, however, did agree to refuse hunting licenses to boys under fifteen. Things seemed better in 1912, when Pennsylvania legislators approved a bill barring all plumage sales by a vote of 174–0. Vermont and Michigan passed protective laws. "A great year for birds!" *Bird-Lore* proclaimed. Still, in that year, 60,000 dozen (720,000) bobolinks, a delicacy also known as "reed birds," were sold in northern meat markets, and southerners, though beleaguered, were successfully fighting rearguard actions to preserve their right to shoot birds for their cherished "robin pie."

The enforcement of protection laws was the dubious responsibility of the local game warden who, one historian has said, was a man "seldom to be looked up to in his community. Rather he was the village loafer who could swing a few votes at election time. He usually liked to hunt and fish but as an enforcement officer he just didn't rate." Missouri made things even worse by giving enforcement powers to local sheriffs and deputies. "Pernicious," cried *Bird-Lore,* pointing out that these men would, of course, be reluctant to arrest a friend or neighbor for taking a few birds. As an innovation, the Audubon Society appointed its first lady warden as guardian of Klamath Lake, a huge water-bird preserve on the California-Oregon border where a hunter, selling grebes at twenty cents each, could make thirty dollars a day. This proved a brilliant move. Mrs. L. H. Bath was not only convincingly firm with abashed hunters but also got local boys to stop throwing stones at the birds and feed them instead.

Everywhere birds were condemned as destructive of one thing or

another. Robins in New Jersey were guilty of eating cherries. Ducks
in Arkansas and Texas gobbled rice. In Arizona mourning doves ate
the alfalfa crop and in California meadowlarks were at the grape vines.
In Utah cedar waxwings despoiled fruit. Herons and grebes were
charged with raiding fish hatcheries, and during the First World War
pelicans were accused by southern fishermen of invading the fishing
grounds and eating millions of pounds of fish, seriously harming the
war effort. "Kill the Pelican or the Kaiser will get you" was their
rallying cry. When the federal food administrator ruled that pelicans
could be shot, a small ornithological expedition traveled along the
Gulf Coast from Florida to Texas, forcing pelicans to regurgitate their
catch, which they do when alarmed. Assessing what 3,428 pelicans
threw up, researchers discovered that only 27 had taken any useful
food fish. Mostly they had eaten menhaden, a junk fish. A somewhat
embarrassed food administrator revoked his ruling.

In the North, the Audubon Society marshaled itself against what
it called the "great menace to our wild life . . . the immigrant population from Southern Europe." The society had received many complaints about "the shooting of robins by Italians and Hungarians."
Accustomed in their homeland to catching songbirds and eating
them, the newcomers were open about their bird hunting. Two were
arrested in upper New York State after having made a meal of boiled
flickers and robins—a "real luxury" for them, said the warden who
brought them in. Unable to pay the $105 fine, the malefactors went
to jail. *Bird-Lore* published a photograph of a string of flickers with the
caption: "Shot by Italian hunters," and another of a thrush, a warbler,
a cowbird, two woodpeckers and seventeen robins with the caption:
"Contents of an Italian hunter's game bag." This latter illustrated the
account of an alert warden in Portland, Maine, who arrested the
violators in the act of plucking the birds. The hapless hunters found
themselves in court guilty of violating not only local laws but also an
international treaty. They were fined $25. In a woods in Jamaica, Long
Island, Frank Aldano, caught shooting robins, turned his gun on the
warden and killed him. A *Bird-Lore* editorial, entitled "Italian atroci-
ties," declared that "no unnaturalized Italian should own a gun."
Massachusetts heeded the call with a wonderfully contrived piece of
discrimination: a law forbidding any alien to kill any bird unless he
owned $500 worth of real estate.

There seemed to be no controversy over the baldly ethnic bias of
this campaign. There was plenty when it came to dealing with an
even more heinous criminal: the cat. The controversy over cats and

what to do with them occupied members of the society over many years—and still does. Most of the discussions have been more emotional than factual, but in 1915, Edward Howe Forbush, state ornithologist of Massachusetts, made a systematic survey of cat owners in forty-three Massachusetts towns and villages, studying the habits of 559 cats. Tabulating the answers to his questionnaires, he found that 227 cats were known to kill birds (43 of them, moreover, did not make up for it by also killing rats); 405 roamed at night, when mother birds were on their nests, and in the early morning, when the birds went out for food. The average kill was 2.7 birds per day per cat; 125 species of birds were victims. Robins were most vulnerable—272 reported killed—followed by sparrows, warblers, thrushes. Most cat owners, however, blamed the neighbor's cat for the killing, not their own.

Katherine Parson of Cambridge replied with a fiscal defense of the cat. By killing mice and rats, she said, cats save the country $9,000,000 a year. There are 5,000,000 rats in the United States, she estimated, and each rat does $5 damage every year; there are at least as many mice in the United States and each one does $2 damage per year. There are 1,000,000 cats in the United States: if each cat each year kills one rat and two mice, it saves the country $9. Multiply this by a million cats and you get an annual saving of $9,000,000. "Preserve the cat," she pleaded.

The lady's analysis was refuted by the superintendent of parks of Rockford, Illinois. Agricultural economists, he said, say that birds are worth $1 a year to farmers in eating insects and weed seeds. A cat eats on average fifty birds a year, thereby doing $50 worth of annual damage. This comes to $50,000,000 or so for all the country's cats, far more than Mrs. Parson's $9,000,000 worth of feline good works. (From the sidelines, *The Oologist,* journal of egg collectors, chimed in with "a screech-owl is worth a dozen cats and not one cat in 20 will tackle a rat.")

The anti-cat crusade had some victories. New York passed the first state cat law: any officer could shoot a cat hunting protected birds or with one "in its possession." Massillon, Ohio, imposed a curfew on roaming cats: they could not be outdoors from 7 p.m. to 9 a.m., from April 1 to September 20, the bird breeding season. The owner of any violator of the curfew would be fined $2 to $5 and trespassing cats could be killed. Cat-control measures were introduced and passed in several state legislatures. Some are on the books today. In 1985, in New Jersey, a game warden invoked the state's law after he was arrested for shooting a cat that came into his yard and made his dogs bark. A judge found him innocent.

Still another battle engaged the Audubon Society and its allies. In 1919, E. I. du Pont de Nemours & Company, ammunition makers, inaugurated a National Crow Shoot. Anyone who shot twenty-five crows in 1919 would get a bronze button. More impressive state and national prizes for bigger bags were promised. Taking a government survey out of context, Du Pont tried to appease birders by saying that crows were destructive of nesting birds and deserved to be killed. Besides, Du Pont pointed out, crows were not protected by law. There was the expected outcry from birders but a less predictable response came from the highly esteemed bird painter Alan Brooks. During the fifteen years he had been living in western Canada, he wrote, crows, attracted by the newly farmed areas, had increased their population from a scattered few to flocks that stretched from horizon to horizon in bands two hundred yards wide. Among their many bad habits, they killed off grouse. Birders, he concluded scornfully, were deluded by a foolish new doctrine—the "little bedtime stories of some of our ornithological leaders dealing with that figmental phantasy the 'Balance of Nature.' "

To the members of the Audubon Society the conservation fights were, of course, only a byproduct of their first interest: watching birds. In the pages of *Bird-Lore* they exchanged their worries, their indignations, their confusions and their proud little stories of avian oddities. Sometimes, from reading the anecdotes, one got the impression that the country was overrun with albino robins, blessed many times over with blue jays and crows of remarkable sagacity, populated by sparrows that tapped on windows when the bird seed had not been put out that morning and serenaded by mockingbirds that performed miracles of mimicry. A listener in East Cleveland heard one mocker imitate the songs of the bluebird, oriole, phoebe, killdeer, cardinal, titmouse, whip-poor-will, nighthawk Cooper's hawk and several others she wasn't sure of. In the Arnold Arboretum in Boston, reported E. H. Early, a mocker engaged a catbird and a brown thrasher (all three are in the same family, called mimic-thrushes) in a battle of song. The mocker, "easily outpointing" the other two, rubbed it in by stopping once to do a few somersaults "for the edification of his rivals."

Worries of all kinds beset bird watchers; for example, the growing number of well-intentioned people who put out feeders for birds during the winter. Would this not make birds more and more depen-

dent on man? And lose the freedom which was their most precious
asset? And give up eating their natural foods, such as harmful insects,
which made them so useful to man? Henry Oldys had words of com-
fort for the worries in an article entitled "Pauperizing the Birds."
Their worries were needless, he said. Birds might use feeders because
they were so convenient but they could get along without them. For
downy woodpeckers, he said, "pecking into suet" at a feeder may be
"an agreeable diversion" but this will not distract them from digging
out bugs. In Germany, he said, caterpillars that had devastated a large
area did not get within a quarter of a mile of the orchards owned by
Baron Berlepsch. He had devotedly put out food for birds and they
repaid him by standing constant guard over his fruit.

Like people who insist that winters are never so cold or snowy as
they used to be, Audubon's birders were always sure that birds were
fewer than they used to be. The distinguished ornithologist Robert
Ridgway said there were fewer in Illinois than when he was young, and
Rolla Warren Kinsey of Lathrop, Montana, agreed with this: too much
land had been cleared by new settlers. On the contrary, Charles A.
McNeil wrote, birds were "unusually plentiful" around Sedalia, Missouri. A. H. Thayer of Monadnock, New Hampshire, a theorist of
birds' protective coloration, did not see much difference at all and
cited Dr. Hugo Munsterber, professor of psychology at Harvard, who
explained that birds represent pleasant memories, and as people grow
older, they are always inclined to exaggerate the pleasures of the past.
Therefore the professor did not trust "impressionistic records" that
there were more birds then than now. The editor of *Bird-Lore* came
out on the side of the professor, remarking that older people hear
and see less well and adding, rather gratuitously, that age "dulls the
keenness."

Watchers could hardly count the reasons why they cared for birds.
M. H. Herbel of Citrella, Oklahoma, was deeply affected by the example of a male cardinal which, having taken a one-legged mate, faithfully brought food to her. Eugene Swope, the Audubon's field agent
in Ohio, eulogized birds because they gave him "a life of more spirit
. . . less days which I seem to have lost along the way." And true
birders found it in their hearts to love everything that gave service to
birds. E. A. Doolittle of Painesville, Ohio, wrote a paean to the stag-
horn sumac, a weedy tree whose virtues are generally regarded as
negligible. It always bears fruit, Mr. Doolittle explained, and keeps its
berries through the coldest seasons—partly because nothing is interested in eating them. But in the depths of winter, when snow has

frozen over the ground and the trees are icebound, then bluebirds
and robins and flickers and phoebes come to eat them as a meal of
last resort. In his devotion to science and to birds, Mr. Doolittle
himself tasted the berries and found them "sour—very, very sour."

A quarter of a century after its formation, the Audubon Society
could point with pride to the political power that bird watchers had
gained. In 1920, Warren G. Harding, Republican candidate for president, sent *Bird-Lore* a telegram saying he favored bird protection. The
candidate, said the editor, "is wide awake to the need of conservation." The magazine was also puffed up by the way advertisers were
courting the birders. A tire maker was giving out pamphlets on birds.
"A certain fountain pen" was advertised, said the editor, as being "as
beautiful as a scarlet tanager." A sewing machine maker was giving
out bird identification cards and so was a chewing gum company.
"When we absorb bird lore with chewing gum," gloated the editor,
"the ornithological millennium is approaching."

RUFOUS HUMMINGBIRD

An All-purpose Artist

Older generations of American bird watchers carried two images in their heads: one of the bird as they saw it, the other of the bird as Audubon had shown it to them. Later generations of birders also ventured out with two images—one of the bird they saw, the other as another artist, Louis Agassiz Fuertes, showed it to them. The finest bird painter since Audubon—and surpassing him in accuracy—Fuertes was the bird watchers' all-purpose artist. As children, they were beguiled by the lively likenesses he painted for their beginner books—Mabel Osgood Wright's *Birdcraft,* Olive Thorne Miller's *The Second Book of Birds,* Thornton Burgess's *Bird Book for Children*—and for *St. Nicholas Magazine.* As grown-ups, they would admire his full-scale portraits in Forbush's *Birds of Massachusetts* and Elon Howard Eaton's *Birds of New York,* and his sketches for John Burroughs' nature books. If they were serious birders, they studied his anatomical illustrations for Coues' revised *Key* and for both Frank Chapman's and Florence Merriam's handbooks. And if they had never bothered much to look at birds before, they might be nudged into interest by his portraits on a hundred or so little cards that were given away as premiums with boxes of Arm & Hammer baking soda.

Fuertes had been set up in his career by Elliott Coues, whom he met in 1894 when he was a sophomore at Cornell. Coues saw an extraordinary quality in the drawings the self-taught young man had been doing since he was a boy, when he collected specimens with a slingshot. The famous ornithologist preemptorily took over young Fuertes' career, showing his work to other ornithologists and commissioning him to illustrate his book *Citizen Bird*. When Fuertes complained that doing the work was hurting his college grades, Coues commanded him: "Never mind your school work. What matters is what you are doing for me." When the book proved an instant success, Coues generously wrote his protégé that "this great hit is mainly due to your pictures."

From then on, Fuertes never stopped painting birds until his early death in 1927, when his automobile was hit by a train at a railroad crossing. "He painted more bird portraits than any artist had ever attempted," says his biographer, Robert Peck, in *A Celebration of Birds*. The vast amount of work never diluted its quality. The children's illustrations had a simple intimacy that made the birds readily recognizable. The technical illustrations had an almost undisputed accuracy; they were taken as articles of faith by scientists. The beautiful large paintings were drawn meticulously down to the last feather fleck. They had an immediacy, as if the bird, at ease in its environment, were less perched at rest than poised for sudden flight. And the reason for this immediacy is shown in the drawings—Fuertes' field sketches —that appear at the head of the chapters in this book. They show how accurate he was as a field naturalist and how deft he was in catching a bird's identity.

Fuertes himself, burdened with piled-up work, was always poised for flight—to Alaska, the Yucatán, the Bahamas, Colombia and Abyssinia— lured by the chance to see a bird he hadn't already seen. "Fuertes in possession of a freshly captured specimen of some bird which was before unknown to him is wholly beyond the reach of all sensations, other than those occasioned by the specimen before him," Frank Chapman once wrote. "His concentration annihilates his surroundings. Color, pattern, form, contour, minute detail of structure, all are observed and assimilated so completely that they become part of himself and they can be reproduced at any future time with amazing accuracy." But beyond the intensity was another feeling that the best of birders have and on which his genius rested. Often, a friend wrote, Fuertes would sit with some new specimen for a long while, "crooning and purring over it, stroking its feathers in a detached ecstacy."

Within the illustration, handwritten notes read:

April 18, 1923
Ithaca
(S. McNiel)

Red Breasted
Merganser
Monroe, Mich., Mar 27, 1909 (Bad)
Shot by Constant Brandreth.

R.A.F.

RED-BREASTED MERGANSER

HOUSE SPARROW

Chestnut-Sided Warbler.
Dendroica Pensylvanica (Linn.)
Male — Female.
May 16th 1895.

CHESTNUT-SIDED WARBLER

SLATE-COLORED JUNCO

PEREGRINE FALCON WITH GREEN-WINGED TEAL

PILEATED WOODPECKER

BURROWING OWL

WILD TURKEY

GYRFALCON

8

The Good Fellows

"The ornithologist is almost always a good fellow; he can hardly be otherwise . . . the elusive grace and charm of the wild bird is not for the morose or mean man. Of course, the ornithologist is a good fellow; he cannot help himself."

When he said this, Witmer Stone could not have been thinking of his noted predecessor, the brusque John Cassin. Nor of the thin-skinned Dr. Brewer, or the loose-tongued Dr. Coues, or the touchy Dr. Abbott. Nor of any number of his contemporaries whose devotion to good fellowship dissolved on occasion into scientific insult and personal scorn. He was certainly too modest a man to apply the definition to the one whom it fit almost to a pin feather: Witmer Stone himself. One colleague eulogized Stone as a

naturalist, scientist, faithful custodian of collections, biographer and historian of scientists and their science, interpreter of the rules of zoological nomenclature, protector of birds, writer of exceptional beauty and vigor, helpful adviser, delightful companion and valued friend. . . . The merry twinkle of the eye, the clever quips or even the touch of whimsey . . . would show that beneath the grind of editorship, the often monotonous

routine of curatorial duties and the piles of sometimes point-
less correspondence there was a spirit fully in tune with his
fellow man, akin to their problems, their joys and their para-
doxes.

The deceased, of course, always get good speeches, and memorials like this usually have to be discounted. Stone, happily, left a convincing memorial of his own, *Bird Studies at Old Cape May.* As good a
regional bird book as any ever written, it is a lovely work, with an aura
of patience and kindliness, full of a feeling of place, the expression
of a bemused watcher who feels that credit for all he sees and sets
down should be given not to him but to the Cape and its feathered
inhabitants.

A point of land that juts out at the southern end of New Jersey
between the Atlantic and Delaware Bay, Cape May has drawn birders
from the days of Wilson and Audubon. It is one of the three or four
spots along the Atlantic that seems to have been created for the
convenience of bird watchers. Pasture and woodland border on
marshland and ocean to provide a habitat for almost any bird species.
Migrating birds, funneled into its narrowing strip by the bordering
stretches of water, crowd the Cape in spring and fall. In fall, especially, strong winds will often ground them there for days in a row.
Today's arrivals pile up on yesterday's, and tomorrow's come in to
create a kind of avian gridlock, a nuisance perhaps for migrants but
a wonder to birders. A watcher, Stone wrote, "may awake some morning to find that with a change in the wind, the whole country is
deluged with birds," and, the wind shifting, they drift away. In one
day, September 1, 1920, he saw eighty-six species.

Stone was what might be called, in his own terminology, a "visitant" to the Cape, going there first around 1890 and continuing for
almost fifty years. Something of his own style is reflected in the place
as he described it, a kind of unassuming elegance and easy beauty:
"weatherboarded houses, windswept and bleached," shaded by silver
poplars with "smooth gray branches stretching up like the arms of
some great supplicant giant . . . deep green foliage ever quivering
. . . hedge pear trees, loaded with fruit until the branches break with
their burden . . . paths all bordered with rows of conch shells . . . bay
berry and sweetbriar . . . oyster tongs and seines hung about the farm
buildings or a basket of duck decoys," a throwback of a place where
the oldsquaw duck was still called "south-southerly" and the knot
"robin snipe."

"One never knows what he may see," Stone remarks, touching on the suspense that keeps any birder taut with hope, "some straggler may come down farther than any of his kind has come before . . . some waif may be driven in from far out on the ocean." He gazes out over the endless stretch of tossing waves and ruefully wonders, "How many birds the casual observer does miss. . . ." Always, the unseen bird is sweeter.

Stone would stand at the edge of a farm, a grassy pasture on his left and tidal stretches on his right, and watch the songbirds on one side, the marsh birds on the other, as if some territorial line had been drawn between them. Looking out from the beach one day, he noticed an odd bird that did not quite look like a tern and swam out to an Audubon's shearwater that had been driven in from the open ocean —the only one he ever saw at the Cape. He could almost, but not quite, touch it.

There was a mechanism in him for being both objective and subjective and a certain patient clarity. In an artfully precise way he makes the reader as well acquainted with a bird as any drawing or catalog of field marks can. For example, when he tells about the way sanderlings behave on the beach:

> They manage to keep an eye on the incoming wave and just in time they will turn and scamper back, going only far enough to avoid a wetting. Then they once again face the sea and rush back with the outflowing water, picking up such food as is being carried along with it. As a bird slows up before turning for the rush, its humped up attitude gives one the impression of shrugging the shoulders. The sallies are usually made on diagonal lines so that the birds are always making progress along the beach while if anyone follows them they run directly parallel to the shore line. When convinced that no harm is intended, they begin again to follow the waves, glancing once in a while over the shoulder to see that their confidence is not abused. As they fly, the head and neck are bowed over as if straining every muscle to increase their speed, when they alight one might suppose that the bill touched the sand as soon as the feet so quickly is it in action again. . . . [Scuttling away when approached] their bodies glide so smoothly over the sand that it gives one the curious impression that they are impelled by some other force and are not connected with the rapidly moving legs. [The note of the sanderling] is a continuous twitter

. . . a sociable conversational sound fitting for birds of such
eminently gregarious habits.

Life histories and keys to identification were not his purpose. It
was to tell what he saw so that others might see as he did. So he
details the shapes the neck of the American egret (great egret) takes:
"When viewed from the rear the neck does actually seem to bulge
either on one side or the other. . . . When wading in a strong wind
the neck is often blown considerably out of plumb . . . in flight
looped out in front and head settled back on the shoulders . . . as
the momentum increases . . . the neck, at first loosely curved in an
S, is quickly contracted." He calls attention to the "dove-like beauty"
of a laughing gull floating in a channel; to "a whirlwind of tree swallows" or a single purple martin hovering in a strong wind over the
roof of a hotel for half an hour, just for the fun of it; to a kingfisher
slamming a too-big sunfish on a stump to get it down to edible size;
to a male tern keeping a fish in his beak and giving it to the female
only after they had mated. Or the way a black-billed cuckoo eats
caterpillars: ". . . seize the caterpillar just behind the head and switch
it violently back and forth until it became perfectly limp and would
wrap around the bill like a piece of string. The cuckoo would then
raise its head and gulp the insect down sitting perfectly still for some
minutes after." Looking at a flock of black terns, he tells himself how
like a nighthawk's one bird's flight was until "to my astonishment I
realized that one of the birds was actually a nighthawk," a moment
familiar to every birder who sets his mind on what he expects to see
rather than what he sees.
    One of his triumphs was, oddly enough, spotting a Cape May
warbler. The bird had been given its name more than a century before
by Alexander Wilson, who had been given a specimen shot in a Cape
May maple swamp. It was never recorded again at the Cape, Stone
notes, "until September 4, 1920, when I recognized one in a shade
tree on Perry Street." The birds, he mused, "had doubtless always
been passing the Cape and the lack of any records has been due to
the lack of ornithologists." His affection for all the Cape's birds did
not extend to the bald eagle—"a thick set, short legged bird with great
ill fitting wings, a degenerate member of the eagle tribe." And his
patience with birders did not extend to those who did not bother to
distinguish among the differing songs of the Maryland (common)
yellowthroat. "If one thinks that all yellowthroats sing alike," he says
with a touch of asperity, "it will pay him to jot down some careful

records of their songs." And, not trusting the dilatory birder to do this, he does it for him, dividing the songs by groups:

GROUP I

1. *Tsu-za-wit'sky, tsu-za-wit'sky, tsu-za-wit'sky.*
2. *Tsivit-swee'ah, tsivit-swee'ah, tsivit-svee'ah, tsvit.*
3. *Chit-wissa-whit', chit wissa-whit'.*
3a. *Chissa-wissa-whit', chissa-wissa-whit'.*
4. *Chissa-wit'so, tsu-wit'so, tsu-witso.* [*tsu-wit'so*].

GROUP II

5. *Wisset, see'-wisset, see'-wisset, see'-wisset.*
6. *Sit-see-a, weet'-see-a, weet'-see-a, weet'-see-a.*

GROUP III

7. *Tse-wit'sa-see'a, tse-wit'sa-see'a, tse-wit'.*
7a. *Tse-wit'sa-see'a, tse-wit'.*
8. *Tse-vit'-sa-vi'a, tse-vit'-sa-vi'a, tse-vit'.*
9. *Tsi-vit'-sa-re'ah, tsi-vit'-sa-re'ah, tsi-vit'-sa-re'ah.*
10. *Tsi-vit'-sa-wee', tsi-vit'-sa-wee', tsi-vit-sa-wee', tsi-vit-sa-wee'.*
11. *Tsu-wit'sua-wee'ah, tsu-wit'sua-wee'ah, tsu-wit'-su* [*or tsu-wit*].

It was "quite easy to identify individual birds after their songs had once been memorized," Stone concludes disarmingly.

How Stone found time to do so much bird watching is hard to see. In 1888, shortly after graduating from college, he took up an association with the Philadelphia Academy of Natural Sciences that lasted all his life. As curator and director, he built up John Cassin's collection from 26,000 bird specimens to 143,000. Though his responsibilities broadened into other branches of zoology, birds were his abiding interest. He prepared a fine regional book, *The Birds of Eastern Pennsylvania and New Jersey,* an early study of bird migrations. He was a final authority on nomenclature and a leader in the movement to protect birds. In 1890, with half a dozen Philadelphia friends, he organized the Delaware Valley Ornithological Club, serving as editor of its journal, *Cassinia,* until, some years later, he assumed the editorship of the AOU's *Auk.*

Even among the bird clubs, which were originally pretty exclusive groups themselves, the Delaware Valley Ornithological Club (DVOC) was considered to be *the* exclusive birding club, a reputation which persists to this day. Anyone "interested in ornithology considered in its widest sense" was eligible for membership. However, a unanimous vote of the fifteen active members—the only category permitted to hold office—was required to admit a member, while only a two-thirds vote was needed to throw him out. In practice, the active membership was restricted to a fairly tight circle of men, most of whom could not be considered snobs socially but were rather fussy about whom they met with ornithologically. Members were required to pay close attention to their birding. An active member who missed four successive meetings was reduced to the rank of associate member.

There was one clear basis for the charge of exclusiveness in the club's policy towards women members: there weren't any. In defining who was eligible to belong, the club's constitution specified that members must be "male persons." Other birding societies were, in practice, all-male groups at first but after a few years most began admitting women. The DVOC acknowledged women's right to watch birds individually and collectively, but not within the club's territory. With the DVOC's blessing, several women who had been active in the Pennsylvania Audubon Society set up a birding society for themselves, calling it the Spencer Fullerton Baird Club. Though it had the active encouragement of Witmer Stone, it seems to have led a desultory life and simply faded away after a couple of decades. Moves to admit women to the DVOC were unsuccessful until 1982, when the word "male" was deleted from the membership requirement clause and, after ninety years, the DVOC took in some women. (The Nuttall Club would not admit women as resident members until 1974, after its centennial celebration. Several male members have not attended meetings since then.)

Like meetings of any birding society the DVOC's were taken up with local reports on birds: disappointment at the scarcity of red-breasted nuthatches, delight at the news that twenty snowy owls were wintering in the area. The most entertaining meeting was the one at which a bird imitator whistled the calls of several dozen birds for the edification and amusement of members who, one would think, would not have put up with imitations. William Baily reported that, thanks to William Penn, members could enjoy a "convenient way of observing fall migration without losing any time in the field." In 1899, to celebrate a fair, the statue of Penn that stands on top of the Philadelphia City Hall was festooned with lights. Attracted or confused by them, migrating birds flew into the statue and fell to the ground. In two months, Mr. C. H. Slaughter, the tower electrician, whose name seemed sadly appropriate, picked up 529 fallen birds, most of them young warblers on their first trip south. A red-tailed hawk that frequented the tower got to many birds before Mr. Slaughter could.

At the AOU meeting in 1889 Stone met another ornithological good fellow, Charlie Pennock, who was to become one of his best friends and one of almost everybody's favorite birding companions— and who is an extraordinary example of how tight a hold birds can have on those who watch them. Charles J. Pennock tried to get away from the world he lived in but never could because he could not get away from the birds that he loved. His gentle obsession gives him a special place in the world of bird watchers.

At college—Cornell and Princeton—Charlie Pennock took courses in ornithology and he became an early member of the Linnaean Society. (He was also pitcher on the varsity baseball team, although never in a class with his nephew, Herb Pennock, the famous left-hander of the great New York Yankee teams of the 1920s.) Settling in Kennett Square outside Philadelphia, he became a successful though restless businessman. His letterheads read at various times: "Carnation, Rooted Cuttings and Plants"; "Lumber Coal Feed Grain and Straw"; "Real Estate, Loans and Investments." An industrious civic servant, he was chief burgess of Kennett Square and justice of the peace. He sat on the board of the Philadelphia Academy of Sciences, where he served as curator of oology and endowed the academy with his own egg collection, one of the finest in the East. Major Bendire, the preeminent oologist, was pleased when Pennock gave him a Cooper's hawk egg that the major coveted.

Pennock was elected to membership in all the leading birding societies and, joining the DVOC, served for several years as president. When the American Bird Banding Association was formed to systematize the practice of bird banding, he served as secretary and recruiter. Delaware appointed him its state ornithologist—it was a nonpaying post but Pennock was clearly the man for it. "Not much of anything rare and desirable gets into Delaware that gets out again without leaving [him] a record of itself in the shape of either hide or note," wrote an admirer of Pennock's diligence. His bird counts were sometimes phenomenal. On a late-winter stay in North Carolina he bemoaned the fact that cold weather kept down the migrations, but still listed: one woodcock, one Bewick's wren, two nighthawks, 16 prairie horned larks, 112 mockingbirds, 191 turkey vultures, 331 pipits, 364 meadowlarks, 414 mourning doves, 680 cowbirds, 1,196 cedar birds (cedar waxwings) and 1,714 juncos—although, he noted cautiously, the juncos were in flocks of up to a hundred and he might have counted the same bird more than once.

The best ornithologists of the time liked to have Charlie Pennock along when they went out into the field. He took Witmer Stone out into the Delaware marshes to find Lapland longspurs. He showed Arthur Bent, editor of the most comprehensive set of life histories of American birds, how to make friends with owls. Out in a rowboat, he summoned up an owl with his hooting, and floated downstream with the owl following, answering hoot with hoot. When the bird lit on a limb thirty feet above the water, Pennock pulled underneath, "talking to him," Bent wrote, "in an ordinary tone." As Pennock drifted along, the owl followed, stopping whenever Pennock stopped and hooted. When the boat went into open water, the dialogue stopped and the bird went off.

Then one day in 1913, Charles Pennock disappeared—vanished completely, leaving no word, no reason, no clue. What finally brought him back after years of mystifying absence was his passion for birds which he could never, no matter what, tear from his life.

On the night of May 15, Pennock left a meeting of the DVOC complaining to Witmer Stone that he was not feeling too well. He went off to the railway station but did not arrive at Kennett Square that night. Nor the next day. He was nowhere to be found in Philadelphia. The police sent out a missing person bulletin: Charles J. Pennock, 55, 5 feet 10½ inches tall, wearing dark suit with gray stripes, standup collar; had close-cropped whiskers and was somewhat gray; had had two marriages, three children.

The family was baffled but expected him to return—he had once gone off without telling anyone but came back after a couple of days. A memory lapse "from inflammatory rheumatism," it was explained. This time the absence grew longer and longer. After a while, his son wrote the DVOC asking if he would be dropped from membership if his dues were not paid. (No, said the club.) After several years, the family stopped hoping and Mrs. Pennock gave his collection of 1,800 bird skins, along with eggs and books, to the Philadelphia Academy of Sciences.

Meanwhile a new name began showing up in all the bird journals. John Williams was sending first-class reports on the birds of northwestern Florida, from the village of St. Marks in Wakula County. Such informed reporting from one of the richest birding spots in the country was welcomed by editors and John Williams quickly was elected a member of the American Ornithologists' Union, the DVOC, the Wilson Club.

The *Wilson Bulletin* published his seven-page article "Some Florida

Herons," full of careful observations. Mortality was high among herons, Williams wrote, because young ones had an unhappy habit of falling out of the nests. Some were hanged to death, their long necks caught in branch crotches as they fell. Nests were raided for their eggs by crows—"jackdaw dearly loves his eggs in the shell." John Williams was prolific, contributing articles on buzzards, kingbirds, red-backed sandpipers (dunlin), black rails, purple martins, turkey vultures. As his name began appearing in the membership lists of various clubs, the name of Charles Pennock was being put in a special asterisked category: "*Deceased Member."

In hindsight, it seems odd that no one made the connection—the inexplicable disappearance into nowhere of one of the country's most eminent birders and the abrupt emergence out of nowhere of a hitherto unknown birder with superb qualifications. Nobody seemed to wonder about this until, in 1919, Witmer Stone was given a manuscript by John Williams. Something about it struck him as familiar. But he dismissed his suspicions as ridiculous. Then he thought again. "I recognized it as being in Pennock's handwriting," he later wrote, "confirming an earlier suspicion as to the identity of John Williams based on the character of some of the published notes, and the sudden appearance of such a trained ornithologist in such an out of the way place as St. Marks—a man of whom nothing was previously known." He confided his suspicions to Pennock's brother-in-law and suggested he go down to Florida to look into his hunch. The brother-in-law made his way to St. Marks, a small village with a fish cannery and a turpentine still, and there was Charles J. Pennock, who, almost without surprise, came up and shook his brother-in-law's hand and, in the way that such adventure stories seem to go, told him what had happened.

On that night in 1913, he had left the meeting feeling troubled—depressed, fatigued and overworked, believing that he should "bury" himself. Instead of taking the train home, he took one to Baltimore. He had about a hundred dollars with him and he made his way south by stages, studying outdoor life, as he put it, until he came to the backwoods hamlet of St. Marks, south of Tallahassee, a spot he had explored many years before as a young birder studying short-tailed hawks. It had long been known as a good birding spot—Colonel McCown, one of Cassin's correspondents, had got an ash-colored flycatcher and a rufous-winged lark there. Now, Pennock shaved off his beard and moustache, assumed the name of John Williams and, living in a three-room shack, set out to re-create in this backwoods village the very same kind of life he had made for himself in the cultured environs of Philadelphia. Up there he had been a business-man in several fields, an active civic servant and, of course, a constant birder. In St. Marks he became bookkeeper for the local fish cannery, accountant for the turpentine distiller, and substitute lighthouse keeper, while serving as county commissioner and notary public, dril-ling troops during the war and establishing a community of bird-houses for purple martins. And, of course, he watched birds, though, he apologized later, his notes were "noticeably irregular and incom-plete due in the main to lack of spare time from regular occupation."

Still, he must have been the most contented of watchers, studying birds he rarely if ever saw up north, collecting eggs, writing reports for birding journals as well as for the U.S. Biological Survey. The village was half a dozen miles from the Gulf, near the confluence of the St. Marks and Wakulla rivers, a first stop for many birds migrating across the Gulf in spring. On both sides of the river were open mar-shes with wide, draining creeks and wide bare mud flats at low tide.

"The gray kingbirds (*Tyrannus dominicensis*)," he wrote for the *Wil-son Bulletin,* "find almost countless members of kindred assembled when they come on weary wings from across the broad waters after a winter's distant sojourn. Here are willets (*Catoptrophorus semipalmatus*) already mating and Wilson's plover (*Ochthodromus wilsonius*) on nimble feet." He came to admire the local black vulture, which he could observe intimately when temporarily tending the local lighthouse. They were so graceful in the air, he wrote, expressing perhaps his deep urge to escape, that "one might almost be willing to be a buzzard to fly like that." Becoming patron saint of the local purple martins, which found the mouth of the Wakulla River a good landmark in spring, he put up a nesting box for them and two pairs settled in. That brought, he wrote, "a civic awakening to our town. Several boxes have been put up around the village and considerable interest manifested in the birds." The next year, eighteen pairs nested and the following year Pennock heard a "tumult at my boxes" and happily saw thirty birds setting up quarters.

All the while he was making these observations and writing about them, other birders were in the region. Journals of the period contain reports from the area by members of the Biological Survey to which Williams contributed. The noted birder Ludlow Griscom, who must have met Pennock at some time, took a bird census in Goose Creek, just ten miles from St. Marks, in 1915. None of them seemed curious about John Williams—not enough, at any rate, to look him up, although he had, by filing so many reports, established himself as a birder worth consulting. There was no indication that Williams tried to conceal himself. In fact, it seemed sometimes as if he were trying to attract somebody's attention.

When his brother-in-law finally did show up, Pennock seemed almost to be expecting him and agreed that he should come home. First he dashed off a note to Witmer Stone. "You sure fixed the lone fisherman for fair," he told his old friend and rescuer. "I will be forever indebted to you for straightening out the web. Am sending some boxes of skins in your care." Resuming his life back in Kennett Square, as if nothing had happened, Charlie Pennock attended DVOC meetings, wrote for birding journals, went on bird walks and gave talks to local groups. "I had a good time going over my St. Marks notes," he wrote Stone, and went back to the village to show Mrs. Pennock where he had been all those years. Resuming his conversations with owls there, he called on some burrowing owls ten times a day and the female "in amiable mood would greet the caller with cheery twitter or a winsome curtsey." He had lost none of his gift for conversing with owls and told of one bird that responded to his calls with "a rather musical throaty rippling trill, with a flutter of the feathers of the throat."

He was, however, becoming a little crochety and got into a petulant argument with the loyal Witmer Stone over some of the skins and books his despairing wife had given the academy. Would the academy please return the books and the skins of the ivory-billed woodpecker, Carolina paroquet (parakeet) and passenger pigeon, all now extinct and therefore more valuable. This has "placed me in a very embarrassing position," Stone replied, uncomfortable at having to deal sharply with his friend. The academy spent time, trouble and money preserving them, else "there would have been no collection whatsoever by the time you came back from Florida." Stiffly Pennock said that if the academy preferred "to hold the word of the Academy for less than the value of three birdskins, I will let the matter drop." Apparently the matter was settled amicably: the academy kept the skins, the books were returned to Pennock.

The disappearance and the return of Pennock-Williams caused a confusion in ornithological publications. The *Auk,* in its 1915 annual AOU list of "Deceased Members," listed "Pennock, Charles John (Disappeared)." In its October 1919 issue, the *Auk* published "Notes from St. Marks, Fla." signed by "John Williams" while "Pennock, Charles John" was still listed as deceased and disappeared. The *Wilson*

Bulletin, in the 1918 Wilson roster, listed as a member "Williams, John, St. Marks, Fla." and on the same page listed "Deceased Member, Pennock, Charles John." In 1921, Pennock was an active Wilson member (no explaining that he had previously been deceased) and there was no mention of John Williams, who left the membership as abruptly and inexplicably as he had appeared.

Indexes of bird books and periodicals were also complicated. In the *Wilson Bulletin,* the Pennock listings were followed by "(see also, Williams, John)" and the Williams listings were followed by "(=C. J. Pennock)." The bibliography in Arthur Bent's *Life History of Marsh Birds* lists him as Pennock, while the index calls him Williams. Completely unembarrassed by all this, the *Wilson Bulletin,* in 1924, in its "Newsy notes about members," reported that "Mr. C. J. Pennock, with whose Florida writings our readers are quite familiar, is spending the winter again in Florida," never remarking that the familiar writings were mostly signed by John Williams. In 1922, after Williams had left St. Marks and dissolved into Pennock, Ludlow Griscom and Maunsell Crosby went to the village and, in recording 109 species, cited John Williams' list of the area's birds as the standard for the region—an irony that the most enduring of Charles Pennock's works should be credited to his short-lived alter ego.

In 1934, Charles J. Pennock went on a different list in *Cassinia,* the DVOC journal: "Retired Member." He was seventy-seven. When he died the next year, *Cassinia,* which had years before listed him as "Deceased Member (Disappeared)," now simply put him down as "Deceased Member."

9

The Collectors

In 1902, a little pamphlet by an indignant birder pecked at the conscience of the birding community. The writer, Reginald Robbins, an occasional contributor to ornithological journals, gave his essay a noncommittal title, "Bird Killing as a Method in Ornithology," and began: "1) The subject is of much importance in the present practice of ornithology. 2) No ornithologist will feel any sympathy with the writer's extreme position."

After this deadpan beginning, Robbins went on into a hot-tempered attack on the accepted practice of collecting, i.e., shooting birds. He cited the contents of the October 1901 issue of *Auk*. Of eight leading articles, six involved killing birds. Of eighteen general notes, ten recorded killing birds—and two apologized for not having done so. Ornithologists, Robbins said, speak up for protecting the lives of birds but, "using turgid talmudic arguments," they exempt themselves from this duty, practicing "murder and criminal curiosity." If a bird is familiar, the kind that comes to the same place repeatedly, the ornithologist will not bother to kill it. But let a different one come in and it is promptly shot. This, he maintained, can deprive the race of an innovation and lead to the suicide of ornithology.

Robbins' paper cogently summed up arguments that had occupied the birding community for some years. As he prophesied, few ornithologists showed any sympathy for his position. "Abstruse," one critic called it, an "extreme position." But Robbins had hit a very tender spot and his pamphlet presaged a bitterness that was to infect bird watchers more and more during the next decades. And, as a matter of fact, not only bird watchers.

Nothing so expresses the ambivalence that Americans have historically felt toward nature than the attitude birders have shown towards their subjects. The American has wanted in his heart to preserve nature, contributing money to set up nature sanctuaries, paying taxes for parks, joining societies for the protection of animals and becoming more devoted to protecting land, air and water. But he has waffled. If a new highway had to go through a virgin woodland to save him a quarter of an hour's driving time, he would—a little uneasily, perhaps—let the road go through and not mourn too long the loss of a few-score trees. If a marsh had to be filled in to build an industry that would bring local jobs and reduce taxes he would not oppose the fill.

And so it has been in bird watching. Audubon was appalled at the commercial egg hunters in Labrador whose depredations gravely endangered many species, and he was saddened at the passing of the great auk, killed by man's thoughtless greed. "Nature herself seems perishing," he wrote in his later years. But he could also make that remark, already cited, about shooting a hundred birds a day and note, in writing about Zenaida doves: "In less than an hour I shot nineteen individuals." In the journals of his last western expedition, he wrote: "Today shot 18 meadowlarks, 11 sparrows, 34 bobolink..." and from that trip he brought six thousand bird skins back home. Often he did hold back, refusing once to continue shooting marbled godwits in the Florida Keys "although the temptation was at times great and they flew over and wheeled around for a while." He had, of course, a reasonable purpose in his shooting: he needed specimens to study and assure detailed accuracy in his art. Yet, did he need eighteen meadowlarks? Didn't his hundred-a-day bags include many duplicates of what he already had? In his shooting how much was he the careful scientist, how much the irrepressible hunter?

But these are the questions of later generations. Collecting was, and long continued to be, a sanctioned practice of ornithologists and they showed few compunctions about it, except for the word "shooting." They rarely used it. Instead of being shot, a bird was "collected" or "taken." There was, to be sure, a distinction. If you shot a bird and lost it among the trees, you didn't collect or take it. It seems pretty certain, however, that "shooting" was avoided not for semantic reasons but to hide some secret doubt about the act, or even shame. Elliott Coues, who defended what he called the "shotgun school" of ornithology, himself expressed the doubts. After listening to the "curious music" of some warblers, he killed one and suddenly, he admitted, he thought of the act as "inevitable tragedy, for tragedy it is and I cannot, after picking up warm, bloody little birds for years, make anything else out of it or learn to look on with indifference." William Brewster once watched a hawk tear at a purple martin it had caught and found himself "moved by deep pity and fierce wrath to an extent surprising on the part of one who, like myself, has killed thousands of birds without suffering more than an occasional slight qualm."

No man wrote more understandingly or voluminously about birds than Arthur C. Bent, in his many volumes of life histories. He would inveigh against the "sordid minds" of the commercial plume hunters, yet one of his cherished memories was of "the thrill" he experienced after shooting a (northern) saw-whet owl, how "surprised and delighted" he was when he looked at its "exquisite soft plumage and its big yellow eyes."

Like so many ornithologists and birders of the time, Bent was a game hunter as well and saw no anomaly in being both. "I was born and bred to be a coot shooter," he wrote, "inheriting the instinct from three generations ahead of me and I only wish that I could impart a small fraction of the pleasure we have enjoyed in following this fascinating sport."

"There is pleasure to be derived in the pursuit of what is difficult to obtain," he begins in a section on how to shoot the sandhill crane. "Cranes give plenty of opportunities to practise patience, skill, and ingenuity in outwitting them." From the "standpoint of the epicure," he says, talking of game birds, "I cannot think of any more delicious bird than a fat young brant roasted just right and served with a bottle of good burgundy. Both the birds and the bottle are now hard to get; alas, the good old days have passed . . . now that we can shoot only in the fall," he winds up, making in his text, at least, no connection between the shortage and the good old days.

A double standard seems to weave through his work. "I have lived to be nearly 50 years old, before I saw my first wild swan," he complains. "If the insatiable desire to kill had not so possessed sportsmen, I might have seen one earlier in my life." Yet he speaks admiringly of the quaint shooting feats of Frank Forester, who shot 125 woodcock in one day, 70 the next—"joyous occasions" laced with applejack. And he tells blandly of a farmer who shot 56 sharp-shinned hawks while sitting in a chair in his front yard.

These instances may seem to belabor a point but the pertinent thing about them is that they represent the open feelings of a wise and dedicated generation of birders, not of thoughtless or venal hunters. The world of bird watchers is filled with men who shared Bent's ambivalence, who took great pleasure in hunting, boasted about their bags and then, in a 180-degree turn, became the most effective of bird protectors. An extraordinary example was George H. Mackay, one of Bent's most helpful contributors. Born in Boston in 1843, he went into the East India trade for the family firm, rounded the Horn fourteen times and shot seabirds while on his voyages, giving his specimens to the Smithsonian. Well-off in his own right, he married a Nantucket Starbird and could afford the time and expense of long and frequent hunting trips. They became the center of his life and the subject of his book *Shooting Journal of George Henry Mackay 1865–1922.* "This book," his introduction starts, "is intended to show the numbers and kinds of game shot by my friends and myself. The scores represent the numbers actually bagged, not shot down."

The entries, which actually start in 1861, go this way.

> From Oct 1 to 27, 1861. Marblehead Neck, Mass. This is a sum total of the game killed for 26 days. My friend Joe Kendall being with me most of the time. 203 coot (scoters), 4 golden plover, 5 Beetle head (Bufflehead)—212.
>
> From Oct 2 to 16 1862. Rockport, Mass. 243 Coot, 1 Canada goose—244.
>
> March 17 1863. Went alone to Martha's Vineyard. Miserable time, no fowl, no luck. Came home disgusted. 20 sheldrake, 4 black ducks—24.

At Lake Champlain in 1865 he complained that he had no decent decoys or guides and in two weeks shot only 105 birds, including 11 snipe. At Lownes Plantation, near Pocataligo, South Carolina, in January 1867, on what a companion called "one of the most agreeable ducking raids I have ever engaged in," 95 birds were bagged in two days despite the fact that hunting time was lost because his friend Joe

Kendall fell overboard and had to change—"36 birds were bagged on the 29th, and 59 on the 30th."

On that same trip, the hunters came on a rice field with thousands of ducks and geese and made the "necessary preparations for the slaughter." With enough ammunition "to take a reasonable sized city" they set decoys and "the next half hour before daylight was one of the most exciting of my shooting experience. Surrounded by hundreds of fowl, calling, quacking and whistling within a stone's throw we had a sort of dread to break the stillness by firing the first gun. It was load and fire. . . . Shot down about 100, able to land about 70. 33 baldpates." A gale on a following day was "music in my ears." Standing knee-deep in a mudbank, doubled up by the wind, he found the shooting "splendid. The score below is sufficient commentary: 96 baldpates." On the trip: 191 baldpate [American widgeon], 100 green-winged teal, 68 shovelers, 54 sprig-tails or pin-tail ducks, 26 mallards. And so on:

> Palmetto Island, South Carolina, Feb 24 1866. The shooting lasted only two hours, 105 long-billed curlew, 28 great marbled godwits.
>
> Spring 1867, Bush River, Maryland. In all, 205 in five days' shooting. (Big.)
>
> Bridgehampton, Long Island, July 4–15 1870. A total of 77 woodcock.
>
> May 23, 1871. We went in for a pie today and shot everything: 16 white birds, sanderling and pipers, 1 black-breasted [black-bellied] plover, 1 red-breasted sandpiper, 1 red-backed sandpiper [dunlin], 7 chicken birds, turnstones, 5 peeps [sandpipers], 5 ringnecks. 36.

At St. James, Minnesota, in August 1871, in two days' shooting, he and his partner shot 252 prairie-chickens. Pausing to sum up, he made "A List of American Birds Shot by George H. Mackay": osprey, turkey, vulture, barn swallow, six kinds of warblers, bluebird, cardinal, oriole, ruby-throated hummingbird, passenger pigeon, great northern diver or loon, herring gull, mockingbirds . . . and so on for more than five pages, 190 different species.

In the 1890s something happened. The entries skipped from 1897 to 1904 and then there was a gap of almost twenty years. Perhaps a reason for the gap is tucked in a letter he wrote William Brewster,

whom he often provided with specimens (and charged him properly
for them, e.g., $1.50 for a king eider). "Birds are scarcer than ever on
Nantucket," he wrote Brewster on July 20, 1892. "I note great change
in this respect since my advent on that island."

There was also a great change in Mackay and it is suggested in a
comment dropped in an article for *Auk.* "To see them on their breeding grounds in such countless numbers," he said, writing about terns,
"cannot fail to create in the mind of the ornithological student a
profound and most lasting impression." And he talked about the
"pleasure to be derived from companionship of these beautiful and
interesting birds." Mackay had moved from hunter to bird watcher
and had begun writing less about shooting and more on birding and
birds, and on protecting them, a matter that from then on absorbed
him. His credentials as a collector gave him a special standing as a
protectionist. "The present year," he wrote in 1892, "a vigorous
effort had been made by inhabitants of the adjacent islands Nantucket
and Tuckernuck to obtain a repeal of the present law for their protection to take the eggs for food purposes. Having taken an active part
with some friends in the bird's defense, the objectionable petition was
not granted and the satisfaction I have taken in seeing the results
amply compensate me for the part I took in the matter."

The depredation of eggs and feather hunters was threatening to
kill off another seabird on Nantucket, the laughing gull. The authoritative Edward Howe Forbush reported:

> At one time there were not over 12 pairs of laughing gulls left
> on the island. The species would soon have vanished but for
> Mr. Mackay's influence in state legislation for the protection of
> birds and in the town affairs of Nantucket. Mainly through his
> good offices the town authorities were induced to employ a
> warden to guard the birds during the breeding season on the
> island. . . . Since this guardianship was assumed, the birds have
> increased, slowly indeed for the first ten years but more rapidly
> since until now (1923) there are thousands of laughing gulls on
> the island; and they appear during the summer in numbers not
> only for miles around but also on the coasts of the three south-
> ern New England states, in places where for many years they
> were seldom or never noted.

Writing for ornithological publications, Mackay showed himself to
be as skillful an observer as he had been a hunter. In April 1892,

watching double-crested cormorants off Newport, he noticed a large number of curious balls on nearby rocks which appeared to have been ejected by the birds. After studying them, he could report accurately on the cormorant's diet: the balls were composed almost entirely of the bones of young parrot fish and drumfish. He solved a problem that had puzzled loon watchers: how did the birds manage to swallow fish much too big for their mouths. Wrote Forbush:

> Mr. George H. Mackay on April 18 1890 on West Island, Sakonnet Point, Rhode Island, saw a Loon preparing to swallow a flounder about 5 inches in diameter. The Loon dropped it on the water, pecked it and bit it. . . . When the fish escaped the bird dived after it and thus kept at it for fully five minutes; then stretching up his head with the bill pointing toward the sky, swallowed it. Mr. Mackay says he could hardly have believed this possible had he not seen it.

His ornithological observations were still tinged by a hunter's bias. "Stupid," he called the white-winged scoter: it could be "attracted by anything resembling a duck, even a plain black block of wood, and seemed to consider itself safe in the company of the most grotesque and clumsy and unnatural of wooden decoys." For years Mackay seems too busy watching and protecting birds to have anything to enter in his hunting journal until, sixteen years before he died, he made one of his last entries:

> October 7, 1921. With the exception of one day many years ago when I shot 16 yellowlegs and a black-breasted [blackbellied] plover, I have not shot a gun for 24 years. So today I thought I would try again with my son George Jr. If I could have a little practice, I feel I could come back to my old shooting form fairly well. 3 black-bellied plover, 1 American golden plover, 1 longbill, 1 grayback, 1 red-backed sandpiper [dunlin] . . .

By that time collecting in America was being rather stringently regulated. New York had passed a law in 1886 requiring anyone who wanted to shoot certain birds to have a scientific reason and a license. While some old-line ornithologists looked on this with some alarm, feeling that science was being persecuted by sentimentality, the birding community in general approved of such regulations and often proposed them. William Brewster, who, in 1881, had held that "a bird's life should count as nothing against the establishment of a new fact," spoke differently twenty-five years later when noting that it was "becoming more and more difficult to obtain specimens." It was, he acknowledged, "because of the ever-increasing and in the main, wholesome feeling against killing for whatever purpose."

The last, unyielding bastion for collectors was the Cooper Ornithological Club (now called Society) of California, at least as represented by its sage and strong-minded leader, Joseph Grinnell. The club was founded in Santa Clara, California, two decades after Brewster and friends had organized their club in Boston. But the name itself recalled a significant earlier epoch in American natural history. James G. Cooper, the club's namesake, was the son of William Cooper, namesake to a hawk and one of the men who had made New York City a center for naturalists. James Cooper was one of Spencer Baird's army medical corps ornithologists in the contingent mapping a railroad route from St. Louis to Puget Sound. His contributions to the biographies of western American birds, Baird said, were the most valuable since the time of Audubon. After serving during the war in the California volunteers, Dr. Cooper stayed on in the state, writing *Ornithology of California,* producing the first good work on the distribution of plants and animals in the West and informally instructing a young generation in ornithology. Taking his students out into the country, he would sit on some convenient rock or log and use the birds that flew about them as texts for his lessons.

He was a much-loved man and when a birders' club was organized in 1893, it was automatically named after him. Its journal was named after the region's most spectacular bird, the condor, and an early article told of two railroad trackwalkers, one of whom captured a condor by hitting it with a shovel and then had to flee to safety on a big boulder while the enraged bird, its wing broken, stalked around him. The two men managed to knock the bird down with a pole, tie it up, set its broken wing and put it in a pen. But the bird, reversing roles, intimidated its captors, who had to keep a safe distance, toss its food into the pen and were relieved when, after a year, the bird escaped, leaving them free men again.

The pages of *The Condor* repeatedly declared the West's independence of eastern birders and showed a touchiness at being looked on as provincial. The club's president, Frank S. Daggett, complained that the American Ornithologists' Union considered only two or three of Cooper's ninety members fit to join its ranks. Even when the AOU liberalized its membership rules Mr. Daggett was not altogether appeased because AOU members didn't fraternize with Cooper members, and their new rules gave the impression that the AOU was conferring an honor on the westerners in considering them for membership. The veteran members of the AOU, he charged, had become increasingly inactive. Their names were still something "to conjure with but their life work is behind them. The Union will be dominated by a handful of men, if it has not already reached that point."

The Californians would not let up on anything, even accusing the AOU of unjustly omitting many western subspecies from their check lists. But the strongest and longest-lived differences between the Californians and the easterners were over collecting. The Cooper club was as firm as any group about bird protection, initiating, supporting and helping enforce legislation. But its membership included many unreconstructed collectors, fiercely against any rules that would limit an ornithologist's right to shoot birds as he saw fit.

When the AOU's Committee on Bird Protection proposed in 1903 that collectors put up a bond when applying for a license to shoot birds, *The Condor* attacked "the particular zeal" of the committee, which, it pointed out, was made up of erstwhile collectors, that is, backsliders. Under such laws only three permits to collect could be in force in any one state at any one time, an outrageous suggestion. "As a prominent bird man recently said," the editor wrote, " 'I would rather see 1,000 birds killed through lack of laws than have one ornithologist discouraged through hardship imposed by arbitrary legislation. Fortunately our own state is still free.' "

J. A. Allen, the usually soft-spoken editor of *Auk,* seemed a little shaken by what he termed this "most surprising outburst of criticism and abuse, so evidently prompted by selfishness." "The proposal," he said, "had been originally drafted in 1886 and adopted by New York that year and today the only objection comes from liberty loving California." To which *The Condor* reported that Allen had turned the "artillery of his strenuous rhetoric" on *The Condor*. If its own mild editorial was an "outburst," what "special epithet" should be applied to Allen's?

The arguments grew furiously transcontinental. After P. M. Silloway had reported that, for his studies of the Holboell's grebe (red-necked grebe) in Montana, he had taken all the eggs from a colony of nests in Swan Lake, William Dutcher of the Audubon Society sternly questioned whether it was right "to sacrifice twenty-eight young birds and the consequent distress of the parents." One typical

set would have been ample to establish the fact that the Holboell's
grebe breeds in Montana. "Wasteful and reprehensible," he called
the taking.

Silloway gave no ground:

> It is the mission of lower animal life to minister to the gratifica-
> tion of the higher. This law of nature is enumerated in the
> Great Book and has ever been the basis of man's dealings with
> inferior creatures. It is my creed that if a set of eggs can minis-
> ter to the pleasure of any number of observers, there is no
> question of the collector's right.

And, having established his biblical claim, Silloway explained that he
had gone back to Swan Lake and found the grebes nesting again with
a second clutch of eggs in their nests. So, he declared, he had done
no ultimate harm.

"Theorists," said Chester Barlow, the editor-in-chief of *Condor,*
are "as useless as a fifth wheel on a coach" and attacked the "ambitious extremist" who within his "narrow mind evolves a whining article" on bird protection. No one person, of course, spoke for the entire
membership, and this was too much for a dissenting member, Garret
Newkirk of Pasadena. The "unflinching destructive disposition of
even some of the better class of collectors," the belief that "the only
good bird is a dead bird," was abhorrent to him. Collectors kill "beings who love and mate, who build homes with marvelous wisdom and
skill; these are hunted, robbed and killed without any consideration
of their rights." He cited an article by Barlow. "Eighteen specimens
were taken," he had reported.

"The writers handle their English deftly," Newkirk remarked.
"They never say killed, slaughtered or murdered but 'taken' or some
such gentle word. For example [Grinnell had said that] on a succeeding visit to the same field the mother bird appeared 'but was extremely
wary. She flew past the bush and alighted but would not go to the nest.
Then she flew up the hill again when I collected her.' Now I should
like to say seriously why one dozen birds should not have been sufficient, leaving six at least to enjoy life; also why the bright little mother
should have been 'collected' merely for dissection to show that her
nest of eggs was complete." He quoted *Bird-Lore*'s motto, "A bird in
the bush is worth two in the hand," and pointed out that *Bird-Lore*'s
editor, Frank M. Chapman, had once been a collector himself.

One reader took exception to the paraphrase of the saying that the only good Indian is a dead Indian. "The late Major Bendire," he declared, "hunted Indians and birds in the same country and killed both with equal lack of compunction when the blood of murdered settlers cried aloud for vengeance or the authorities at the National Museum wanted positive identification."

When Ernest Thompson Seton, nature writer and artist, suggested that only museum experts be allowed to collect, *Condor* summoned up two patriarchs of birding: "Shades of Audubon and Coues! This approaches pretty near the limit." Many ornithologists had no connections with museums—almost all of them west of the Mississippi would have been out if the Seton proposal had been put into effect: "The editor has little patience with the wild fights of ultra enthusiasts" who preach "total abstinence." With more patience than the editor, H. S. Swarth, curator of the Museum of History, Science and Anthropology, explained rationally why collectors felt they had to shoot several birds of the same species. "Being desirous of obtaining a specimen of the linnet in fresh fall plumage I shot into the birds at random," he reported, and was rewarded by seeing red markings on two females. The markings had been observed before only on males and this chance collecting provided new data.

A League for the Extermination of Amateur Ornithologists was proposed by Dr. Harold Gifford of Omaha. He would not kill off "the mere bird lovers" or professional ornithologists who were "a necessary minor evil" but the man "who collects birds, skins and eggs as a boy collects stamps," who is "sure death to any rare bird that crosses his path . . . the no-specimen, no-record man who will sacrifice anything that flies for the satisfaction of clinching his claim to an unimportant record"; included also was that "noxious by-product, the collector for money, who may make rare birds extinct and should be put in the same abhorrent category as plume collectors." Tolerantly printing this, *Condor* noted that "the above does not, of course, represent to any degree the views of the Editors." It is the "view of the extreme bird protectionist whose field of vision is narrowed until he can see optimum good only in the conservation of each and every individual bird." He does not realize that "with the extermination of amateur ornithologists scientific ornithology is doomed to die out inside of a generation."

The Cooper Club itself was officially divided on the issue. Its northern division, based in San Francisco, where Grinnell taught, passed a resolution opposing restrictions on collecting eggs and nests that were being imposed under a new law. No permits at all were being issued, it asserted. The southern division, based in Santa Barbara, rejected the resolution and supported the effort to "prevent the ruthless slaughter of birds and destruction of their nests." Permits, it said, were held back only from hobbyists and commercial collectors. Serious members of the club "have been very fairly treated."

Commercial collectors, who were being made everybody's villains, had long been a respected part of the birding community. John Bell of New York and John Krider of Philadelphia were looked on as elders of the science. Though many commercial collectors shot birds for people who simply wanted to build little private museums, and were interested more in owning specimens than in studying them, the responsible professionals collected only for serious students and museums. They were cited in ornithologies, consulted by museums, looked on as authoritative contributors to the science. One of the most highly regarded was Wilmot Brown who worked in the West and, along with specimens, sent very interesting notes. A long and wearing search for Heermann's gull took him to Isla de Fonso in the Gulf of California. There were fifteen thousand birds on the island, he reported, "so occupied with lovemaking, they paid little attention to us. They would hold their bills in a tug of war, talking to each other in low love tones." After patiently waiting for the lovemaking to result in eggs, Brown obtained "a very large series." Collecting Craveri's murrelets cost Brown many nights' sleep because the murrelets were such noisy nocturnal birds, "butting" into "the tent walls in their amorous frolics," he reported. One pair in their excitement hit head onward, thrashed to the ground, into the tent and into his bed, where Brown threw his blanket over them. "This is the first collecting," he confided to Brewster, "I have ever done in bed."

These same arguments over collecting, of course, were taking place in other birding groups but were generally conducted more discreetly than in California, which proclaimed its differences openly and heatedly. In part this was the doing of the almost undisputed leader of California birding, Joseph Grinnell, a professor of zoology who, when he was not actually heading the Cooper Club as president, was still its most influential voice as editor of *The Condor*. A man with a gift for imagery—to him the varied thrush was the "Mesmer of the woods" whose song had the "quavering twang of a banjo string on a cracked bridge"—he also had a many-sided talent for dispute, involving the club in controversies both relevant and irrelevant to birding. At one time he proposed that *The Condor* expand its field to include all other vertebrates. "Brief poignant comments are invited," he said in announcing a postcard vote on his proposal. The vote was two to one in favor but the comments apparently went far beyond the poignant. The "vigor" of dissent, Grinnell said in announcing the vote, and the "threats of subsequent dire calamity" caused him to "hasten to cover with our little scheme." The magazine will continue "on its feathered career, unblemished with any glint of fur or scales."

He was more persistent and less lighthearted in another crusade —for simplified spelling. It was, he wrote, giving fair warning on what he was up to, "a wid-spred movment which is essentially progressiv" using such words as "geografical, publisht, redy, dismist, discust, altho, fesants, krinkled. . . ." But, as he put in a 1914 editorial, this had put the editor "in a quandary." Readers had complained that he was using the magazine to satisfy a personal whim and denounced the spelling as an "eyesore." He called for a mail vote which would ask: "Simplified Spelling, yes. Simplified Spelling, no." If reversed, he said, apparently to ease any fear of reprisal, he would "defer meekly" to the will of the majority and would hold no personal grudge against those who disagreed with him. Possibly members might have been tempted to vote no just for the rare chance of seeing Grinnell behave meekly about anything. The first vote from Californians gave Grinnell a narrow victory but when the vote from all members came in it was sixty-three no to forty-four yes. "The editor was disappointed in his cherished hope," he wrote and, forgoing meekness, went at cautious people who were averse to abrupt change, even a good one.

But Grinnell's great battles were fought in defense of collecting and he summed up the arguments for the practice in an essay entitled "Conserve the Collector." He has watched the decrease in collectors, he said, with "considerable apprehension" since the "skin record is essential." The "opera glass student" cannot be depended on to take the place of the collector. It is true, he said, barely acknowledging what had been going on, that collectors perhaps "in some instances behaved indifferently toward people who are sensitive to bird killing." But ornithology as a science is threatened and it should not be allowed to lapse wholly into the status of a recreation or a hobby "to be indulged in only in a superficial way by amateurs or dilettantes."

The tendency towards "extermination of the collectors" is related to the "increasing number of extreme sentimentalists," he charged. Conservation began as a good cause but lawmakers yielded to "militant sentimentalists," ignoring the needs of ornithologists. Sure, Grinnell said, give permits only "upon avowed sincerity or purpose" and put limitations on rare species (his own average was twelve a day).

Collectors are entitled to equal rights with sportsmen. There is "no more practical reason for shooting a snipe for sport than for shooting a savannah sparrow for a specimen." Collectors, he added, kill the predacious blue jay and the predatory Cooper's and sharp-shinned hawks, which kill other birds. Collecting is self-limiting because it is hard work. It is more demanding than hunting: the collector must show "industry and artistic skill and the naturalist's gift." The collector's satisfaction is more enduring than the hunter's: he observes many things while stalking and his specimen has more value because it adds to knowledge. Kept as "an object of study and appreciation" instead "of being merely eaten, it becomes a joy forever."

The club, of course, had other things on its mind, encouraging and publishing definitive studies on western birds and opening to general knowledge the immense ornithological riches of California. *The Condor*'s editors could sometimes relax and turn irony on themselves, as when they reported that Theodore Jesse Hoover, brother of the president, for whom a subspecies of warbler is named, went out to hunt for fossil birds in the ancient tar beds at Independence, California. "From force of habit," *Condor* noted, "Mr. Hoover took a gun with him." Perhaps to collect archaeopteryx?

The collector gave ground steadily, if grudgingly, to the force of law and birder opinion. Eventually what made it easier for him to give up his gun was the increasing use and reliability of field glasses. For most of the nineteenth century glasses were hardly used at all by watchers. Alexander Wilson first tried one—a monocular glass, or telescope—only two years before his death in 1813. Audubon used one from time to time, finding a seaman's glass particularly helpful when he was off the rocky islands near Labrador to get a close-up look at gannets on the crowded ledges. In 1853, Henry Thoreau, after having birded in Concord for some twenty years, debated with himself over the value of getting a glass. "In some respects methinks it would be better than a gun. The latter brings them nearer dead. The former alive." Two months later he bought one and his notes indicate that he used it frequently and successfully. "I have come with a spyglass to look at hawks," he wrote in his journal and, observing a red-tailed hawk, he wrote: "Resting the glass in the crotch of a young oak, I can see every wink and the color of its iris."

The telescope was awkward to use since, as Thoreau discovered, it needed some support. After the Civil War the binocular glass began to replace the monocular. At first, watchers went out with opera glasses, dainty affairs that required delicate handling in the field. They were two-powered, i.e., magnified the image only twice (today's glasses are three or four times that powerful), and their lenses, not too faithfully ground, distorted colors. A young Japanese student in Massachusetts, introduced to watching by a group of local birders, began by collecting birds with a slingshot but, as he wrote a friend, "a law was passed that if I shoot any more I shall have to pay $10. I have an opera glass lent to me but sometimes the rainbow forms around the bird and it is impossible to tell the color."

The most profound result of the use of the glass was, quite possibly, the ways it opened bird watching to women. Florence Merriam in 1890 said that though opera glasses "were very imperfect and of small magnifying power" they made it easier for women bird watchers to make field observations "despite the cumbersome clothes they then had to wear." By that time, birding journals were reporting that "the field glass is more and more coming to replace the gun" and one convert reported that "my list of acquaintances passed the hundred mark and all without a gun. Try the field glass. It works." Acceptance, however, was tentative. One advertisement in a birding journal, inserted by a watcher who apparently hedged his bets, went: "Wanted: a good shotgun, 12 gauge, and a good field glass."

As might be expected among watchers, the introduction of the field glass also introduced a whole new area for argument. Old-line birders, even after good field glasses were available, always referred sneeringly to "opera-glass advocates" and insisted that sightings made with the glass could not be trusted because they tempted observers to make snap judgments and left no proof in hand. "Which does the most harm?" asked H. R. Taylor in a letter to *Condor,* "a spyglass ornithologist with a ready imagination who describes things never heard of before (and which never really happened) or a sane student of birds who is obliged to use a gun and whose writing may be depended on for information and not for imagination." Other collectors cited the British birding maxim: "What's shot's, history; what's seen's, mystery." The nature writer and guide John Burroughs used to scold his students for using a glass. "Don't ogle through a glass. Shoot!," he would tell them, until—like George Mackay—he turned ardent protectionist. William Brewster, amiably straddling the issue, proclaimed that the glass was for diversion, the gun for study.

By 1900 four-powered glasses were being widely used. In the years that followed, the introduction of prisms instead of multiple lenses made field glasses more powerful, more accurate, more convenient and less expensive. In 1922, a writer in *Auk* announced that "the

majority of bird lovers now happily use the glass instead of the gun,"
and Witmer Stone declared that "what is now needed is descriptions
of our birds based on field characters as seen through glasses, not
from birdskins in hand." Still, he thought, birders who use glasses
should "carry a gun also, just in case." In 1933, as if signing off an
era, Frank M. Chapman, who had himself once been an active collector, wrote: "Let not the field student of today, who never knew the
gun, forget that his glass has won its standing on a foundation which
could have been laid only with the aid of the gun."

10

A Pastime for Chums

One very popular aspect of collecting went out of favor not with fits of anger but with a kind of nostalgic regret. Until the early decades of this century, collecting birds' eggs and nests—oology—was as common as bird watching and listing is today. Scientists and serious students were involved in it but for the most part it was the pastime of boys at the age when collecting—almost anything—was an end in itself.

It was a popular enough hobby to support a magazine called *The Young Oologist* (later *The Oologist*) which was filled with advice, encouragements to swapping and stories which had an idyllic, boys'-book air of innocents going out to seek prize and adventure. In "A Day with a Young Collector," Benjamin Leigh in 1886 told of his quests. "Every Saturday my chum and I were in the habit of going on a walk for the purpose of collecting eggs and usually had the most miserable luck. The last day we were at school we determined to go out in a new direction. I saw a Baltimore oriole and its nest in the top of an old pear tree. My chum volunteered to climb for it. When he got half way up, the old birds commenced to halloo 'bloody murder' and we felt badly to take their nests but could not help ourselves."

The tree bent under the weight, the tale goes on, but they got the

nest and four light-gray eggs. Being careful oologists, they noted that
the nest was made of grass, threads and bits of wool. While Ben was
climbing, a pair of kingbirds made noises at him, leading them to
suspect that they had a nest in a nearby tree. Putting the oriole eggs
carefully away, "I climbed into a tree and found my conjecture was
right," wrote Ben, and took a nest with three fresh eggs.

After this fine start they ran into a sparse spell—nothing but a
catbird's nest, not worth bothering with. Then Ben's companion
called out to come quickly: he had found a wood thrush's nest with
three eggs, two almost hatched. Their luck continued. A country boy
asked what they were doing and led them to a nest which turned out
to be an ovenbird's with five reddish-brown eggs—a great find. Then
he showed them a flicker's nest on top of a high dead stump with three
pure white eggs. It was a happy day: six nests, twenty-two eggs.

It was not always so good. R. R. Reardom and his chum—in these
accounts the friend was always called "chum"—took the train from
Philadelphia to Fort Washington on May 28, 1887, and nothing went
right. They spotted an oriole's nest way out on a branch of a button-
wood tree but couldn't get at it. They saw a warbling vireo's nest but
decided to take it on the way back. They got close enough to a
red-eyed vireo's nest to see the red in the female's eyes before chasing
her off and taking her four eggs. An owl's nest had nothing in it and
"of course we did not take" eggs from a robin's nest. In a towhee's
nest they found a cowbird's egg and then happily came on a tanager's
nest—their first—with three eggs. Though there were lots of birds
around, nests were hard to spot. They started to dig into a sandbank
for a kingfisher's nest but it was several feet in and, while they were
arguing over whether it was worth going after, it started to rain,
making a bad day worse. They had to turn back and felt too tired to
go after that warbling vireo nest they had passed up, so they decided
to go fishing instead and caught one eel.

Most young collectors never went beyond taking common eggs—
robin, catbird, pewee, chipping sparrow—which they would pierce
with a pencil, blow out and hang up on a string. Oology was simply
a chance to climb, collect, swap and fairly soon throw out their boxes
of unlabeled eggs and dried nests as a part of a vanished boyhood.
Those who kept on knew they were following in the steps of many
distinguished ornithologists. Brewer, Baird, Brewster, Coues, all collected eggs when they were young and kept on through their lives.
The serious young oologist was methodical about the eggs he took.
He pierced them carefully with a drill, blew out the contents with a

little pip, washed them delicately with water, marked them to identify the bird, put down the number of eggs in the nest and the date taken and then packed them carefully in cotton-lined containers—usually cigar boxes—to be taken out again and again and admired or offered up for exchange.

The advertising pages of the *Oologist,* which went through several changes of name and ownership, were full of tempting offers for robin's eggs at two cents each to roadrunner's at forty cents and bald eagle's at a prohibitive five dollars. The editorial columns were full of advice, often conflicting. Go alone, said one instruction: companions make noise and scare birds off. Take a kid brother along, went a more cynical piece of advice: you can get him to do the hard climbing. Tell him: "No, it's not too high. The tree is sound, it will hold you. No, the wind isn't blowing much . . . No, don't come down now!" Take a fishing pole along to reach distant nests. And an old hat to carry the eggs in—you can hold it in your teeth as you climb, leaving your hands free. The advice dealt not just with technique but also with ethics. Limit your take to five sets of eggs of any one species in a season. Collectors who take twenty or thirty sets a season or enlarge their collection with robin's and catbird's eggs are "Egg Hogs." Don't collect for money: it gives the pastime a bad name and builds prejudice against oology from "cranks" who hale collectors to court.

At the serious level, of course, oology was and still is a purposeful, necessary study of an important part of a bird's life. It involves knowledge of the way birds use materials and choose sites, when and how they lay their eggs and incubate them, the shape and size and color of the eggs. An oologist, in a way, goes at birding in reverse. While most birders identify nest and eggs by looking first at the bird, the oologist can look at nest and eggs to identify the bird. Does the nest hang from the end of a branch? It is an oriole. If it is in a field amid briars, has an open instead of an arched shape, and has weed stems woven into it: a field sparrow. Does it have corky bits of wood in it: a black-throated blue warbler. A grass tunnel leading to it: a meadowlark. Song sparrows nest under tufts of grass, great blue herons in tallest trees, kingfishers in a sand bank, swifts in chimneys. Ospreys may build on telephone pole crossbars, wrens in the fold of a blanket hanging from a line or anywhere else. Some birds are fussy builders, like the cliff swallow, which makes a carefully molded nest of mud. Some are slapdash, like the robin, which builds a bulky mud-walled nest lined with coarse grass. Some are secretive, like the winter wren; some offhand, like the killdeer, which simply lays eggs in a hollow in the ground. Some are set in their ways, like the oriole, which will take any bit of white wool or string that may be around but will usually pass up colored pieces. Some are adaptable, like the crested flycatcher, which prefers to line its nest with snakeskin but nowadays will settle for the more available plastic wrapping.

The scholarly oologists are concerned with egg structure, shell thickness and strength, weight and shape. The shapes are defined as generally elliptical, long elliptical, short elliptical, subelliptical, long and short subelliptical, spherical, oval, short oval, long oval, pyriform (one end pointed, the other broad), long pyriform and short pyriform. The shape holds meaning for both the oologist and the bird. Seabird and bobwhite eggs, for example, are pyriform, in one case to keep them from rolling off the cliffs on which they are commonly laid, and in the other because a bobwhite lays as many as twenty eggs in a nest and that shape allows all of them to fit in.

The patterns on shell surfaces are described as wreathed, capped, overlaid, scribbled, scrawled, speckled, streaked, marbled, spotted, dotted, blotched, splashed. The aesthetic pleasure oologists take in the eggs is suggested in the subtle vocabulary they use to describe the infinite gradations of color: tawny olive, greenish glaucous, aniline lilac, Quaker drab. Only a few eggs—woodpecker, owl, petrel among them—are pure white. Most surfaces are smooth, although the hawk's are rough and granulate. The woodpecker's are glossy, the cormorant's are chalky and the passerine's (perching birds) are lustreless.

The oologist wanders off into a territory of odd facts that other birders miss. Northern nesting birds lay more eggs than southern nesters of the same species. A horned lark on the tundra, for example, lays four or five eggs, on the prairie it lays only two or three eggs. A reason: longer summer days in the north means that parent birds have more time to hunt for food for their young and so can support a larger brood. Some ducks are indiscriminating layers: they will lay their eggs in any convenient nest, not necessarily their own. One wood duck's nest was discovered to contain forty eggs laid by five females. "A dump nest," it is called. One oologist engaged in studying the contents of a rock wren's nest found that the bird had turned the tables and had become a collector of mankind's artifacts. By painstaking count the nest was found to contain: 67 Supreme paper clips, 1 Ideal paper clip, 628 Gem paper clips, 69 Star paper fasteners, 87 matches, 4 toothpicks, 1 screw top from LePage's glue. An oologist of Paw Paw, Michigan, told of finding a vireo nest lined with Sunday school lessons, which, he said, spoke well for the morals of Paw Paw's birds but not for those of its careless schoolboys.

The urge to find and possess eggs has driven men to distant and dangerous places. For years oologists were mystified by the Harris' sparrow, a bird named by Audubon in 1843, because they had no idea where it nested. Finally, almost a century later, George M. Sutton flushed a pair near Hudson Bay and was finally led to a nest. Kneeling to examine the eggs, Sutton felt "a thrill the like of which I never felt before . . . at my fingertips lay treasures that were beyond price." (Admiral Peary did oology a good turn when, on his trip to the North Pole, he stopped at Cape Sheridan to photograph the nest of the red knot, whose nesting place had up to then been unknown.)

Some quests ended in disappointment. Maurice Thomson in 1889 found the nest of the rare ivory-billed woodpecker, hacked thick growth away to get at it and saw "five beautiful pure white eggs, almost transparent, vastly fragile and in the eyes of a collector extremely valuable." But when he pulled at the branch, the eggs rolled out and his treasures broke.

There were more mortal tragedies. William C. Crispin, going after peregrine eggs, fell from the end of a long rope: his fate was discovered by three ladies picking wildflowers nearby who saw a rope dangling empty in midair. Francis J. Britwell, out on his honeymoon in the Sierras, climbed into a pine tree after a nest. When a heavy wind came up, he called for a rope and when he tried to put it under his armpits, it slipped over his neck. Losing his grip, he fell and, his bride watching, he choked to death. Richard P. Smithwick, digging into a sandbank after a kingfisher nest, had just reached the nest, seven feet in, when the bank caved in; they found Smithwick, smothered, his legs sticking out of his excavation.

Egg collecting had its indoor attractions—poring over the hard-gotten prizes and checking them against price lists to see how much they were worth. Master price lists were issued every few years. The last was done in 1922 by the *Oologist,* with the advice of twenty-five respected ornithologists whose interest testified to the high standing of oology at the time. Leon Dawson, author of *Birds of California,* and Arthur Cleveland Bent, the life history authority, were among them. Their suggestions were codified by a Committee of Final Values, which set the prices. They ranged from flicker, cowbird, chipping sparrow, redwing and others at the bottom price of ten cents, through the spoonbill sandpiper at $60, California vulture (condor) at $75, the vanishing ivory-billed woodpecker and vanished passenger pigeon at

$100. Some were so rare that the committee could set no price: whiskered auklet, "blue" goose, masked duck, stilt sandpiper, wandering tattler. The prices were not the actual cash value. They were rather more than the egg actually would bring but they gave comparative values. These were the basis for egg exchanges among collectors who got almost as much reward and spent almost as much time swapping eggs as hunting them.

Buyers and traders had to be wary of fakes. W. J. Wirt, a well-known dealer of Albion, New York, was accused after selling phoebe eggs as those of Wright's flycatcher. Letson Belliat of Des Moines, also known as Dean Schooler, sold mourning dove eggs as those of saw-whet owls. I. E. Miller of Huntington, Indiana, using the alias of Dr. Boyde, sold meadowlarks' eggs as woodcocks' and common terns' as plovers'.

The birding community found it easier to disavow the collecting of eggs and nests than it did to give up shooting specimens. The fact that it was so often dismissed as a boy's hobby gave egg collecting an undeservedly low rating as a science. Some grown-up collectors gave it a bad name. One expedition boasted of having taken five hundred great blue heron eggs in the Thousand Islands, another of taking three thousand eggs in the mangrove swamps of Florida. Worried oologists denounced this and tried to repair the damages being done to their discipline. They proposed that studious collectors be allowed to continue unhampered, that others be encouraged to photograph eggs without taking them from the nest, and that "those who collect only to possess eggs and proceed with insatiate greed to add and add" —especially small boys—be dealt with harshly. In 1904, Chester Reed, whose guides were the beginning books for most birders of the time, spoke sternly to his readers: "At some time during youth the desire to collect something is paramount. It is frequently a passing whim, concerned with quantity regardless of kind. Knowledge does not imply possession and the study of oology is neglected in the desire to possess. Knowledge is better than an empty egg shell or a stuffed bird skin."

While oologists would not defend "rapacity . . . and the collecting mania," they considered collecting eggs better than shooting specimens. "All I know," wrote Leon Dawson, "is that a dead bird sings no songs and lays no eggs; where a hen deprived of her egg presently lays another and cackles as merrily as before. I belong to that humble class which finds in the collecting of birds' nests and eggs a solace and an inspiration." Not every oologist was so poetically philosophical.

R. P. Sharples denounced the Audubon Society and its crusading protectionist ladies. "We are unreasonably persecuted," he declared. Taking eggs is altogether permissible because many birds are too numerous and besides, he went on swinging wildly, there is too much female bossing. "Women want to boss us at the polls, temperance advocates boss us when we are thirsty." Now after fifty years of collecting eggs he was fed up with being bossed. "I am going to move out if this thing keeps on," he threatened.

In many ways, it was generally acknowledged, the egg and nest collectors were the most knowing of birders—more careful, perceptive, patient than those who simply watched. Joel A. Allen, editor of the *Auk,* remarked that, though he did not himself collect, he admired the science. Through it, older ornithologists gained an intimacy with birds that field glass users do not get. "Of course," he went on, "in collecting eggs they destroyed the possibilities for further study of the birds which they robbed" but they gained "a knowledge of birds and their ways that is greatly to be envied."

By the 1920s, taking bird eggs and nests was frowned on by ornithologists and forbidden by law. It has remained an important part of the science and the Western Foundation for Vertebrate Zoology in Los Angeles amassed the world's largest collection of eggs and become a centre for the studies. From their researches in embryology, protein content and the structure of shells, the oologists have served not just ornithology but the common good. In the 1940s, it was discovered that the wide use of pesticides, infecting birds' food, was making egg shells so thin and fragile that they broke before hatching. Some species, notably birds of prey, could not reproduce and were in danger of being exterminated. This discovery, more than any other, stimulated the investigations of the effects of pesticides and the eventual outlawing of such materials as DDT—and led indirectly to the strength of the modern environmental movement.

By that time, oology was already obsolete as a pastime. In 1941, R. Magoon Barnes, for years its spokesman as publisher of the *Oologist,* closed up shop. There were only a couple of hundred active oologists left in the country, he explained, and he had more and more trouble getting contributions to his pages. Where his magazine was once full of stories of boys going out after eggs, it was now full of reminiscences of the old oologist who could do little more than remember those long-ago springs when, climbing out on a shaky limb with an old hat clenched in his teeth, he shared his treasures and adventures with his chum.

11

A Friend of Bird and Birder

When people talked about Edward Howe Forbush, they always mentioned "his friends" or "his many friends" or "his host of friends." Probably no birder ever had more of them and none, in turn, was better served by them than he was. His classic three-volume *Birds of Massachusetts and Other New England States* is a kind of anthology of his friends, of people who were fond both of birds and of Forbush and sent him their observations and adventures, set down exhaustively and accurately and charmingly. Going through his volumes is like going along on a long bird walk, getting to know birds through the eyes and ears and feelings of scores of birders—all their perceptions filtered through the mind of one of the finest and most literate ornithologists the country has ever known.

And when you have been with the book and its author for a while you realize that Forbush's friends are, as much as his contributors, the birds themselves. "Birds," he says, brooking no contradiction, "may be ranked among the noblest forms of life" and leaves the strong impression that he is going out of the way to be courteous to the other forms.

A man spare in appearance and habits, moderate in expressing himself, attentive to the opinions of others but firm in his own, For-

bush served as state ornithologist in Massachusetts from 1891 to
1929. To help him in his work, he enlisted his friends—hundreds
of the region's bird watchers—and sent them carefully prepared
questionnaires. These were designed to establish reliable data, but
anecdotes, discursions and opinions were also welcomed. From
the responses, Forbush compiled an encyclopedic body of information about the birds of New England, which represent about half
of the country's species.

His *Birds of Massachusetts* is a most beguiling encyclopedia, telling
a great deal about how birds behave and almost as much about how
bird watchers do. It is done as a series of life histories, a method of
presenting information on birds which evolved during the nineteenth
century. The life history is as standard a form as, say, the classical
sonata, but it permits individual styles to vary it. With Forbush it took
on a very personal tone and even in its required setting down of data
on "Description, Measurements and Molts, Field Marks, Voice,
Breeding, Range, Distribution," it carries an air of delight.

The life history of the blue jay, for example, starts out formally,
"Cyanocítta cristáta cristata (Linnaeus). Blue Jay," then goes on to a
detailed description which makes any bird watcher—who generally
thinks of the blue jay as just being blue and mostly as having a raucous
call—feel that he has been color blind and tone deaf for not having
been aware of the permutations of the color blue and of the bird's
vocalising. The top of the jay's head, and other top parts, Forbush
begins, are "grayish-violet-blue." The front of the head is sometimes
"bluish-white." Side of head, chin and throat are "very pale bluish-
gray." Parts of the wings and tail are "dark azure-blue" and the wing
linings are "dusky-blue."

The section "Voice" starts out stolidly: "Ordinary cry represented
as *jāy jāy, djāy djāy, djáh djáh* or *däh däh*," then it goes on enthusiasti-
cally to "a great variety of notes—a scream very like that of the red-
shouldered Hawk [remember how Brewster was fooled], a sound like
a toy trumpet, and other notes rendered . . . as *pa-ha, pa-ha, piuh-piuh,
tink-tink, hash, hash, side-light, side-light, side-light, sid-lit, sid-lit, hilly-hilly-
hilly, peedunkle, peedunkle, too-wheedle, too-wheedle, heeweeo-heweeo-heweeo,
chillac-chillac-chillac, w-e-a-u-g-r, whēeo whēeo whēeo, keo-eyeo, we-hue*" and,
reluctantly bowing out with an "etc," he remarks that the jay "chatters
and gabbles softly for many minutes at a time, warbles at times, and
imitates songs and calls of other birds; its sweetest common note is
a pensive, bell-like call full of pathos."

He takes equal pleasure in cataloging the subtleties of the jay's eggs: "ground color varies much (sometimes on a single egg) from cream to olive-green, olive-buff, vinaceous buff, pea-green or even pale bluish-green or grayish-green, but usually olive or buffy, spotted and blotched irregularly with various browns and lavender or drab and sometimes with a few small spots of blackish also."

Since he was, by profession, an economic ornithologist, Forbush comes, as he does in all his life histories, to "Economic Status." The jay is given good points for its thrifty way of burying nuts and seeds in the ground and thereby doing a job of reforesting. It does, however, have the deplorable habit of killing some small birds and stealing farmers' corn. From his "point of view," declares Forbush, who balanced his job as protector of the farmer with his role as guardian of the birds, "it is ethical for him to steal corn, for he is not supposed to know the grain is not his. It is only when judged by human standards that we find him lacking in virtue."

All in all, he finds the blue jay "an engaging rascal. Where there are Blue Jays, there always is action . . ." It creates "great uproar in the woods" just for excitement. It brashly teases a sleepy owl and gangs up on a hawk—until the hawk counterattacks, at which point the jay flies "screaming, away to cover . . . it evidently prefers the role of a live coward to that of a dead hero . . ." After this disparagement, he permits one of his correspondents to speak in defense of the jay's character. "Mr. Charles J. Anderson told me of a cat," he writes, "that was tied to a tree to prevent it from killing birds, but it happened that a pair of Blue Jays had young in a nest concealed in that tree. When the cat attempted to climb the tree, both parent birds flew at him and drove him under a bush near by, where he cowered in fright."

Forbush's friends were always eager to show birds in their best light, seldom bothering to hide their bias. Sometimes, in their admiration of the birds' many merits, they sound as if they were measuring them by that basic catalog of virtue, the Boy Scout oath. Their bravery, for example, is praised by William H. Moore who, as he told Forbush, came near the nest of a goldeneye duck and was met by an old male which "talking, fluttering and doing his best to draw my attention" led him away. When Mr. Moore went back, the male "again went through his antics" and, in a comment which speaks as much about devoted bird watchers as about devoted birds, he said: "I followed but did not bother him any more as I had seen how attached he was to his duties."

Birds are loyal, wrote Freeman B. Currier, who saw a crow fall into the Merrimack River. With its feathers soaked, it was unable to rise.

Its alarmed cries brought a flock of brethren and, "after much cawing one bird flapped down to the surface, seized the half-submerged one in its claws, and flew toward shore, dragging the unfortunate along." When the rescuer's strength gave out, another crow took over and, one after another, they got the waterlogged bird to shore. "It . . . spread out its soaked pinions in the sun" while the others stood by. When the feathers had all dried, the party flew off to the woods.

Birds are self-reliant. Frank Mosher, who worked for Forbush as his "very careful assistant," gave a day-by-day report on how a chestnut-sided warbler used available material to build her nest. She started by placing straw and plant fibers in the fork of an arrowwood bush, went over to a tent caterpillar colony and tore off some web to bind the forking branches around this foundation and framework, then brought more straw and grass to build up the sides, more caterpillar web to tie around them and finally lined the nest with soft grasses, fine rootlets and fibers. (Mosher also clocked scarlet tanagers as they ate newly hatched gypsy moth caterpillars. The average rate, he found, was 35 caterpillars a minute, which meant 630 in eighteen minutes.)

Birds do good deeds, according to the testimony of Dr. Herbert Friedmann. Keeping watch on a robin's nest in Ithaca, New York, he saw a female cowbird come up when the parents were away and sit on the nest. One of the robins, on returning, gave its distress call and drove the cowbird off. The other robin came up accompanied by "two Catbirds, three Yellow Warblers, and one Blackpoll Warbler," and they chased after the cowbird, "each calling its loudest." One of the robins, seeing the cowbird egg in the nest, jabbed its beak through it and, with a jerk of its head, tossed it out. "Although there were two male Cowbirds in the near vicinity," Dr. Friedmann added, "neither of them appeared during the fracas" and their only response was a few squawks from one of them.

Birds are resourceful. Arthur Harrison saw two female song sparrows building nests on the bank of the Merrimack River, one about six feet above the water, the other about twelve feet. To his surprise, he saw both birds lay their eggs in the higher nest and take turns at sitting on them. He found out why when a rainstorm raised the river water level and submerged the lower nest. The upper nest was well above the water and yielded eight young.

They are thrifty. Sydney Chase watched a Nantucket loon dive, stay down a full minute and come up with a flounder six inches across, far too big for its beak. Instead of discarding it, the loon took the fish by the head and kept biting at it until it was crushed enough for him to get it completely in its bill. Then he swallowed it head first, took a little water in his mouth, shook his head and dived again.

They are kind. Herbert M. Warren was touched by the behavior of some blue birds at his back door. When the female was killed, the male took over care of the family until, in a few days, he found a new mate who helped care for the young until they "finally left the box accompanied by their father and stepmother." Not all birds, Forbush observed, "have the kindly disposition of this admirable stepmother."

They are obedient to duty. George O. Welch took eggs, one by one, from a bobwhite nest: "The bird laid forty and then died."

Wilbur B. Smith even found a trustworthy hawk, a bird often accused of raiding chicken coops. Keeping tabs on a red-shouldered hawk that frequented a barnyard, Mr. Smith found it a well-behaved raptor: though there were chickens and pheasants all around, not once did the hawk strike at them, even at a rooster which once recklessly stood only four feet away from him. It just went on eating rats and mice.

There were birds, of course, that did not come up to these standards; for example, the cedar waxwings observed by John Willison, whom Forbush called "my young friend." John reported that "one warm day last fall, I was walking with a chum," when they came on a flock of cedar waxwings in a chokecherry tree eating the berries ravenously and behaving very oddly. It looked "as though their feathers had been drawn or brushed the wrong way. . . . The birds did not seem to notice us and we soon came near enough to easily catch them with our hats." " 'Why, they're drunk,' " the chum exclaimed. They had, evidently, been gorging on overripe chokecherries. "Their actions were very comical," the story continued. "Their crests were erect. . . . Some tumbled to the ground . . . others tottered on the branches with wings continually flapping, as though for balance . . . they kept up a continual hissing noise, as a family of snakes might do. We caught several to inspect, and finally left them in peace."

Certainly the female tree swallow whose nest Dorothy A. Baldwin was watching did not set a good example. While the male was away getting food, another male came "to the hole and began to chatter to the female inside. She came to her door and opened a conversation with her caller, who when her husband returned beat a hurried retreat." This happened repeatedly and the husband, when he "found the stranger in close communion with his mate fell upon the interloper furiously while the unfaithful wife chattered excitedly in her doorway. Finally one day she was seen to come out and fly away with the stranger, never to return. Her mate mourned for a day and then too disappeared, leaving the eggs cold in the deserted nest." "Inconstancy," wrote Forbush, saddened, "is a failing common to birds as well as men."

And the sandpipers that Caroline Hamilton was watching should never have betrayed such a trusting friend. Out on a beach Miss Hamilton was distressed when she came upon a flock of semipalmated sandpipers. She wrote Forbush:

> Each one in the small flock, had but one leg. They all seemed rather stupid or under the weather, just standing in one place or at times hopping a bit. . . . We felt they had been left behind when the main flocks flew away because of their injuries and we were indignant over the brutes who had shot off their legs. Finally every last one of those little frauds put down a second perfectly good leg, ran off a short distance and then flew away.

The watchers themselves revealed their own virtues. Thornton W. Burgess, the author of many children's bird books, was helpful. One day "while fishing at Moosehead Lake," he told Forbush, "my attention was drawn to a curious object flopping shoreward about 100 yards out. I presently recognized it as a Chimney Swift. It came steadily in with a series of flops, and I picked it up on the shore. It was taken into the kitchen of the hotel and dried off and then set free, when it flew away with no sign of injury." Burgess also told of an enormous bullfrog which caught a barn swallow that was flying low over a pond. A girl, seeing the bird's wings sticking out of the frog's mouth, caught the frog and made it disgorge before it could swallow the swallow.

Forbush himself, constantly interrupting his friends with his own observations, showed a split point of view. As an economic ornithologist, he emphasized birds' usefulness to man yet could not repress his non-utilitarian feelings for them. Answering accusations that the purple finch ruins fruit crops by eating fruit buds in peach orchards, he says that it actually produces larger crops by thinning the buds. Anyway, he goes on, the finch devours weed seeds and injurious insects, which "should prejudice us in its favor," then adds, "to say nothing of its song and beauty."

It was not a casual afterthought for, like so many others, Edward

Forbush had, early in life, suffered that Wordsworthian shock of surprise that carried birds into his heart. As a Massachusetts farm boy familiar only with the common birds, he went on a May morning—"a day never to be forgotten"—into "an old pinery and heard strange notes on all sides. . . . There came into view close by in a little opening where the sun shone in, a brilliant male . . . his green back, yellow cheeks and black throat flashing in and out as he moved among the dark branches. I thought it the most beautiful bird in the world and longed to possess it." It was a black-throated green warbler.

At first his interest was all in possession, in collecting eggs and nests, bagging birds with home-made bow and arrow and slingshot until, for seventy-five cents, he bought an old muzzle-loading musket. This was so efficient that he was forced to learn how to preserve his specimens. Already, the ambivalence of the bird collector had assailed him. When he was fifteen, "I came to believe myself a hunter naturalist but even at that early age the excitement of the chase was sometimes followed by reaction and remorse at the death of the lovely creatures slain, as I fondly believed, in the interests of science." He took up taxidermy and in 1891, when he was thirty-three, he was appointed director of Gypsy Moth Suppression in Massachusetts, where the country's first gypsy moth plague had hit. Forbush's work suppressed the moth in local areas, although that, as events proved, was not really enough. He went from there into his lifetime job as state ornithologist. His *Useful Birds and Their Protection* was an important early work of economic ornithology, a branch of the science which he, as much as anyone, helped establish. With his findings and arguments, familiar today but not readily accepted then, he tried to persuade farmers that birds, though they might damage some crops and poultry, performed an essential service in eating insects, weed seeds and rodents.

He made a good case for the crow, which was the perennial villain both of farmers, who charged it with damaging their crops, and of birders, who saw it as the murderer of young birds. Forbush told about a sheep raiser on Martha's Vineyard who thought crows were killing his newborn lambs and offered a bounty of fifty cents per crow. "The native hunters," wrote Forbush, "under the stimulus of this bounty had killed nearly all the Crows" in the neighborhood. "Notwithstanding my objection he continued to offer the bounty, although he expressed some fear that the expense would leave him bankrupt." About three years later he complained to Forbush that something was wrong with his pasture grass. Pulling up some sod, Forbush found that white grubs were eating the grass roots. In the absence of crows, which feed on them, the grubs had multiplied. Chastened, the farmer gave up on the bounty, the crows came back, and, eventually, so did the grass.

Here again, Forbush found in the crow some virtues that had nothing to do with economics. "If a person knows only four birds," he says, "one of them will be the Crow. . . . He is well worth knowing. Each Crow is a character." One crow he knew imitated the clucking of a rooster so well that hens came running when he called, and Forbush listened with pleasure to the variety of crows' calls: the repeated *"clockety-clock, clockity-clock"* of one bird, the cooing *"aaaou, cou, cou, cou, aaaou, coucoo"* of another, the *"hollow-ollo-ollo"* of an amorous crow out courting.

By man's standards, Forbush admits, few birds are perfect and they are constantly warring on each other. But, he advises, leave them alone. The great horned owl, though it raids barnyards, also attacks crows, which prey on smaller birds like robins, which damage fruit crops. If you destroy the great horned owl, then crows increase injuriously. If you reduce the crow, then robins will increase, with consequent damage to orchards and vineyards.

There were some birds even Forbush would not defend, most particularly the Cooper's hawk, whose "fierce 'cucks' are the most merciless sounds of our summer woods." When they "ring through the sunny, leafy woods of June, the hush of death pervades everything. All erstwhile cheerful thrushes and warblers become still and silent." Examination of 133 Cooper's stomachs gave damning evidence: 86 contained wild birds and poultry, 11 contained mammals, only 5 contained frogs, lizards or insects. "From an economic standpoint, this Hawk stands near the foot of the list," Forbush concluded sternly. "It is not a bird to be protected." Such a judgment, untypical of Forbush, seems archaic today when the credo of balance of nature forgives every bird its apparent sins.

Still, if ever there was a birder who tried to be evenhanded, it was Edward Howe Forbush. Launching into a little homily on nature's balancing act, he starts with the skunk. The skunk is often denounced for taking the eggs and young of ground-nesting birds, like grouse. Yes, it does do this, Forbush admits, but don't forget that it serves as a protector to young water birds, in this roundabout fashion. The young birds are safest in shallow waters where there are no big fish to eat them. In the shallows, however, lurk snapping turtles, "cold-blooded monsters" which grab the young birds by the legs and pull them under water to devour them.

But here the skunk comes to the rescue. It sniffs along the shore and unearths the eggs that turtles deposit in the ground. Forbush once watched turtles lay their eggs on a river bank and within twenty-four hours skunks had dug up and eaten every one of them. But Forbush cannot stop here without trying to vindicate even the turtle. Perhaps, he says, turtles can be considered an unwitting friend of the birds because, in laying eggs that skunks eat, they provide a "tempting supply" of eggs and this distracts the skunk from raiding bird nests. And so, feeling that all's right in his world, Forbush ends his apologia for God's creatures.

Some birds, to Forbush, are utter paragons. The quail is "the most democratic and ubiquitous of all our game birds . . . friend and companion of mankind; a much needed helper on the farm; a destroyer of insect pests and weeds; a swift flying game bird, lying well to a dog; and, last as well as least, good food, a savory morsel, nutritious and digestible." When he comes to the mallard duck, he is jubilant. "Economically," he announces, "the Mallard is by far the most important duck in the world": for its great numbers; its use through the ages as food for man; because "it comes well to decoys and is an excellent table bird . . . is the progenitor of most of the domestic ducks the world over." It is also, he adds, highly destructive of mosquito larvae. In fact, when once matched against some goldfish in a controlled study, they completely outate the fish, ten mallards clearing a pond of virtually all mosquito larvae in forty-eight hours while the goldfish made no dent at all on the larvae in their pond.

Again and again, he is astonished by birds. "The Nighthawk is a wonderful bird," he exclaims. "It wanders in migration from the islands of the Arctic Ocean to southern South America. It feeds and flies indifferently at any hour of the day or night . . . has an enormous stomach . . . its mouth . . . opens far back under its ears and forms a yawning trap to engulf unwary insects, while its long and powerful wings enable it to overtake them with ease. It lays its eggs . . . exposed to the blazing summer sun, where it seems as if the young bird must be roasted alive, but nevertheless it seems to reproduce its kind with fair regularity." And, to be sure that man will not just admire but also be grateful, Forbush adds that the nighthawk "gourmandizes on such pests as the Colorado potato beetle and the cotton-boll weevil."

Fairly strict about keeping his correspondents to the business in hand, he permits himself some moments of unabashed sentiment as in his passage on some least terns that he disturbed on a beach. The male took flight, and [the female] nestled over the chick nearest me, coaxing it [with her bill and] a gentle twittering, and the male bird alighted with a tiny, bright, silvery fish. A little one stuck its head out from beneath the mother's wing, the father bird courteously passed the fish to the mother, and she fed the chick which begged with open mouth for it. Again the provider winged his way over the sunny sea to return with another fish. The little ones were now asleep under the breast of the mother. He offered her the fish; she refused; he flew away, but soon alighted and politely proffered it again, only to be refused again. At last, having full assurance that his family needed no more, he swallowed the fish himself. Where shall we look to find a lovelier picture of happy, harmonious family-relations than that shown here on this sandy beach beside the roaring surf?

And he permits himself bursts of poetry:

Loveliest of all water-fowl [he begins his hymn to a duck] the Wood Duck stands supreme. Deep flooded swamps where ancient mossy trees overhang the dark still waters, secluded pools amid the scattered pines where water-lilies lift their snowy heads and turtles bask in the sun, purling brooks flowing through dense woodlands where light and shade fleck the splashing waters, slow flowing creeks and marshy ponds— these are the haunts of the Wood Duck. See that mating pair on the dark and shaded flood of a little woodland river; they seem to float as lightly as the drifting leaves. The male glides along proudly. . . . She coyly retires; he daintily follows . . . they glide along close together, she clothed in modest hues, he glowing and resplendent. He nods and he calls in low sweet tender tones and thus, she leading, he pursuing, they disappear into the shadows.

Forbush's years are studded with remembered visions. Some are ethereal—"the day when, as an impressionable lad, I first saw the Bald Eagle wheeling majestically up the sky . . . to a height almost beyond the utmost compass of my straining vision, and . . . sailed away until it vanished in the vast spaces of the upper air . . . as lightly as a drifting cloud."

Some memories are less idyllic—of a heronry in the overheated sand dunes of Cape Cod where the "windless air was stagnant and fetid; swarms of stinging midges, deer-flies and mosquitoes attacked at will; and vicious wood-ticks, hanging from the vegetation, reached for me with their clinging claws, and crawled upon my limbs, seeking an opening to bury their heads in my flesh"; he envied "the young birds . . . [in] the tree tops high above that pestilential hole . . . where they could . . . get a breath of the free air of heaven." At night there was "pandemonium." If the birds

> sleep at all, they must slumber in relays or take cat naps. In the twenty-four hours that I remained within hearing, there was not a minute when the sound of their voices was stilled . . . the babel of sounds increased as the night grew darker, until a nervous person might have imagined that the souls of the condemned had been thrown into purgatory, and were bemoaning their fate . . . a succession of most dismal groans, as if . . . suffering slow torture.

Other memories are comic.

> At one of my lonely wilderness camps in the month of March a pair of Barred Owls . . . made night hideous with their grotesque lovemaking. . . . Their courting antics, as imperfectly seen by moonlight and firelight, were ludicrous in the extreme. Perched in rather low branches over the fire they nodded and bowed with half-spread wings, and wobbled and twisted their heads from side to side, meanwhile uttering the most weird and uncouth sounds imaginable . . . soft and cooing and more expressive of the tender emotions . . . maniacal laughter . . . chuckles interspersed between loud *wha whas* and *hoo-hoó-aws*.

And then there was a vision of the birder's Eden he found on the winter beaches at Cape Cod:

> gulls may be seen in countless myriads, mile upon mile, as far as the telescope can bring them into view. . . . Flocks of Brant pass high overhead. . . . Bunches of scoters, sheldrakes and Old-squaws speed by before the wind . . . a few Black Ducks. Great Loons, Red-throated Loons and Grebes float near the shore. Gannets are fishing in the bay. . . . Horned Larks and Snow Buntings flit by. . . . Myrtle Warblers, Flickers and Cat-

birds move about in the thickets, and a . . . Pigeon Hawk
. . . on the wings of a driving gale. . . .

And a "monstrous great Arctic Owl" he has been stalking regards him
with "a tigerish glare." Then she turns away because she sees something in the sky. "Whatever she sees there is beyond my ken, for I can
find nothing there even with the binoculars." And even in this
watcher's paradise Edward Howe Forbush is unsatisfied for there is
something that he cannot see. "Oh," he wails, voicing the discontent
of every birder, however blessed, "Oh, for the eyes of an owl!"

12

The Independent Midwest

For many years, watchers in the Midwest had almost no way to get together and talk about their doings. Their main meeting place was the pages of *The Wilson Bulletin,* the organ of the Wilson Ornithological Club, which, though it had its beginnings in 1886, never held an annual meeting until 1914.

In its first form the club was a group of young birders, part of a proposed national Young Ornithologists Association, which never came to anything. In 1888 it became a Wilson Ornithological Chapter of the Agassiz Association, a loose aggregation of nature groups inspired by Louis Agassiz of Harvard, who, through his teaching and lectures, had done more than any other man to spread an interest in nature study in America. That association fell apart. After a few disorganized years and loose alliances with birding magazines, the group asserted itself in 1902 as the Wilson Ornithological Club. By that time it had established its midwestern character and independent ways. It held to them all from then on and often, like the Cooper Club in California, had its back up against what it considered the exclusive eastern birding establishment, though many easterners were among its members.

By 1910, the club had some 140 members widely scattered but still mostly in the Midwest. What held them together was their quarterly magazine, *The Wilson Bulletin,* and what held the *Bulletin* together was its forbearing editor, Lynds Jones, who for some thirty-five years ran the *Bulletin* almost uninterruptedly out of his office on the campus of Oberlin College, where he taught science and natural history. His editorial columns were always apologizing for issues that were late or small, impartially blaming himself for being dilatory and scolding members for not sending in contributions—one issue was late "from a lack of copy and for no other reason." The province of the club had been set as "the life history of the bird from the time it leaves its egg" and this gave the *Bulletin*'s pages an anecdotal quality, homier and less academic than other publications. Esther Craigmile reported that at Sparks, Nevada, deep in the Sierras, she did her birding from a hammock and had seen three dozen species, including many nighthawks. Benjamin T. Gault of Glen Ellyn, Illinois, reported that a young prairie-chicken had settled in his poultry yard but found the roosts too noisy and left. Agnes Chase said that when walking through Washington Park in Chicago carrying her field glasses, as was her habit when going to work every morning, she came upon a half-dozen young hoodlums and stopped them from stoning the resident downy woodpeckers. Maunsell Crosby told of an orphaned owl which, after its mother was killed, hooted—as no owl should—in broad daylight. "By loss of his mother," Mr. Crosby observed, "his education was incomplete."

With the advance of technology Marion E. Sparks addressed herself to the question: "Does the extension of interurban trolleys affect birds?" Studying the new trolley line at Urbana, Illinois, she came to a surprising conclusion. Though fewer ovenbirds nested along the line and the sora (rails) seemed confused by the passing cars, she found more ruby-crowned kinglets and robins, observed that an unconcerned cardinal still busily gathered food for his nesting mate though trolleys passed only twenty feet from his nest. In 1903 Miss Sparks counted only sixteen species along the line. The next year there were thirty-seven, the newcomers including a brown creeper, indigo buntings, downy woodpeckers, flickers and a ruby-throated hummingbird.

The first wintering mockingbird ever recorded in Lincoln, Nebraska, was seen by Dr. F. B. Holleneck in his yard at South Twentieth Street. Fifty-six wild ducks were killed by a bolt of lightning on Jacob Bremer's farm in Chillicothe, Ohio. They fell in the barnyard and Mr.

Bremer gave them away to his neighbors. Albino robins were reported at Texas A&M University, an albino goldfinch at McCook, Nebraska, and a white cowbird at Norman, Oklahoma. There were many stories about tame birds—the pet robin which left home to fly about in the trees all day but always came into the house at night to roost, and the venturesome nuthatch who flew into the kitchen looking for butter and cheese.

Though he tried to keep the *Wilson Bulletin* pages free of rancor, Jones could not suppress the members' xenophobic feeling towards easterners. In 1910 W. F. Hennier protested that the AOU's third *Check-list of North American Birds* showed sectional bias by misplacing midwestern species in its classifications and by giving inaccurate geographical ranges. "If the pages of *Wilson's Bulletin* had been consulted," the list would have had things right. Keeping after the prejudiced easterners, Mr. Hennier sent them a corrected list but they never published it.

An uncontroversial paper on bird diet turned somehow into a regional dispute. In 1912 Ira Gabrielson, just starting a career that was to make him years later a notable head of the Fish and Wildlife Service, studied the feeding habits of brown thrashers and catbirds in Montana. He observed parent thrashers feeding their young 773 meals. The male fed them 292 times, the female 481. When they found some raisins from a spilled box, the male ate them himself, while the female fed them to the young. A typical meal consisted of two grasshoppers, one moth, three mayflies, one earthworm, one raisin. The catbird's food, Gabrielson found, included mosquitoes, house flies and stable flies.

This study brought a skeptical review from the *Auk,* which was run pretty much by easterners, accusing Gabrielson of "over-enthusiasms"—a patronizing way of charging scientific sin—in his unbacked identification of the insects. Gabrielson defended himself spiritedly: the parent bird had been held in his hand while he counted the number of mayflies in its beak, the flies had been checked with an entomologist, the mosquito had been swatted by the observer. He did admit difficulty with some birds: while most carried worms crosswise in their beaks, making identification relatively simple, the rose-breasted grosbeaks carried them front to back, covering up most of the clues. The critic's proposal that food intake be checked by tying bags over the "anal orifices of young birds" was waved aside as "highly amusing," with the implication that this was to be expected of eastern dudes.

Lynds Jones himself became involved in argument, with the West rather than the East. Usually he did his birding in and around the college, and few areas of the country were more closely watched and counted. On the Oberlin campus itself he and his students made a study of the grackles, mapping their roosting spots, discovering that they ate insects, blackberries and green corn and were scared to death by the Fourth of July fireworks. One summer, exploring new habitats, Jones and a friend, William Leon Dawson, took a railroad trip to California watching for birds out the window and at station stops, when they would dash out, keeping one ear open for bird songs and the other for the engine's warning departure bell. A washout in Montana held the train up for three days, but while the other passengers fretted, Jones delightedly found two birds he had never seen before.

His report brought a rebuke from the editor of *The Condor* for listing birds that had been seen on the wing, not collected and thus verified. To which Dawson replied mildly that, while they certainly made a few mistakes, they did not subscribe to the theory that only the collector could make accurate identifications. Besides, they were not out doing errands for science but watching birds for their own pleasure. Though they were happy to have added 181 species to the list of those they had already seen, they had reservations about the growing spirit of competition among birders over the length of their lists. "If rightly conceived" they could be "a source of legitimate satisfaction," he believed, whereas "the accumulation of such a list, if it were merely for the sake of numerical comparison with some rival observer, would be as vulgar as a collection of tobacco tags."

At the Wilson Club's first formal meeting in 1914, members heard that for the first time in its history it had a surplus in the treasury: $43. Along with solvency, the club gained a number of valued members, among them a pillar of midwestern birding, Dr. Thomas S. Roberts of Minneapolis. In the days when birding had been dominated by easterners, Dr. Roberts had been a most respected outlander—at its founding, the AOU had immediately elected him a member. Considered in the medical profession to be one of the country's best diagnosticians, Dr. Roberts had to wrench time from his busy practice to watch birds. When he was fifty-seven, he gave up medicine entirely for ornithology. Working at the University of Minnesota and directing its natural history museum, he produced a landmark work, *The Birds of Minnesota.*

A diligent scientist, Dr. Roberts was also a delighted bird watcher. He tells in detail of following an indecisive phoebe, as she picked a place to nest in an abandoned house, from a downstairs window to an upstairs back bedroom and finally to a chimney-pipe hole, where at last she settled. He would interrupt a fact-packed life history with a little poem to "The Eaves Swallows." And he sought out birders throughout the state for their knowledge.

Dr. Johann Hvoslek, a country doctor, shared the results of his fifty-four years of daily watching with Dr. Roberts, and Almira Toregson, a schoolteacher, gave him her observations on a thirty-eight-year-old colony of cliff swallows. All types of people contributed findings to Dr. Roberts: Edward Addison Everett, whom he described as a "successful merchant miller"; Tom Miller, "a canny Scotchman who shot for market, entertained hunters and bred fine horses"; Whitfield Harrison, "an untutored man," who for nineteen years was engineer on a railroad bridge across the Mississippi at Lacrosse and took notes on the prothonotary warblers that nested in his engine room. Dr. Roberts marveled that the birds, which usually nest in the "seclusion that reigns in the depths of the pathless bottom land," had chosen to rear their young "within a few feet of the thundering trains, clanking machinery and escaping steam." Harrison, in the best tradition of birding, had not only kept scrupulous records but had also "come to speak of these little companions in terms of endearment."

The Wilson Club and the Midwest had their full share of purposeful and productive birders—and they also had one who might have gone on to an eminent career in ornithology save for a bizarre and sensational crime. In 1921 the name of Nathan J. Leopold, 4754 Greenwood Avenue, Chicago, first appeared on the Wilson membership list. He was seventeen at the time but his reports on birding in the city and its environs were being published frequently. In Lincoln Park he saw two dozen Franklin's gulls, rare visitants to the area, and, he wrote, "a beautiful specimen in adult plumage was taken" and put in his growing collection. In the winter of 1923 he noted many titmice at Riverside Park, a great horned owl in Jackson Park and several sandpipers at Wolf Lake. He became one of the younger members of the American Ornithologists' Union. In 1924, Leopold's name disappeared from the Wilson membership list with no explanation. None was needed, of course, because he was by then known as a principal in a shocking murder case. He and a friend, Richard Loeb, had kidnapped and killed a fourteen-year-old Chicago boy, Robert Franks, and had stuffed his body into a culvert at Wolf Lake, the spot where Leopold had once reported seeing some sandpipers.

The police had few clues to follow, except for a pair of horn-rimmed eyeglasses they picked up nearby. They saw nothing distinctive about them until an oculist pointed out that the hinge connecting the earpiece to the nosepiece was of a recently patented type, used when the earpiece was particularly short. The manufacturer in Brooklyn referred them to a Chicago optometrist whose records showed he had sold three pairs of glasses with this hinge: one to an attorney, who had been in Europe for the past six weeks; the second to a woman—who had her pair on when she was questioned; and the third to Nathan Leopold. The police had already talked to Leopold, having been told by a warden at Wolf Lake Park that he went there frequently. Yes, said Leopold when the police asked him. He did go there—to watch birds. The police, checking on this novel excuse, were impressed by what they found. Leopold was indeed a bird watcher, in fact one of the most promising young ornithologists in the country. Only recently he had delivered a long paper at the American Ornithologists' Union's annual meeting. It was entitled "The Kirtland's Warbler in its Summer Home."

Leopold had chosen to go after the bird because it was a most interesting ornithological quarry. The first known specimen had been collected off the Bahamas by Dr. Samuel Cabot, Jr., in 1841, when the doctor was sailing to Yucatán to join John L. Stephens in his great archaeological explorations of Mayan ruins. It was all but forgotten until another specimen was shot near Cleveland in 1851 by Charles Pease, who gave it to his father-in-law, Jared P. Kirtland, who in turn gave it to Spencer Baird, who named it after the donor: "a gentleman to whom, more than anyone living, we are indebted for a knowledge of the Natural History of the Mississippi Valley."

It proved an elusive and finicky bird and it took a half century of hunting before its breeding place in Michigan was found. It nests only in thick ground cover of laurel, wintergreen and blueberry growing under stands of young jack pine. When the pines grow high, their shade kills the undergrowth and the warblers no longer nest there. When forest fires burn down pine groves, new stands grow in to accommodate the Kirtland's warbler. It was still a relatively little-known bird when Leopold, who had studied ornithology at the University of Michigan, went in 1923 to the Au Sable River where the bird bred. Crawling through the thick growth, he came within four feet of a nest and listened to the male's song—*"chip chip chip chip hip wheou"* with crescendos and accelerandos, he wrote. "Every muscle in his body tense" it gives out "a burst of clear bubbling song easily audible at a quarter mile as though the singer's throat will burst from the sheer force of the song."

Disturbed by the intruder, the male pinked Leopold on the thigh and shoe and the parents stopped feeding their young, so Leopold caught some horseflies and fed the nestlings himself. They willingly took seventeen. Gently dealing with the birds, Leopold coaxed the male into eating from his hand. Their food, he wrote, consisted "largely of centipedes, worms and caterpillars . . . also deer and horse flies, grasshoppers, crickets and dusty millers. They drink the white pitchlike fluid which exudes from the branches of the pine." Finding a cowbird egg in one nest, he destroyed the young when it hatched and came to the conclusion, generally accepted today, that the cowbird is the most dangerous natural enemy of Kirtland's warbler.

All this made interesting material for the police dossier but the eyeglasses still had to be accounted for. Confronted with them, Leopold said they had fallen out of his pocket when he had tripped running in his clumsy rubber boots to get a shot at a Wilson's phalarope. The police asked him to demonstrate—and that was Leopold's undoing. "I tripped and tripped and tripped," Leopold later wrote, describing the reenactment, "I just couldn't make the glasses fall out of my pocket." Typewritten ransom notes provided conclusive evidence and the two pleaded guilty. Only Clarence Darrow's extraordinary defense got them life sentences instead of death. Loeb died years later in a prison slashing. Leopold, paroled after serving thirty-three years of his sentence, went to Puerto Rico and worked as the administrator of a leper hospital. When he died in 1971, readers of his obituary must have been puzzled to learn that he spent his last years compiling a *Checklist of the Birds of Puerto Rico and the Virgin Islands.*

There is no record of the effects of the case on the local bird watchers but it may be more than coincidence that the regular "Seasons" department in *Bird-Lore,* to which Leopold was a regular contributor, had no reports from Chicago for several years. Among true bird watchers, however, the Leopold case must have been overshadowed by a quite different sensational charge of murder. The prosecutor was Althea Sherman of National, Iowa, and the defendant was, of all creatures, the much-loved little house wren.

In the March 1925 issue of the *Wilson Bulletin* Miss Sherman presented an impassioned "Case of the People of North America versus the House Wren." She was specific in her indictment. This "tyrannical" bird was "a destructive little demon." It tore apart the nests of other birds. It usurped their nesting places. It pecked holes in their eggs and tossed them out of the nests. It killed their young. Males heartlessly deserted their mates. Let "the felon be sentenced," she demanded, for "its diabolical disposition" and its "nefarious work."

Bird watchers were accustomed to having such diatribes aimed at bullies like the crow or the blue jay. To have Jenny wren thus attacked was shocking, although, in this instance, the shock was mitigated for having been caused by Althea Sherman. They had come to expect the unexpected from her. As one admirer understated it, Miss Sherman had "a rare ability to express herself," which she did frequently and forcefully and in surprising ways. When an ornithologist called the Le Conte's sparrow so "shy, skulking and elusive" that it must be shot on the wing to be identified, Althea snorted that this was nonsense. She knew three of the birds which "sat on a fence awaiting me" and, far from skulking, would feed unconcernedly in her presence on the seeds of ragweed, smartweed, pigweed, wild grass and Spanish needles. At another time, when the Iowa legislature proclaimed a state "Bird Day," most birders were pleased. Not Althea. Why should there be a day only for birds? she asked. Why not for anything in nature— animal, vegetable and mineral? Why not a day for worms? They were, she said pointedly, always with man.

Holding birds to strict standards of behavior, Althea scorned the hypocrisy of the female blue jay in springtime when the courting male starts offering her nutmeats and "she, poor silly creature" accepts "the meats with a great fluttering of wings and a helpless air, as if she had not been able to forage for herself all winter." The female flicker, to Althea, was a "weakminded, inconsistent, frivolous creature that is called from duty by the notes of any stray male. Shakespeare would have written 'Frailty, thy name is female flicker.' " And, however taken she might be by the beauty of birds, she was blunt when she found them ugly. Twelve-day-old screech-owls to her were "repulsive, exceedingly filthy, decidedly repellant . . . perfect miniatures of a doddering, half witted old man . . . the beak, a large hooked nose . . . a low, imbecile forehead . . . bleared eyes. . . ."

Althea Sherman's birding territory, she once explained with cartographical precision, was "situated in northeastern Iowa, 6 miles west of the Mississippi River and 3 miles south of the 43d parallel of latitude." Her parents had settled in the village of National in 1866, and her father, a descendant of Roger Sherman, a signer of the Declaration of Independence, opened a cobbler's shop where he mended boots for farmers and gave them mortgages on their farms. Sticking to both lasts, he prospered and sent his two daughters off to college.

Amelia went to medical school and returned to National to practice. Althea, who was born in 1853, took a master's degree in art at Oberlin and went west to teach. In 1895, she came home to help take care of her parents.

The sisters were a lovingly incompatible pair. Amelia was sternly frugal, dedicated to "industry, economy and self-denial." She shuttered the parlor windows to preserve the wallpaper from fading and saw with satisfaction that, after seventy years, it was still as fresh as new. Althea had no stinginess in her. She donated money to causes and lent it to profligate friends who never paid it back. But she was uncompromising in what she thought was wrong—English sparrows, for example, and the U.S. Postal Service when it shut down the village post office and had the mail handled at the nearby town of McGregor. Althea never acknowledged the change. She gave her address as "National (via McGregor)" and was snippy to correspondents who did not use that address.

When Althea was young and the homestead was being farmed, there were not many kinds of birds around. Mostly swallows, she recalled. When she came back home to stay, the untended prairie acres had grown up in trees and shrubs and undergrowth and now there were many nesting species—catbirds, thrashers, flickers, red-headed woodpeckers and "that hated alien, *Passer domesticus.*"

Helped by Amelia, Althea began to take bird censuses, counting 33 species nesting in her dooryard and 153 in the neighborhood. Her little farm, her barn, her outbuildings, became a laboratory where she studied birds fondly and assiduously. A whole day was taken up observing a catbird's nest two feet from her bedroom window. During her sewing time, she patiently made notes on a mourning dove's nest —"a dreary task," she sighed—and dashed out to toss her scissors at a red squirrel when it raided the nest. She cooked for the birds from her own recipe: "One cupful cornmeal, one cupful lard or chopped suet; half cupful chopped walnuts; 3–4 tbsp. corn syrup, water to moisten; cook for a few minutes."

Not content with her dooryard, her windows, her plum-tree grove and all the other natural vantage points, Althea built a special chimney-swift observatory: a wooden tower twenty-eight feet high, nine feet square, with an artificial chimney two feet square inside. A door and ladder were built into the tower, windows and large peepholes were bored into the chimney. Going into the tower, Althea and Amelia would climb to a peephole and, sticking their heads inside, could watch what the swifts were up to. When one pair built a nest only fifteen inches from a peephole, she was within touching distance of the whole family process: nest building, mating, egg laying, incubation, feeding. "A paragon of perfection," she called the graceful bird. "No evil has been detected in its relations with its own or any other species." Her subjects were referred to as bachelors, widowers, widows, grass widows, and when she once saw a third swift come in to help a nesting pair feed their young she remarked "quite likely an old maid."

When phoebes nesting in the barn became infested with lice, Althea and Amelia set themselves up as a "Board of Health" for the birds. Commercial lice killers proved ineffective so they picked the lice from the little birds by hand—118, Althea reckoned, from one nestling half the size of her thumb. They removed the hair lining from the nest, washed it with a solution of corrosive sublimate, rinsed it, dried it with a warm flatiron and put it back in the nest. "At nest leaving time," Althea wrote proudly, "the young apparently were as clean as phoebes ever are."

Birds became as familiar with Althea as she with them. A sparrow hawk (American kestrel), recognizing her as the creature that sat in a blind near her nest, screamed whenever she came into sight. A red-winged blackbird with three mates was named Brigham—he was "a true polygamist of the Latter-Day Saints stripe" and had a "vindictive, insolent manner" towards her. When she and Amelia followed him into a bog to look at his nest, he always attacked Althea but let Amelia alone. True originals in their research methods, the sisters one day changed clothes. "Brigham seemed nonplussed," Althea reported with some satisfaction, "and sat rather sheepishly on a fencepost but finally hit my sister a few feeble blows." A hummingbird, less hostile, grew so accustomed to drinking the sugar water Althea put out for him that he ignored the nasturtiums he had been feeding from and waited for Althea's sugar water. "One is led to wonder," Althea wondered in a flight of fancy prose, "if the Homeric gods on high Olympus were more deeply stirred by the appearance among them of the youthful Ganymede bearing cups of nectar than the hummingbirds at the sight of their cupbearer."

Althea had an open mind about birds, debunking the dove, which "as an emblem of peace may have been chosen by those who were unacquainted with the mourning dove's fighting qualities." The bad manners of flicker nestlings, which fought each other for food their parents brought, were an unseemly contrast to the well-behaved sparrow hawks' young, which "stand in perfect decorum against the walls of the nest" while the mother "tears the prey and gives each its share."

As spring ended she would heave a sigh of relief that "the grand ball —the mating festival—the noisy dance caused by sex impulses, the same as in human creatures, that has made a pandemonium of the west ravine seems to be about over."

In 1913, Althea extended her birding to the Eastern Hemisphere. She saw coots and parasitic kites at Karnak on the Nile, a golden-backed woodpecker in Delhi, India, crested larks on the way to Marathon in Greece, a lesser spotted woodpecker in Hønefoss, Norway. With a touch of irritation at the end of her report, she regretted that the "conflict of nations" outbreak of war forced her to cut short her foreign watching before she had completed what she set out to do. The war depressed her and an uncharacteristic gloom darkened her usually bright observations. "Every spring," she wrote, "there are so many despoiled nests, so much fighting among the birds that one is made utterly heartsick, especially when the whole of mankind is also waging war." The brown thrashers, she said, pierced each other's eggs, flickers raided each other's nests, grackles and blue jays were "criminals" and "our dear little wrens" spoiled other birds' eggs.

This passage presaged her famous attack, a decade later, on the wren. In 1915 she had little but praise for the bird for attacking English sparrows (she had already excommunicated the sparrow, declaring that it is "never counted among the birds") and for keeping a very tidy house. They always destroyed their old nests when getting ready for a new brood. "Out with your old insect infested beds," Althea's wren would proclaim. "Nothing but clean beds will do for my offspring." But years of further observation opened Althea's eyes to what she believed was the house wren's true character. First in a speech at the Iowa Ornithological Society, then in articles in journals, she attacked the bird and also the birders who encouraged them by putting up wren boxes. The wren is "a deadly menace," she declared, given to "dangerous practices." There are "grades of viciousness," she said, citing the "infamous Jukes family" as an illustration, and it is the wren's "diabolical disposition alone that prompts it to destructive acts. . . . There are people who deny that the earth is round, and there are other people who deny that the house wren is a bad bird. . . . A blacker villain than I had thought," she went on, confessing her early errors. "Why not let children raise rattlers?"

If readers of Althea's philippic were waiting for the whole weight of the birding community's wrath to come down on her, they were disappointed. Just the opposite happened. Letter after letter to the editors hailed Althea for her courage in facing an unpleasant truth

they had always turned away from. Mrs. Charles F. Weigle of La-
fayette, Indiana, praised Althea for telling "the unvarnished truth
about the common house wren . . . Common is the exact word . . . the
most treacherous enemy. It is called 'a fearless little feathered friend'
. . . and how that word 'little' always appeals to our sympathies." She
had seen wrens throw bluebird and titmouse fledglings to the ground
and stab them. The English sparrow, she said, "is a bully and a coward
but never a murderer." The wren, she said, invoking that other villain,
is "even a greater danger than the cat." The wren demands the whole
neighborhood. "Suppose a pair of bluebirds, the most heavenly of all
created things, have come to nest with you . . . the male calls to his
mate in ecstatic warbling tones. She answers in low minor tones
(D-flat and C on the musical staff)." They trustingly lay their eggs and
the wrens promptly come to pierce or smash them. In three years,
Mrs. Weigle wrote, the eggs of five pairs of bluebirds and the fledglings of two were destroyed by Jenny wren. The fledglings, what's
more, had their eyes gouged out.

Willis H. Warner of Canfield, Ohio, from eighteen years of observation concluded that the wren had a "malevolent nature." It pitched
eggs out of martin houses, pierced cardinal eggs, pulled the lining out
of chipping sparrow nests. Harriet Chapman Battell of Ames, Iowa,
watched one wren, singing all the while, impale an egg in a nest.
"Overboard went the egg," Mrs. Battell wrote bitterly, "and out came
the song."

For all her anger, Althea had to admit in her honest way that she
herself was an accomplice for having put up wren houses. In doing
this, she had given the wrens an unfair advantage over other birds,
permitting them to "increase unduly." The wren's "true nature was
not recognized until man had overturned the balance of nature—like
a snake in the garden of Eden." The wren-box craze was not "the fault
of innocent children" who put them up but "the criminal fault of
those fostering for gain the business of house wren making." Teachers and leaders, she said, flailing out at everybody by now, were
"selling the birthright lives of many kinds of birds for their own mess
of pottage. Down with the house wren houses!"

Althea was not, of course, the first to accuse the wren of anti-social
behavior. She cited precedent for her charges. Robert T. Ridgway had
stated that the wren is "tyrannical . . . no small bird can nest in its
vicinity." Otto Widman had called it "as great a nuisance as the
English sparrow," as damning an association as any birder could
make. But criticism had usually been buried in dispassionate life histo-

ries and muted by affectionate remarks for the attractive birds. Forbush, for example, remarked mildly that the wren pokes "his bill into the business of his neighbors and sometimes into their eggs. Nevertheless on the whole he is a fairly good citizen, a good provider and a devoted parent."

A few birders contradicted Althea, speaking up for the wren. O. M. Bryers of Three Rivers, Michigan, said when he put up wren houses the number of bluebirds and purple martins had actually increased from one to thirty-eight within ten years, because wrens had driven house sparrows away. After the first emotional spate of pros and cons, ornithologists felt it necessary to restore calm. Waldo Lee McAtee pointed out that neither "supporters or defamers" had paused to take "a judicial view," so he proceeded to take it. On the basis of its food habits, he said, "the species would receive a very high appraisal for it is almost exclusively insectivorous and that in chiefly commendable directions. The house wren is as worthy of approbation as any of our birds on the score of its food habits. It has a better rank in this respect than most of the species whose eggs it occasionally destroys." Where "serious depredations have been noted" the remedy is to shut up the wren houses that, as others pointed out, had increased the wren population and made it more belligerent in keeping other birds away.

A more subjective approach was taken by *Bird-Lore*'s editor.

> The house wren has become abundant with our help and through the exercise of the instincts which have made it a successful species. But is there any reason why we should call him a criminal? As a matter of fact, we are the guilty ones. Tried in a court of men and he no doubt would be convicted of the charges made against him; but a court of wrens would dismiss the case and commend the culprit. Purely as a matter of justice: which verdict should we take? Should we judge wrens by their standards or by ours?

Althea herself, while acknowledging her own complicity, did not give an inch so far as the wren's character was concerned. In her will, she ordered that whoever got the Sherman homestead was not to allow any wrens to nest on the property. But as she grew older, she could not keep them away. By the time she died in 1943, not quite ninety, they were nesting unmolested again in her dooryard and Althea seems in the end to have made her peace with Jenny wren.

13

The Scientist and Her Singer

No bird watcher was more purposeful or possessive in her pursuit than Margaret Morse Nice, who for a decade kept her eyes and ears on the song sparrows of Columbus, Ohio, as they came, courted, mated, nested, raised their young, developed their songs, departed and returned—following them through the generations, parent to child and even to great-grandchild until sometimes her writings begin to sound like the begetting portions of the Bible except that her birds mostly have names like K34 or K56 or 12M or 128M. Then she put all her exhaustively intimate knowledge down in a classic example of scientific single-mindedness, *Studies in the Life History of the Song Sparrow.*

Her subject with its lilting Latin name, *Melospiza melodia,* or "melodious song finch," was ideal for her "Studies," as, indeed, was Margaret Nice herself. The bird is abundant, friendly, widely distributed, accessible. It starts three or four broods a year, often inhabits the same place year after year and does not seem to mind intrusion. Mrs. Nice was ever present, unobtrusive, soft-fingered, sharp-eared and persevering, taking constant delight in her subjects and achieving a kind of working rapport with them, never seeming to disturb the birds too much by poking into their nests, counting their eggs, capturing and handling them.

And her objective approach and laborious statistical compilations never diluted her delight in her subjects or her ability to see them as distinct personalities. She came to know one of them for seven years, an extraordinarily long time to observe a single wild bird. By the time she got through telling about him she had made him, as the most respected history of modern ornithology puts it, "world famous."

The sparrow 4M—so-named because he was the fourth male she chose for her study—came into her life in March 1928. Like all song sparrows he was about six inches long, striped brown, with a dark tie-pin spot on his chest and a sweet and varied song whose base was three short identical notes followed by a longer one (the rhythmic pattern of the opening of Beethoven's Fifth Symphony). He was one or two years old when he settled in Mrs. Nice's habitat, "a wild neglected piece of flood plain" in back of her house outside Columbus, Ohio. She called it Interpont. There 4M established himself in a territory of about a third of an acre with two apple trees, a pear tree, an elm, a maple and a box elder. He sang loudly to keep other sparrows away and to attract a female. When one came to stay with him, Mrs. Nice named her Quarta, to match 4M's 4.

From then on, 4M and Margaret Nice were busy almost every hour of the long spring days, the one with never-ending chores of siring and raising a family, the other in watching and recording the way he did it. And 4M showed himself to be a responsible and adventurous bird. Having successfully courted Quarta with song and by "pouncing" on her, he chose a nesting site, copulated with her, helped her build the nest, guarded her as she sat on her eggs, and brought food for the young when they hatched. From time to time, he made sorties into the territory of his neighbor, Uno, so-named because he was the first bird Mrs. Nice seriously studied, and was driven off. Then he had to defend his territory from Uno's counterattacks.

When Quarta, after a couple of failures, hatched a brood of four fledglings and proceeded to start another nestful, the young were left entirely to 4M's care. Taking them off to a corner of his territory, he tried to keep them concealed in the brush but they were always calling for food and coming out of the cover while he was forever twittering alarm calls and shooing them back under the bushes. Every time he took a little time out just to sing, they would spring up beside him. Besides caring for them, 4M had to keep watch over Quarta, chase predators—snakes especially—which were raiding nests, and engage in constant warfare with Uno who, taking advantage of 4M's preoccupation with his children, would harry Quarta. Their fights were often desperate, the two birds rolling over and over on the ground. They ended usually in a standoff, although once, 4M gave Uno such a trouncing that, from then on, he stayed where he belonged. At the end of the nesting season, only one fledgling from 4M's four nests survived. Snakes and rats got all the others.

That year saw the beginning of a lasting relationship between 4M and Margaret Nice. It did not come about, of course, entirely by chance. The bird was there because Interpont was an almost ideal habitat for a sparrow—plenty of brush cover for nesting, plenty of weed seed for food—and hence ideal for a serious sparrow student like Margaret Nice. She had been serious about birds since childhood, starting her bird education with a Sunday school script called "Jenny and the Wren," a conversation between a Jenny wren and a Jenny girl. Going on to graduate work in ornithology at Clark University, Nice did an impressive thesis on the feeding habits of bobwhites, based largely on the behavior of a pet bobwhite named Loti, who lived in her laboratory and, wandering through the hallways, became a well-known campus figure. At the University of Oklahoma, she and her husband collaborated on a state bird book and when he took a teaching post at Ohio State they settled at Interpont.

Having surveyed the flood plain and noting how the sparrows divided it up into their territories, she charted the thirty-eight acres in detail, using mimeographed maps which located each bird and its movements. In the spring, she had to make new maps every day to keep track of arrivals. Through the summer, she spent almost all day out in the field or in her laboratory to record data on birds she had lured into her traps and then marked them with celluloid and aluminum leg bands. With these markings, she could know which birds stayed the winter, which left and came back the following year and what territories they went to. Training her ear, she became so adept at recognizing individual songs that she could tell which bird was around simply by listening, without having to look at the bands. A captured bird was weighed in a small cloth bag (which was always weighed separately because on damp days the cloth was heavier), and its dimensions measured with tiny calipers. Males, Mrs. Nice found, were heavier than females except in May when females bore eggs. All birds weighed least in the morning, growing heavier from feeding through the day.

Even the most scholarly bird students sometimes give way to

whimsy and though Mrs. Nice tried hard to keep to her strict M-and-K terminology she could not resist giving some of her birds personifying names—Bluebell, Goldenrod and, to one brother and sister which mated, Siegmund and Sieglinde after Wagner's incestuous siblings. About half her nesting male sparrows were year-round residents. Others wintered in the South. Males were more inclined to stay around for the whole year than females were and they transmitted this habit to their sons. Seven year-round resident fathers at Interpont had seven year-round sons. Four migratory fathers had four migratory sons. Two resident fathers, however, had four migratory sons and five migratory fathers had seven resident sons. (Sometimes Mrs. Nice's sober lists seemed about to dissolve into nursery rhymes.)

The male's first job in February or March is to establish his nesting territory, defined by Nice as "any defended area." He does this by singing loudly to proclaim his presence—his song can carry two hundred yards—and by fighting off other males who come across what he has set as his boundaries. A third of an acre is a usual territory. If another male invades, the resident stands hunched and silent watching the invader, puffs his feathers up, while the invader sings loudly. If his posturing does not work, the defender goes after the trespasser and the two birds spar in the air or roll over each other on the ground. The winner either resumes ownership or takes possession and the loser goes off to find another territory. Sometimes the invader already has a territory nearby and is simply looking for a change. If he loses, he goes back to his old territory and sings loudly at his rival, who sings loudly back. A male will fight harder for his territory than he will for a mate and is nearly invincible on his home ground.

A female returning to the area, usually later than migrant males do, may make for territory where she nested the year before. If she is not wanted, she tries an adjoining territory and, if unwelcome there, she settles in the territory of any male that will have her. Charting fifty-four females, Mrs. Nice found that twenty of them settled in the same territory two years in a row, though not with the same mate, and sixteen settled in neighboring areas. One, however, had to go nearly half a mile before she could find a home.

"By his singing," Nice says dryly, summing up volumes of prose on why birds sing, "the male evokes a negative reaction in other males and a positive one in the female." A female feeling a positive reaction reveals it with a kind of chatter and a nasal *ee-ee-ee.* Mrs. Nice could find no reason why a female chooses one male over another—neither appearance, nor song, nor the territory seemed to be crucial to the choice. If the male is interested he starts his courtship by pouncing: darting at the female, bumping into her, then rushing off with a brief, loud song. Once it is settled that she will stay, the male teaches the female the territorial boundaries by dashing at her whenever she is about to cross them. Copulation takes place just before nest building starts, the male jumping on the female, whose tail is raised and spread wings are quivering, and impregnating her by barely penetrating her anal orifice. When it is over, the male goes off silently while the female gives her *ee-ee-ee* cry. Copulation is repeated during the nest-building and egg-laying period.

While the male chooses the nest site, the female does most of the building, sometimes working and chattering while the male sits over-head, a silent guard. Nice found the chattering very helpful in locating the nests, which are usually pretty well concealed. She would sit by on a camp-stool with a stopwatch, timing the female as she worked rapidly away for fifteen or twenty minutes, then rested for about five. The first nests of the year, built before the foliage has come out thickly, are usually put on the ground under tufts of grass or weeds. When leaves come out to offer more concealment, nests are built higher in bushes. Nice gave the nests grades for concealment, ranging from excellent to poor. In the excellent nests, more than half the young were successfully raised. In others only a third were. Grass, weeds, grape vine, bark, all go into their construction.

During the nesting cycles, Nice noted, male and female are close, the male guarding the nest, singing while the female is sitting in it. Incubation is entirely the female's business. Eggs are laid in the morning, one each on successive days, and incubating on the first one begins before the last is laid. As a result, eggs hatch on different days. The male calls the female off the nest every twenty or thirty minutes with a "signal song" that tells her it is time to go get food. Typically each female lays four sets of four eggs. Older birds lay two five-egg sets and two three-egg sets. In all cases, Nice discovered, the total comes to sixteen eggs. Nice could not make much sense out of eggs and heredity. K187 laid small eggs but her daughter K202 laid "astonishly large" ones. K23's eggs were finely speckled, while her sister K131 laid eggs that were irregularly blotched.

If a male loses his mate before nesting, he can usually get another fairly soon. If the nesting has begun, he finds it harder because most females are taken by then. If a female loses her mate during nesting, a neighboring male sometimes comes over to take his place. Though she would repulse him if her mate were still around, she now is receptive and the male will serve two females, calling at each nest and bringing food to each family. He will sometimes also mate with both but bigamy among sparrows is uncommon.

Once the young are hatched, the male helps feed them diligently for ten days in the nest and for the eighteen or so days after they leave. Both parents clean out the excreta. The young have to be taught how to eat. At the start, according to Mrs. Nice's stopwatch, it takes a parent half a minute to get a seed or insect down the fledgling's throat. By the time it leaves the nest, ten seconds will do it. Bringing up the young is hard work—parents lose almost a tenth of their weight during the feeding period. In the first five days after hatching, they feed the young an average of seven times an hour and then it goes up to seventeen times. Parent birds apparently have to learn how to feed their young. K2, for example, was slow in starting to feed her first two broods, did a little better on the next two and the following year was on the job from the start.

The female starts building a new nest right after the young leave the old (a nest is never used twice) and she starts laying another clutch in about a week. Most pairs are faithful for the season, though they may try out various mates before settling down. K42 joined 9M in February 1931, a little early for mating, then she started to wander. Both 9M and 11M, an unattached male, followed her but she kept them off with threatening notes. On March 2 she stayed briefly with 66M, then for two weeks with her follower, 11M, and finally went back to her original choice, 9M, with whom she finally nested. But she was late in laying and incubating. Mrs. Nice's narrative can from time to time take on the air of a contemporary novel of suburban infidelities. K58 mated with 65M in 1931. The following year she joined 101M but left him to go over to 9M, K42's erstwhile mate. Then, 101M flew over and brought her back home, pursued by 9M, who was the one, Mrs. Nice believed, that K58 really favored, for after a while she went back to him and stayed. Next spring 9M had died and K58 stayed briefly with Nice's favorite, 4M, who had taken over the territory, but after two days she went to 143M and spent the season with him.

Young birds lead a perilous and often a very short life. Snakes eat the eggs. Cats eat the young. Weasels, skunks, opossum, crows, grackles and snakes eat both. In the most successful broods, Nice found, three young survive. But on the average, only 1.4 live to adulthood, and of these few make it past two years. Unpredictable factors affected the birds' mortality at Interpont. In 1930 the breeding season was shortened by a great drought. Three years later, floods drowned out the first nests. A severe 1935–1936 winter killed many resident birds. In 1933 a Depression make-work program cleared and ploughed much of Interpont to provide vegetable gardens for the unemployed. Any change in conditions is bad for the sparrows, which have to spend a third of the year reproducing in order to keep their population stable.

Nice herself was a disturbing factor for some birds. Despite all her care in handling the birds some found the experience traumatic. One male, after having been trapped and then having his territory disturbed by nearby ploughing, deserted both his nest and his territory, highly unusual behavior. Nestlings that were being banded would give loud screeches and the parents would rush over crying *tchunk* or *pu pu pu* at Nice and try to distract her by running off with raised wings. Mostly Mrs. Nice steeled herself to let nature alone but sometimes she could not keep from intervening. She felt guilty when she removed cowbird's eggs from nests or chased snakes away. But she felt altogether justified by taking on the neighborhood boys who, believing that all sparrows were English sparrows and fair game for anyone, shot song sparrows. After "my efforts to educate the boys failed," she noted, she got herself named special game protector of the state of Ohio, a job that came with a big shiny badge. That took care of the young marauders.

The sparrows' songs were central to Nice's research, a key to getting to know her birds, especially the males. Methodically, she wrote down each bird's song in syllables, dots, dashes, curlicues and soon had their songs so well fixed in her memory that she could tell which was which without referring to her notes. She knew when one had just arrived by his loud singing and that by his brief silence he had taken a female and begun mating. Though the singers are individualists, she found, they all follow general rules. They give an "awakening song" half an hour before sunrise on clear mornings, a little later than that when it is cloudy. They vary somewhat: M1 was an early riser, M4 got up later. The existing books had all told Nice that song sparrows had two songs. She learned they had at least six that were frequently used, plus innumerable others. Each sparrow has his own musical style. The repertory of one may have only a half-dozen songs, another's may have twenty-four uniquely recognizable as his. Some are dulcet, others harsh. Usually a song has three parts, the third section repeating the first, with the middle section a variation on the song's theme. Each song is two to three seconds long and given five to seven times a minute, although in territory-setting time it may be sung ten times a minute. While Nice could hear as many as seven notes in a song, she believed there were probably more too high to be heard by human ears. A bird goes through his whole repertory uninterrupted before starting over again.

Sparrow 1M sang a sequence of six sections starting with a *chip-chip-chee-yer, zig-zig-zig-zig,* went on to *chee-chee-chiddle-hair-terpee-terpee-terpee* and ended in the sixth section with *hur-hur-hur-hur-hur-hur-er-ree-state-state-state-er.* Sparrow 4M's nine distinct songs had several subsections. The A section Mrs. Nice described as "determined, almost grim." Section C was given "in a desperate hurry." G was "light, airy, charming," while K was "prettiest of all with the gayest lilt at the end." "One song began *spink-spink-spink-spink-creteree,* went on to *hur-hrreeee-tweet-tweet-tweet-tweet-tweet* through *yip-yip-er-see-wee-er-wippy* and always wound up, at night, with *hee-hee-hee-whinkie-didledere-whinkie.* Females have a short unmusical song, usually given before nest building starts.

A young male starts learning to sing in the fall not with a real song but with a warble. Studying 7M's development in his first adult year, Nice found that when he started on February 5 he had only a warble. The next day he had a short song and two days after he had what Mrs. Nice described as a "spectacular, beautiful, varied" song and within a week he was giving 247 songs in an hour. Nice discovered as time went on that sons do not sing like their fathers. Knowing that they learn largely through imitation, she was puzzled until she realized that they give their first warble in early fall, by which time they have left their nesting territory and the influence of their fathers.

Why do they keep on singing after mating and nesting time is over? Nice asked herself. She dismissed as unscientific piety the belief of one well-known birder that the song is a "message of peace and good will . . . a little prayer of thankfulness sent straight up to heaven by the shortest route." She rather agreed with the conclusion that such singing "was simply an outlet and a pleasurable one, for nervous energy . . ."

Her favorite singer, through his very long life, was 4M, and he is the thread of the continuing story at Interpont. She saw little of him during 1928, his first year at Interpont. The next year, on February 13, he began singing to proclaim his territory, and also Uno's, who had not yet showed up. When he suddenly stopped singing, Mrs. Nice investigated and found that he had attracted a female, Quarta, who—as told earlier in this chapter—stayed with him for the nesting season. The following year 4M mated with a female Mrs. Nice named Quatre and when she was killed 4M began singing to attract a new mate. One came and Mrs. Nice named her Chatvar, which is Sanskrit for "four." Another female had come by and Mrs. Nice, trapping her, discovered that it was Una, Uno's old mate. She did not go back to Uno but settled in an adjoining territory with a sparrow named 5M.

Sparrow 5M was a trouble to 4M. He had managed, after skirmishing, to wedge in a territory between 4M and Uno. Another sparrow, 10M, came and tried to take 5M's territory. This involved a great deal of fighting and flying about and 4M was drawn into three-cornered fights with 5M and 10M all the while he was trying to tend to his own mating business. When 10M settled for a small territory nearby, matters calmed down.

Chatvar and 4M had bad luck with their first nest. Cowbirds laid eggs in it and snakes took Chatvar's eggs. Mrs. Nice and her daughter caught the snake and threw it in the river but then Chatvar, like Quatre, died. She was succeeded by Rosemary and by this time Mrs. Nice had to pay close attention to keep Interpont's intricate domestic arrangements straight. For example, 29M had deserted his mate, Bluebell, who took on 26M, who had, in turn, been left by Rosemary when she went to nest with 4M. It was a happy ending for 4M (and his devoted watcher, of course). Though he had lost two mates that season, he still had time to build a nest and raise a brood.

The next year, 4M's mate was Blueberry, who came back to him the following year. She disappeared, however, before laying a complete set of eggs. Then, 4M's second mate was killed and he had no others that year. In 1933, his mate Sweetbriar also disappeared and 4M, by this time a very senior sparrow, was once again without a mate for the season. In 1934 he mated with Goldenrod and hatched two young. Though he still sang strongly enough to hold his territory, 4M was not breeding as prolifically as the birds around him.

In 1935, with so many young males at Interpont, 4M had trouble attracting a mate. He finally brought in a female Mrs. Nice came to dislike intensely—"a cold old-maidish creature," she called her, "tyrannizing over her fine husband like a veritable Xantippe." She was always edging towards a nearby male, 225M, and 4M was constantly going over and driving her back home. She was always distant towards 4M, foraging and feeding apart from him. Nice was tempted to help her beloved 4M by capturing Xantippe and taking her away. But the bird was wary. Mrs. Nice could find nothing good to say about Xantippe. She was desultory about building a nest. When she finally did build one, she laid only two eggs. Some wrens came along and punctured them and, on May 6, Xantippe left, with Mrs. Nice apparently muttering a good riddance.

It would be going too far to say that 4M thought so too but, at any rate, five days later, on May 11, 1935, he did something that Nice thought was absolutely marvelous—nothing in all her song sparrow studies matched it. Starting before sunrise, he launched into an unprecedented sequence of song that kept on all that long spring day and did not end until past sunset. Mrs. Nice, up at dawn, listened as he began at 4:44 a.m. with song D *(tin-tin-tee-tee-tee-tee-ching)* and then, at the rate of five songs a minute, went steadily through his repertory for an hour. After a half-minute pause, he resumed, singing almost continuously until noon at the rate of 200 to 278 songs an hour, with Mrs. Nice intently noting and clocking. He eased off a little in the afternoon but when he finally stopped at 7:43 p.m. he had sung 2,305 distinct songs.

That outburst was, in a way, his valedictory. He continued to sing in a more restrained way for three weeks without attracting a mate. Instead he became a kind of foster father to the fledglings of a neighbor's mate, Dandelion, who had apparently gone into 4M's territory to retrieve one of her wandering chicks and took 4M back with her to help with the feeding. Later she came over to 4M's territory and nested with him but their brood was destroyed.

Nice could hear 4M sing sporadically through the fall and on Thanksgiving Day she heard him sing a last song. Then she neither saw nor heard him again. During his eight years at Interpont, she had seen him go from spirited youth to sedate old age. He had had seventeen nests and eleven mates, was seven times a widower and raised thirteen young.

All this interest in the personal lives of birds was a byproduct of Mrs. Nice's scientific purpose. She was trying to determine how to look at birds: whether as reflex machines responding only instinctively to their environment or as creatures who can carry out complex processes that require foresight and planning. She went to Europe to study under the bird behaviorist Konrad Lorenz, most widely known for his fabled relations with his geese. She came to the conclusion that Julian Huxley had reached: instinct, not intelligence, was the mainstay of bird behavior. In this way they differ from mammals, which rely more on an intelligence developed by learning through experience. Birds, she concluded, are emotional animals with excellent memories.

Having studied her sparrows in the field until 1936, Margaret Nice spent three years raising them in her house and finally finished her studies. Her approach, she summed up didactically, was "a phenomenological method" but she was somewhat warmer in her definition of what a dedicated bird watcher should be. Though the definition describes her own particular approach, it also applies, in one degree or another, to anyone truly subject to that gentle obsession. "A necessary condition for success," she said, citing an English observer, "is a continuous sympathetic observation of an animal under as natural conditions as possible. To some degree, one must transfer oneself into the animal's situation and"—here she gets about as close to the soul of birding as almost anyone can—"inwardly take part in its behavior."

14

The Imbuers

A reader going through the annals of birddom, the little small-print stories in the old birding journals, comes across a fine old-fashioned word: "imbue." It almost always referred to somebody whose name was prefixed by "Miss" and who was, often, a teacher. Miss Mary Agnes Tillisch imbued the children of St. Paul with a love for birds. Miss Fannie Stebbins imbued the children of Springfield, Massachusetts, with an understanding of nature. Miss Elizabeth Dickens of Block Island, Rhode Island, imbued the local children with an appreciation of their tiny island's bird life.

There were thousands like them who worked through the Junior Audubon clubs, using their ten-cent pamphlets as texts. Their teaching could be sentimental and superficial and their bird walks just an excuse for an outing. Still, they opened the children's eyes to nature and, in the end, helped produce multiplying generations of bird watchers. Except for little pats of appreciation in *Bird-Lore* or in the school columns in local newspapers, these imbuers have been forgotten, though the tradition they set is kept by devoted teachers everywhere in the country today. A few have come into a wider fame than they knew when they were alive. Miss Blanche Hornbeck of Jamestown, New York, trying to tame an unruly seventh-grader named

Roger Peterson, got him to looking at birds and sent him on to become the world's best-known birder. Miss Fannie Adele Stebbins is memorialized by a bird sanctuary near Springfield and Miss Elizabeth Dickens by one on her island.

Some are remembered in local memoirs and through their own reporting. Miss Harriet Abbott of Fryberg, Maine, a lady of great energy who was town clerk, schoolteacher and first woman to serve on a jury in her county, was an oracle to Fryberg's young: "the village children consulted her freely," her obituary said, bringing her their questions, the injured or dead birds they found and their excited stories of new sightings. Miss Bertha Chapman of Oakland, California, was so effective teaching about nature to small groups of children that she wound up in charge of nature study for all the city's schools. Miss Mary Agnes Tillisch, after having taught at an Indian reservation at Fort Peck, Montana, moved to St. Paul and taught for forty years at Miss Wood's Kindergarten and Primary Training School. A tall, quiet lady, she took children out on bird walks, herded them to the natural history exhibits at the University of Minnesota museum, letting them handle nests and eggs and beguiling them with recorded bird songs. Primarily interested, as an imbuer should be, in making them curious about birds, she left, a memoir said, "a wholesome and lasting impression on children and young people."

The children of St. Johnsbury, Vermont, had two women of more than average skills to tell them about birds. Isabel Paddock Carter, curator of the St. Johnsbury Museum, was widely respected for her work on bird songs and cited repeatedly in Frank Chapman's *Warblers of North America* with her often unexpected descriptions: the black-throated blue warbler's song "is hard to express in musical notation. . . . a little like the breath sucked through the teeth." Inez Addie Howe, also of St. Johnsbury, had a gift for telling stories, like the one she passed on to Forbush for his *Birds of Massachusetts:*

> Two Pileated Woodpeckers met in a tree-top, their wings spread at full width, and they danced and balanced before each other and bowed to each other . . . and apparently fed or kissed each other. . . . Their long necks and the opening and closing wings showing the silvery lining made a pretty sight against the sky. . . . [They] went through the prettiest circles with fluttering wings; you could hardly see the motion of the wings, they moved so rapidly. . . . After they circled and sang, they flew off to a higher tree on the hill.

For forty years, Sarah Chandler Eastman shared her feelings with the children of Portland, Maine. In 1906, she mourned the absence of the chickadees: "dearest to me of all winter birds." Another year she had a triumph. After a long search she finally found a Cape May warbler: "Never was a bird more obliging than he. He flitted about us, displaying all his markings to the best possible advantage." Of all her tales the one about Charlie was the most delightful. One day in 1894 in a driving snowstorm, she heard a fallen blue jay "give three cries so piercing and despairing that we sprang to our feet in alarm." When she picked him up, he "turned on me a bright inquiring eye which plainly asked what I intended to do with him." She took him home, named him Charlie and put him in a cage, where he seemed happy and well until he started having fits. A German bird fancier told Miss Eastman, "Dot bird vill haf to die," but Miss Eastman diagnosed the trouble: people were feeding her bird too many sweets. When that stopped, the fits stopped too. Charlie, said Miss Eastman, "sang sweetly in February and March . . . danced with ecstasy" as he sang. Let out of his cage, he would hide until someone said: "Here's something for Charlie." He stole objects and, after watching everybody search for them, would bring them out. When he was fourteen, he flew out a window and, Miss Eastman's story ended wistfully, she never saw Charlie again.

The imbuer par excellence, perhaps, was Miss Elizabeth Dickens, of Block Island, a lovely three-by-seven-mile bit of glacial debris that sits a few miles off the Rhode Island shore and is, like Cape May, so convenient a place for birds to land on during their migrations that it has become one of the best birding spots in the country. Miss Dickens was born there in 1878 and, some thirty years later, began a daily report of the birds she saw. For more than fifty years, she kept it up day by day, compiling an unbroken record of all the birds that came by her corner of the world.

Her entries are very economical: "Jan 19 Canada geese 8 (going east); song sparrows 6 (singing)." She notes the rare visitor: "Coot 1" and the innumerable residents: "Herring gull 100." "Heavy rain" keeps her from sighting any birds one day but the next, despite "Heavy S.W. Gale" she goes out to see "Meadowlark 3, Herring Gull 8, Black Duck 1, Canada Geese 11." At the end of that month there are "Redwing blackbird 4 (first arrival); Canada Geese 8, Holboell grebe, 1,000." On February 28, a single robin and on March 3, a hundred snowflakes. March 11, "earliest record for R.I. of Osprey," and then the spring birds begin: "Grackle 10, cowbird 1, Field sparrow 2 . . . *Big* flight of Canada geese plus Brant," a brown creeper and the first shorebirds, "Greater yellowlegs 4." She would take her eye off the birds to note "Frog 1, Dandelions 4" and along with the first great blue heron were "first violets." Then the birds flood in—sandpipers, a pair of bald eagles, a willet, a red-breasted nuthatch that slept under a hose leaning against a garden post, warblers, small hawks, a rare pomarine jaeger, Wilson's terns (common tern) 50, an oriole (the counting gets breathless), loons 60, a cuckoo, flycatchers, thrashers, grosbeaks. In a dense fog, when she could not see anything, she hears loons and Wilson's terns and, so much an event that it is underlined, a hermit thrush.

In August it reverses. The shorebirds are coming down: "Bartram's tattler [upland sandpiper] 4, Ruddy turnstone 1, white-rumped sandpiper 25, bobolink 50 in a flock. Purple martins hundreds . . . 200 shearwaters cruise by the island" and an enormous visitation: "Myrtle warblers 1,000": the next day "Myrtle warblers 10." On October 9, "Cormorant, big flight" hard to count as they move unevenly across the water. "Vesper sparrow 25, Junco 300, scoter 250, kittiwake 100, whistler [common goldeneye] 2, horned lark 11, pied-billed grebe 1, shrike 1, whistling swan [tundra swan] 6." The statistics abate. On December 9, only "Horned lark 12, meadowlark 9, herring gull 50." On December 17, a wounded bittern. On December 22, nothing. "Acute indigestion," the listing explains.

Her records have been invaluable to ornithology. The Fish and Wildlife Service, to whom she reported, said that ornithology owed to Elizabeth Dickens "practically all the knowledge we have" of the significant place the island holds as a stop-off in the Atlantic flyway. Much more important to Miss Dickens was the fact that the island children owed her practically all the knowledge they had of the island's birds—and a surprising proportion of the island's residents are knowing about their island's birds, if casual about it.

Miss Dickens began teaching the island children in the 1920s, making the rounds of the island's seven one-room schoolhouses. Standing in front of the class, usually wearing a hat, black stockings and high sneakers, she would hold up an exhibit. "This," she would say, "is a meadowlark. He is formally dressed with a black necklace. He whistles four notes and you can remember them because he's saying: 'You can't see me.' " Next was a bobolink, and she would gravely explain: "He dressed in such a hurry he got his clothes on backwards. All his beautiful markings are on his back." She had a captive audience, since she spoke in such low tones that the children had to keep quiet to hear her. Besides, she knew every one of them by name, as she knew their parents and grandparents and sometimes their great-grandparents. The mischievous ones, trying to get out of their homework, would make up bird descriptions or report birds that couldn't possibly be seen on the island. She ignored such foolishness.

They would, sometimes, really find uncommon species. In 1932 she reported to *Auk*—she had been elected a member of the American Ornithologists' Union—on "Rare Birds on Block Island":

> *Fregata magnificens* [man o'war bird]. November 16, two of my former bird study pupils brought me a beautiful female man o war which had been shot and left on one of the fishing wharves at Old Harbor. *Vanellus vanellus* [northern lapwing]. On Nov 20 one of my high school girls brought me fine specimen of a lapwing which had been shot on Block Island. It had passed through many hands before it was salvaged by my little friend. *Chen hyperus atlanticus* [*C. C. atlantica*]. A greater snow goose was shot on the morning of Oct 27 and was secured by a high school boy for the School Collection.

The collection was her particular pride. For years, as pupils brought her dead birds from the docks or beaches, fishermen brought her those they found at sea and the lighthouse keeper ones that had collided fatally with Southeast Light, she would keep them in her house in bookcases on top of the parlor organ. But as they began crowding her out, she got the island ladies to peddle their pies, pastries and jellies to buy glass cases, and she put the collection in the new high school. One year she noted triumphantly that she had made enough "doughnuts to pay the last dollar on the bird cases."

Every winter, she mustered a good portion of the island school population for the annual Christmas bird census, and the children went whatever the weather. One year she marched them ten miles in a 36-mph wind to be rewarded with sixteen species and 368 individual birds, among them 94 horned larks and 3 loons. In 1927, the ground sealed with two inches of sleet, they walked eleven miles, fortified along the way with squares of unsweetened cooking chocolate their leader doled out to them, to find twenty-five species and 1,200 individuals.

Addressing a more mature audience, Miss Dickens contributed to the standard ornithologies. She was the first to report on the historic November heron flight of 1910:

I'll never forget [she wrote Forbush]. In the early morning I was attempting to feed my flock of 75 turkeys when they suddenly all became sky-gazers. Of course, I did likewise and beheld 12 great blue herons circling above the flock. Round and round and round they flew until I was almost dizzy trying to follow their motion with my eyes. At last they seemed to have had enough of this and flew away to the southeast. A little later another dozen came from the west and alighted in a row along the edge of the bluff. 'Twas interesting to see the difference in heights and sizes. Then there came groups of threes and fives and nines and so it continued at intervals all day. In the afternoon came one great flock of just a hundred birds. As they reached land a life-saving (?) crew fired into them and the flock became two bunches of 40 and 60 birds each. I don't know how many herons I saw that day but there must have been several hundred.

Her rarer regional findings, put into the records, included a blue-gray gnatcatcher on September 11, 1919, a dickcissel in June 1922, a blue grosbeak in April 1926. She was a prime source on the grasshopper sparrow, a rather uncommon bird that seems to have had the common sense to nest regularly in Miss Dickens' fields so it could be counted. And among her sober observations was a whimsical entry about the brown creeper, a bird which is accustomed to circle up tree trunks looking for insects. On her end of the island, where no trees grew, Miss Dickens noted a brown creeper "climbing a cow's tail, for want," she wryly explained to Forbush, "of a more promising prospect."

She lived on the family farm with her father and always said that everything she knew about birds she learned from him, while the islanders said everything Lovell Dickens knew about birds he learned from Elizabeth. It was a working farm and when her father died, Miss Dickens took over all the chores and also took in her ailing Aunt Edna. She also kept, separate from her bird listings, a journal of daily events. The journal had a single page for each day of the year but into each page she crammed a dozen years of recorded days. The entries start out at the top of a page in a free hand but as they go down, year by year, the writing gets smaller and smaller until it is barely decipherable, the lines sitting one on top of another, running off at a slant and finally climbing frantically up the side of the page. At the head of each page she wrote a motto, usually of a pious nature and often salted with her own parenthetical comment. The motto "They also serve who only stand and wait" is followed by "(Comforting, isn't it?)" and "All things come to him who waits" by "(That statement is a lie. They do *not* come)."

Each day's entry notes "Eggs 4" or "Eggs 11," the number produced by her setting hens. Usually the weather is described, the health of the horse or cow is reported, visitors and funerals are recorded. Sometimes off-island events or catastrophes are given brief attention and delights get equal billing with disasters. The great hurricane of September 1938 "uproots nearly every large tree on the island. Tidal wave destroys Old Harbor fishing fleet. We lost barn, sheep house and hen house. Many birds."

Jan 1, 1945. Health, happiness and all good fortune attend you all the year. Fog & torrential rain. Terrific south wind. Eggs 6.

Jan 2, 1945. "To endure life smilingly is no ignoble task" (True). Eggs 2. Barge sank off Charleston Beach in last night's storm. 3 lives lost.

April 12, 1945. Plant peas, onion sets and most flower seeds. Eggs 11. Death of President Franklin D. Roosevelt.

Jan 25, 1946. Eggs 7. Wet gale. Fishing boat from New Bedford wrecked at s.e. point; 2 lives lost. Island Light and Power plant burns in early evening.

Jan 3, 1947. Temperature 4! Black Duck 2; Marsh Hawk 2; pheasant 1; starling 3; meadowlark 2; redpoll 11; song sparrow 3. Eggs 2.

Dec 6, 1947. The most exciting day in many years. 1 old Canada goose, 1 gander and 4 grownup young feed just outside the gate.

Tuesday, Jan 4, 1949. Eggs 6. Perfect Day! I have such a good time washing.

She tended a large garden, filled hundreds of canning jars with vegetables, beach plum and raspberry jam and fish heads her fishermen friends brought her. She kept a cow, a horse, a dog, sheep, chickens, turkeys, geese, and took care of everything with her heart as well as her hands.

Friday, April 18, 1947. Eggs 11. Plant parsnips, cabbage, peppers, tomatoes, squash, cucumbers, beans, pole beans, potatoes, lettuce.

Wednesday, April 20, 1949. Eggs 4. I finished planting 1 bushel green mountain potatoes & 1 peck early potatoes. I did it all.

Monday, Jan 28, 1946. Teddy is 12 years old, the best cow on B.I. even though she seems lame all over. [The next year]: Teddy will go to Clarence [the milkman] soon. I shall miss her.

At this point, after seventeen years of entries on one page, she is so close to the bottom of January 28 that all she can cram in is: "Eggs 4. Pay all bills."

Her small shingled house sat out on an edge of the island with nothing to ward off the incessant winds. "Tuesday, February 1: 6 eggs. Blow Blow Blow! Feb 13. Eggs 5. Still she blows. I fall down and skin my knee & break my glasses. March 19. Eggs 11. Don't open an outside door at all! Something which never happened before in my life." January 11, 1956, brought a bad storm and no boats ran to the island: "Our basketball team marooned on mainland since Jan. 6," she wrote—anyone not able to get to the island was considered marooned, even on so solid a piece of ground as the American continent. After five days the boats started running and, she noted with relief, the team was rescued.

Anniversaries are always observed. "Friday, March 4. Eggs 6. This is the day I shot the Black Australian Swan at Dickens Point. The day Mr. Taft was inaugurated president." On June 21: "Eggs 12. Six long years my Papa has been gone. Eggs 12. Hoe and poison potato bugs." October 25, anniversary of the day their house burned down: "53 years is a long time but I have much to be thankful for." On October 27: "Roosevelt's birthday. Good old Teddy. We're proud of of him. Quince jelly." And world events wait their turn. "Tuesday, May 8, 1945. Eggs 8. Paper my clothes press. V E Day!! President Truman, Prime Minister Churchill & Joe Stalin accept Germany's unconditional surrender!"

There were constant visits from island people—Earl Smith bringing grain, Bob Rice to plow, Clarence Lewis to cultivate, Merrill Slate to discuss the bird cases, Arthur Rose to shear the sheep ("paid $6 gladly, it makes the sheep happy"), Mary and Jack Hartnett with ice cream, Arthur Sprague to take her to Old Harbor to pay bills ("If I owe anyone 1 cent I am not aware of it," she would always write— except one year when she admitted she owed five cents), the pastor to talk church finances. (For years, Miss Dickens was treasurer of the Free Baptist Church and nobody could figure out how she kept ac-

counts. Whenever she was told that money was needed she would
think and then say: "I think we have sufficient funds." After her death,
when the church leaders opened the massive safe she kept in her
house, they found it completely empty. A close friend pulled a couple
of egg crates from under a sofa and showed them the church treasury.) Contemporary friends would come with their families; younger
friends with their newborn; ornithologists from Providence or Boston
or Brooklyn to pry into her knowledge. On August 3, 1957, there was
a rare entry: "Don't see a human being to speak to" and, maybe only
half a dozen times is the notation, with an indignant underlining: "Not
one caller."

She had a pioneer's self-sufficiency: "Sept 2 1949. Eggs 9. Pick
beach plum and make juice for jelly. Go to shore & get sand to make
cement and fill rat holes in the cellar and do a few other things." One
day, when she was standing in her doorway talking to Billy Lewis, a
rat started across the yard. Reaching inside the door, she took her
gun, raised it, shot the rat dead, put the gun back without losing a
syllable of what she was saying.

In her later years, no friend was more constant than Billy Lewis,
who lived on the adjoining farmland. His name dots her journal: "Oct
21, 1957. Stove pipe falls apart, oil stove smokes!! Billy to the rescue."
"Jan 23, 1952. Aunt Edna falls out of bed [as she constantly was
doing]. Billy to the rescue."·On Thanksgiving Day, 1945, "One dozen
American Beauty roses from Billy who is in France." In 1949, he sent
roses from California. There was an understanding that after she was
gone, Billy was to be given a first chance to buy her farm. When she
died in 1965, the farm was sold to him and, after a few years, through
donation and sale, it was transferred to the Nature Conservancy and
the Rhode Island Audubon Society. With subsequent additions of
Lewis family farmland, that part of the island is now the Lewis-Dickens
nature preserve.

While Elizabeth Dickens and Mary Tillisch worked in their small
worlds, other women set out to indoctrinate all the country's children.
By creating a special literature and coating science with sentiment,
they taught children to know the birds, to care about them and, most
of all, to treat them with kindness. The men politely, or patronizingly,
left this task to the women and they responded by writing the country's first truly popular and useful bird books.

The women deliberately set themselves apart from their brother writers. They were concerned "not with the science of ornithology" but with arousing "sympathy and interest in the living bird." That was the way the senior among them, Olive Thorne Miller, put it in her *First Book of Birds,* published in 1899. It was her twentieth nature book. The first one was published in 1870, when she was thirty-nine, and her last one in 1915, when she was eighty-four. Eleven of them were on birds.

Men who study dead birds, Mrs. Miller said, "can tell how their bones are put together and how many feathers there are in the wings and tails. Of course," she conceded, "it is well to know these things. But to see how birds live is much more interesting than to look at dead ones." The watcher will be "surprised to find how much like people they act. After studying living birds he will never want to kill them. It will seem to him almost like murder."

Mrs. Miller took on her young public face to face, going around talking to schoolchildren. "Birds," she would tell them,

> seem to be the happiest creatures on earth, yet they have none of what we call the comforts of life. [A bird] cares nothing for a roof to cover him . . . he has the broad green leaves to shade him . . . his neat feather coat is like a waterproof that lets the drops run off. He does not need a dining room because he eats where ever he finds his food . . . and he prefers his food raw. He can sleep on any twig—the whole world is his bedroom. He has only one suit of clothes at a time and he washes and dries that without taking it off. He wants no fire to keep him warm for when it is too cold, he flies to a warmer place. A bird really has no need of a house, excepting when he is a baby.

In *Bird-Ways,* which paraphrased her talks, she divided birds into rather arbitrary categories. The robin was a "Bird of the Morning" and "If every bird has his vocation . . . that of the robin must be to inspire cheerfulness and contentment in man" with "his *'Cheer up up! Cheer up! Cheery, Be Cheery, Be cheery'* poured out in the early morning." The hermit thrush is the Bird of Solitude which in its song speaks "irrepressible words of endearment, ineffably sweet and tender." Mrs. Miller did not stop, however, with a poetic generality. She went on to analyze the thrush's song: "a prelude of three notes on an ascending scale," then a "deliberate rest, followed by three other and different notes" and ending "in a rhapsodic trill." Having dutifully given the details she felt free to remark that each of the thrush's notes is "as perfect as a pearl . . . lofting the soul into the region of poetry and drama." This is not to be dismissed as overdone rhetoric. Everyone who has listened to the thrush's song will share Mrs. Miller's feelings, though they might phrase their own a little more sparsely.

Mrs. Miller was aware that her books were often the only texts teachers had and she was respectful of the strictures of ornithology having studied Coues, Ridgway and others. Adapting their life histories, she gave them a cosier tone, moralizing in instructive ways about birds' manners. The male kingbird, she said, always jumped up politely whenever the female returned to the nest, and in feeding his children he thoughtfully held a dragonfly in such a way that the young could nibble off bits small enough for them to swallow. She praised birds' behavior, telling of the little chickadee which, unable to draw an egg collector away from her nest, refused to budge from it, shaming the nest robber until he slunk away. There was the tale of the bereft Jenny wren which, with no nestlings of her own, pitched in to feed a brood of sparrows. She told of the pigeon that loved a cat, of the goldfinch that loved a scarlet tanager and of the disobedient baby crow which would not come when its mother called until she flew over and, with one swipe, knocked him off the branch: after that, he came when called.

Mabel Osgood Wright shared Olive Miller's credo and stated it firmly. "Nature is to be studied with the eyes of the heart," she declared in her 1895 *Birdcraft,* quickly adding, lest any of her readers think that feeling was all, that the heart is not enough. Birding requires "keen eyes and a pocket full of patience." Her book, which was subtitled *A Field Book of Two Hundred Song, Game and Water Birds,* might have tested that patience. Her descriptions, though complete, were rather dense and her method of identifying birds kept the reader turning back and forth from category to category: e.g., "Brown or brownish birds of various sizes and markings; Tree climbing birds of various sizes seen up on the trunks and branches." Still, it was so needed in its time that *Field Book* went into seven printings within a dozen years.

Mrs. Wright had another best seller in *Citizen Bird* but she owed a good deal to her collaborators—Elliott Coues and Coues' protégé, Louis Agassiz Fuertes, whose animated and accurate illustrations for *Citizen Bird* were his first major work. The book told about a patient naturalist and four eager children who badgered him for facts about birds and then argued with his answers. Coues himself couldn't stand the children he and Mrs. Wright created—"I could have swatted them into the middle of next week," he said, but he decided it was worth putting up with them since the book was "a phenomenal success with a sale averaging 500 copies a day." On her own Mrs. Wright went on to her most important work as editor of the children's section of *Bird-Lore*.

The best seller of this group was Neltje Blanchan, whose *Bird Neighbors* sold some 250,000 copies. (Her husband was Nelson Doubleday, the publisher.) Concerned with "nature sympathy, the growth of the heart" rather than "nature study, the growth of the brain," *Bird Neighbors* seems better suited to sympathy than study. Its method of identification included such cumbersome classifications as "Birds of the Air Catching Their Food as They Fly" (flycatchers, kingbirds); and "Birds that Show a Preference for Pines and Other Evergreens" (chickadees, nuthatches); and "Birds that Choose Conspicuous Perches" (shrike, blue jay). Her color categories were catchall, i.e., "Brown, Olive or Grayish Brown, and Brown and Gray Sparrowy Birds."

Mrs. Blanchan was shameless about endowing birds with human traits. Woodpeckers are "phlegmatic," waxwings "gentle, courteous, elegant," the cardinal "a shining example of self-conscious superiority." Bluebirds, which are "undemonstrative, matter-of-fact lovers" when they are looking for nesting places, undergo an emotional change when the female starts sitting on her eggs. Then her mate "looks with wondering admiration" and "applauds her with song." The catbird with its "glorious song . . . hateful catcalls and squawks" is "the 'Dr. Jekyll and Mr. Hyde' of birds," while the mockingbird was the "angel that . . . the catbird was before he fell from grace."

For all their sentimental style, these authors were not gushy dilettantes. Their simple, clear writing was buttressed by trustworthy fact. They were members of the leading ornithological societies and moved comfortably in literary circles, contributing regularly to such magazines as the *Atlantic Monthly*. They kept an eye on man's doings as well as birds'. In a sly aside during her description of the white-throated sparrow, Mrs. Blanchan remarked " 'I-I, Pea-body, Pea-body, Pea-body,' are the syllables of the white-throat's song heard by the good New Englanders, who have a tradition that you must either be a Peabody or a nobody."

Florence Merriam, the best pure ornithologist among the women writers, diverged from writing books on birds to do a provocative book on Mormon women which struck a perceptive balance between the demands of Mormon precepts and the rights of Mormon wives. Miss Merriam had begun her birding at Smith College, where, inspired by George Bird Grinnell's short-lived attempt to form an Audubon Society, she organized a campus chapter laying "deep wily schemes," she wrote, to get other students to give up wearing birds' plumes in their hats. Her scheme, which involved taking classmates out to watch living birds and show them the errors of their millinery, worked far better than she had expected. After a few bird walks, the town milliner was besieged by students wanting to de-feather their hats.

After Smith, Miss Merriam found that she vastly preferred birding "to the most abhorred and abhorrable occupation" of housework. To relieve herself somewhat of the hateful chores, she wrote articles on bird identification for Grinnell's magazine, put them together in *Birds Through an Opera Glass*. She had studied "the perplexities of nearly forty young observers" at Smith, she explained, and she intended now "to furnish hints that will enable young observers and laymen to know the common birds." She does go off into dubious ornithology with such passages as this one of the robin: "Everything about it bespeaks the self-respecting American citizen. Sitting on a branch and whispering a little song to himself, his sentiment is the wholesome every day sort, full of contented appreciation of the beautiful world he lives in." But the book is a workmanlike guide, making identification somewhat easier with all kinds of clues: a field color key, lists of visible markings, classifications by locality, size, color, song ("singers and trillers").

A forced reprieve from housework came to Miss Merriam when, suffering from tuberculosis, she was sent west for her health and used the time to write a breezy book, *A-Birding on a Bronco*. Recovered and returned to the East, she married a naturalist, Vernon Bailey, and made birds her whole career, writing her most popular book, *Birds of Village and Field*. She was the first woman member of the American Ornithologists' Union, of which her brother, Clinton Hart Merriam, the distinguished zoologist, was a founder. Forsaking her young public, she wrote *Handbook of Birds of the Western United States*, which for years was the authority on the subject, and a classic regional work, *Birds of New Mexico*. In these books, she served science, not sympathy, taking for granted that serious birders using them would collect birds. Her chatty, familiar style peeks out frequently from behind the veil of science—as when she writes about the cowbird which, though she is to be scorned for her undomestic and polygamous ways, should be looked upon "with some charity" because she always "takes pains to place her eggs where they are most likely to be hatched"—a bit of sisterly understanding beyond the ken of her brother birders.

15

The Great Connector

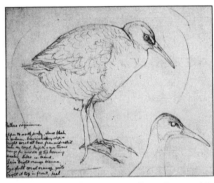

John Burroughs, the most famous nature writer of his day, was also an imbuer but on a grand scale, leading Americans by the hundreds of thousands out into nature to notice birds and pay attention to them, to enter into their lives and let the birds into their own. "The bird has added to the resources of my life," Burroughs confided. "It has afforded me another beautiful object to love and helped me feel more at home in this world." A bird "is hot, ecstatic, his frame charged with buoyancy and his heart with song," he said, opening his readers to his own raptures.

And then he would open to them a panorama of birds and nature:

When the mating or nesting high holes (flickers) are awakening you in the early morning by their insistent calling and drumming, they are doing the same to your neighbors nearby, and to your fellow countrymen fifty, a hundred, a thousand miles away. Think of the myriads of dooryards where the "chippies" are just arriving; of the blooming orchard where the passing, many-colored warblers are eagerly inspecting the buds and leaves; of the woods and woody streams where the ovenbirds and waterthrushes are searching out their old haunts. . . . I fancy that on almost any day in mid-May the flickers are drilling their holes into a million or more decayed trees between the Hudson and the Mississippi; that any day a month earlier, the phoebes are starting their nests under a million or more wood-sheds or bridges . . . that several millions of robins are carrying mud and straws to the sheltered projections about buildings or to the big forked branches in the orchards.

For half a century, from 1870 to 1920, Americans eagerly turned to Burroughs' nature essays in magazines, reread them again in his two dozen books, envied the lucky ones who made pilgrimages to his home on the Hudson, and were impressed by the great men who sought his company. "Not since Audubon had a naturalist achieved this sort of fame," writes Robert Henry Welker in his seminal book *Birds and Men,* "and never before had the birds of America been granted so renowned a champion." He was regarded as gentle "John o' Birds," the gray-bearded sage of nature who lived in a bark-sided cottage and found wisdom in wildflowers and warblers. It was a plausi-ble portrait except for what it left out: that Burroughs was a man of intellectual firmness, of acute literary discernment, and that he was, in the matter of birds, a great connector of men who were anything but gentle in mind or manner—the most rambunctious poet of his day as well as the most rambunctious president and most rambunctious businessman.

He met the poet Walt Whitman in 1863 in Washington, D.C., where Burroughs had gotten himself a job in the currency division of the Treasury Department. Brought up on a farm in the Hudson Val-ley, Burroughs had managed to scrape together an education for himself, reading omnivorously and teaching school to pay for a few months at a small college. His only suitability for the Treasury job was that he was a good Republican, although he did have an ancestral recommendation: his great-grandfather had set up the original U.S. currency system for Alexander Hamilton. (Another ancestor was hanged as a wizard in Salem in 1692.)

Whitman was working for an army paymaster and spending much time as a volunteer nurse in army hospitals. He and Burroughs were introduced to each other by the proprietor of an army supply store where they were shopping. They became good friends, getting to-gether two or three times a week over a mug of ale and a peck of oysters and, on weekends, going out for country walks. Burroughs was already familiar with Whitman's *Leaves of Grass.* "I did not have to wait for somebody to say to me, 'This is great,' " he said. "I knew it as soon as I read it." Having expected to find what Emerson had described as "half song thrush, half alligator," he found instead a man "as vast as the earth and as loving and noble . . . the wisest man I have ever met." In 1867, Burroughs published the first full-length critical appreciation of Whitman, *Notes on Walt Whitman as Poet and Person*—with considerable help from the subject of the book, who edited it and wrote some supplementary notes himself. Still it was Burroughs' own book, his first, and it was a clear-eyed if totally admiring evaluation of the controversial poet.

On their country walks, the two would watch birds, Burroughs identifying and talking about them while Whitman, who was a constant note-taker, jotted down Burroughs' remarks. During one walk in 1865, Burroughs was describing the hermit thrush's song, "the voice of that calm sweet solemnity one attains in his best moments," as he later wrote, "a peace and solemn joy that only the finest souls may know." He told Whitman about the bird's reclusive habits and solitary ways and said that, to him, the bird's song evoked the words "Holy, holy, holy." Whitman's notebooks contain Burroughs' comments on the thrush: "His song is a hymn . . . in swamps—is very shy, never sings near the farmhouse—never in the settlements— is the bird of the solemn primal woods and of Nature, pure and holy."

"That's my bird," said Whitman, and Burroughs reported that "Whitman told me that he has largely used the information I have given him in one of his principal poems." This was the great dirge "When Lilacs Last in the Dooryard Bloom'd," in which the "information" came out this way.

A shy and hidden bird is warbling a song.

Solitary the thrush,
The hermit withdrawn to himself, avoiding the settlements,
Sings by himself a song.
. . . . . .
Sing on, sing on you gray-brown bird,
Sing from the swamps, the recesses, pour your chant from the bushes,
. . . . . .
Victorious song, death's outlet song, . . .

> *As low and wailing, yet clear the notes, rising and falling,*
>   *flooding the night,*
>
> . . . . . .
>
> *Covering the earth and filling the spread of the heaven . . .*

Burroughs did not actually introduce Whitman to birds. The poet had been observing birds since his boyhood on a Long Island farm —during one spring migration he listed forty birds he had seen. Whitman studied *The Birds of Long Island,* by Jacob Post Giraud, and as he did with Burroughs, made poetic use of Giraud's observations. In passages in "Song of Myself," he wrote:

> *. . . the wood-drake and wood-duck . . .*
> *They rise together, they slowly circle around.*
>
> . . . . . .
>
> *. . . the razor-bill'd auk sails far north to Labrador,*
> *. . . I ascend to the nest in the fissure of the cliff.*
>
> . . . . . .
>
> *Where band-neck'd partridges roost in a ring on the ground with their*
>   *heads out,*
>
> . . . . . .
>
> *Where the yellow-crown'd heron comes to the edge of the*
>   *marsh at night and feeds upon small crabs . . .*

All these observations, as Welker points out, are readily traced to Giraud, who notes that the wood duck "would slowly rise and perform a circuit in the air"; that the auk nested "chiefly in the fissures of the rock"; that partridges when roosting "adopted the form of a ring with their heads out and lying thus in a close body received the mutual warmth of each other"; that the yellow-crowned night herons fed "principally on small crabs."

Like so many other watchers, Whitman had one of those ever-remembered childhood encounters. In "Out of the Cradle Endlessly Rocking" he recalled the time he came upon a mockingbird nest:

> *Up this seashore in some briers,*
> *Two feather'd guests from Alabama, two together,*
> *And their nest, and four light-green eggs spotted with brown,*
> *And every day the he-bird to and fro near at hand,*
> *And every day the she-bird crouch'd on her nest, silent, with*
>   *bright eyes . . .*

"Never disturbing them," the boy kept watch, "cautiously peering, absorbing . . ." After the female disappeared, the boy heard the male singing all summer long. (There is, incidentally, a borrowed phrase in this passage—"four light-green eggs spotted with brown" were Giraud's words.)

Where such experiences awakened others to birds, this awakened Whitman to himself as a poet. "Never again," he continued, would he be

> *the peaceful child I was before . . .*
> *[for] The messenger there*
>
> . . . . . .
>
> *arous'd, the fire, the sweet hell within,*
> *The unknown want, the destiny of me.*
>
> *Demon or bird (said the boy's soul,)*
> *Is it indeed toward your mate you sing? or is it really to me?*
>
> . . . . . .
>
> *Now in a moment I know what I am for, I awake,*
> *And already a thousand singers, a thousand songs, clearer,*
> *   louder and more sorrowful than yours,*
> *A thousand warbling echoes have started to life within me,*
> *   never to die.*

In the body of the poem, there is a long section that paraphrases the mockingbird's song, not in any exact imitation of the sounds but a kind of poetic inference of the singing style, monosyllables at the start of the verses introducing longer phrases: *"Shine! Shine! Shine! / Pour down your warmth . . ."* and *"Blow! blow! blow! / Blow up sea-winds . . ."* It is, remarked Burroughs, "altogether poetical and not at all ornithological, yet it contains a rendering or free translation of a bird song . . . quite unmatched in our literature."

But poets who watch birds write about them as poets, not as watchers, and Whitman was concerned with being poetical rather than ornithological. For all his specific details, Whitman used birds as vehicles for his deeper and subtler feelings, as symbols of thoughts almost inexpressible. Having heard the mockingbird *"near at hand, inflating his throat and joyfully singing,"* he later hears himself singing *"Democracy! near at hand . . . a throat is now inflating itself and joyfully singing."* In birds he found a homely, hopeful metaphor for the Civil War:

> *If worms, snakes, loathesome grubs may to sweet*
>   *spiritual songs be turn'd*
> *If vermin so transposed, so used and bless'd may be,*
> *Then I may trust in you, your fortunes, days, my country*

Whitman had his faults as a birder. He was not always properly behaved, breaking the rule that a birder must be quiet and diligent. *"The spotted hawk swoops by me and accuses me, he complains of my gab and my loitering,"* he confessed. And he was, Burroughs said, "none too accurate." With Whitman, Burroughs was indulgent—a poet, Whitman had declared, "must not know too much or be too precise about birds."

Burroughs read other poets, however, with a schoolmaster's eye, praising good works and scolding mistakes. "I am in want of more victims," he once said. "I catch them all napping." William Cullen Bryant was caught putting a bluebird up in an elm tree: an oriole would be much more likely, Burroughs pointed out. That did not lessen his admiration for Bryant, whose poetry, repeatedly derived from birds, finds in them illuminations of moral truths. Moralizing, however, never blurred the pleasures that birds gave Bryant—when he heard *"The gossip of swallows through all the sky"* or when he watched *"the new fledged bird"* taking wing *"half happy, half afraid"* or when *"the wood thrush sings down the golden day / And as I look and listen the sadness wears away"* or his fetching celebration of the bobolink in "Robert of Lincoln":

> *Merrily swinging on briar and weed,*
> *Near to the nest of his little dame,*
> *Robert of Lincoln is telling his name:*
> *Bob-o'-link, bob-o'-link,*
> *Spink, spank, spink;*
>   *. . . . . .*
> *Braggart and prince of braggarts is he,*
> *Pouring boasts from his little throat:*
> *Bob-o'-link, bob-o'-link,*
> *Spink, spank, spink;*
>   *. . . . . .*
> *Six white eggs on a bed of hay,*
> *Flecked with purple, a pretty sight!*
> *There as the mother sits all day,*

> *Robert is singing with all his might:*
> *Bob-o'-link, bob-o'-link,*
> *Spink, spank, spink;*
>
> . . . . . .

Watchers who wave this off as anthropomorphic exaggeration miss the point. Bryant was a good observer and as specific in his descriptions as more prosy writers. *"Six white eggs on a bed of hay, / Flecked with purple,"* would satisfy any oologist.

There is one poem that would not endear Bryant to watchers, "The Old World Sparrow," written when the English sparrow had been newly introduced to America and was welcomed as a gardener's friend.

> *A winged settler has taken his place,*
> *He meets not here, as beyond the main,*
> *The fowler's snare and the poisoned grain*
> *But snug-built homes on the friendly tree*
> *And crumbs for his chirping family*

Then comes a catalog of the bugs the sparrow will decimate:

> *The insect legions that sting our fruit.*
> *A swarming skulking ravenous tribe*
>
> *And the dreaded canker worm shall die*
> *And the thrip and slug and fruit moth seek*
> *In vain to escape their busy beak*

Birders can take some satisfaction in noting that this feathered nuisance could inspire nothing better than doggerel from a usually poetic watcher.

Burroughs had approving words for James Russell Lowell as both bird watcher and writer. "Singularly true to the natural history of his own country," he said, having forgiven Lowell his lapse when, as ambassador to England, he had fallen unpatriotically in love with British birds. The singing of the blackbird and nightingale, Lowell had said, "beat any of ours." Recanting when he came back home, he declared that "the best singer in the world" was Bryant's friend

> *that devil-may-care, the bobolink,*
> *Remembering duty, in mid-quaver stops*
> *Just ere he sweeps o'er rapture's tremulous brink,*
> *And 'twixt the winrows most demurely drops,*

Some phrases that Burroughs admires in Lowell's poetry—*"the thin-winged swallow skating in the air"*—have the authentic quality that could come only from someone who was at home with the birds, as Lowell was. A somewhat lonely child, living on a secluded estate, he made companions of the birds, protected them—he once climbed out on a precarious pine branch to free a young blue jay entangled in some string—and kept his eye on birds all his life. The first-hand feeling comes through in such lines as:

> *Through the dim arbor, himself more dim,*
> *Silently hops the hermit thrush.*
> *The withered leaves keep dumb for him*

and

> *The bluebird, shifting his light load of song*
> *From post to post along the cheerless fence*

His work is bejewelled with contrasting images, sometimes austere as in

> *A single crow on the tree-top bleak*
> *From his shining feathers sheds off the cold air*

and sometimes glowing as in

> *My oriole, my glance of summer fire.*

Lowell's mind carries him to unseen images:

> *As if a lark should suddenly drop dead*
> *While the blue air trembled with its song*

With a nice wit he remarks:

> *The owl, belated in his plundering*
> *Shall here await the friendly night*
> *Blinking where'er he wakes and wondering*
> *What fool it was invented light*

And as well as any birder ever did, he tells why he is so possessed by them: *"A bird is singing in my brain."*

Burroughs found Henry Wadsworth Longfellow the least exact of poets, complaining of the lines in "The Skeleton in Armor":

> *As with his wings aslant,*
> *Sails the fierce cormorant,*
> *Seeking some rocky haunt,*
> *With his prey laden,—*

"No bird of prey sails with his burden," frowned Burroughs. "He flaps laboriously."

Aside from accuracy, Longfellow gives an interesting illustration of the American ambivalence towards nature. In one of his stories from *Tales of a Wayside Inn*, Longfellow tells the familiar story of farmers who, to avenge themselves upon the birds that had been eating their grain, killed them all in "a St. Bartholomew's massacre," and found, next year, that their crops were devoured by caterpillars. The chastened farmers, of course, welcomed the birds back to eat the caterpillars.

Yet in *The Song of Hiawatha*, Longfellow described with almost bloodthirsty satisfaction how his hero dealt with birds that were eating his corn:

> *Kahgahgee, the King of Ravens,*
> *Gathered all his black marauders,*
> *Crows and blackbirds, jays and ravens,*
> . . . . . .
> *And descended, fast and fearless,*
> *On the fields of Hiawatha,*
> . . . . . .
> *But the wary Hiawatha,*
> *Ever thoughtful, careful, watchful,*
> *Had o'erheard the scornful laughter*
> . . . . . .
> *"Kaw!" he said, "my friends the Ravens*

> . . . . . .
> *I will teach you all a lesson . . ."*
> *He had risen before the daybreak,*
> *He had spread o'er all the cornfields*
> *Snares to catch the black marauders,*
>
> . . . . . .
> *Soon they came with caw and clamor,*
>
> . . . . . .
> *To their work of devastation,*
>
> . . . . . .
> *All their skill in wiles of warfare,*
> *They perceived no danger near them,*
> *Till their claws became entangled,*
> *Till they found themselves imprisoned*
> *In the snares of Hiawatha.*
> *From his place of ambush came he,*
> *Striding terrible among them,*
>
> . . . . . .
> *Without mercy he destroyed them*
> *Right and left, by tens and twenties,*
> *And their wretched, lifeless bodies*
> *Hung aloft on poles for scarecrows . . .*

Only the king, Kahgahgee, was spared and the gentle poet gave
him a merciless reprieve. Hiawatha let him live, tied to the

> *ridge-pole of his wigwam.*
> . . . . . .
> *Sitting in the morning sunshine*
> . . . . . .
> *Croaking fiercely his displeasure . . .*

The poets had their own way of embedding birds in the minds of
Americans. The familiar, much loved poems were read aloud at home
and memorized in class. No one can count the times that Robert of
Lincoln's *spink, spank, spink* was recited, with expression, at school
assemblies. And thousands of schoolchildren, remembering the poem
better than any bird description, could have told you, from Robert of
Lincoln's nest, how many eggs the bobolink laid and what color their
spots were.

Burroughs might legitimately pick at the errors in other writers' works because he himself was a fine field naturalist. He had watched birds since he was a boy of six or seven when he saw "a bird that so fired his imagination that he resolved to know more about birds." As he recalled it later, "gazing vaguely up into the trees, I caught sight of a bird that paused a moment on a branch above me, the like of which I had never before seen or heard of. I saw it a moment as the flickering leaves parted, noted the white spot on its wing and it was gone. How the thought of it clung to me afterward! It was the revelation. It was the first intimation I had had that the woods we knew so well held birds that we knew not at all." (That bird, he later learned, was a black-throated blue warbler and years afterward he became the first birder to discover its nest in New York.)

In 1863, while teaching school near West Point, he wandered into the academy library and came across Audubon's *Birds of America* and, from that point on, his main interest in nature was birds. He was a founding member of the Linnaean Society and a member of the American Ornithologists' Union. By the time he went to Washington, his nature essays were being published. The first collection appeared in 1871, bearing a title Whitman insisted on—*Wake Robin* (which confused many innocent readers unaware that the wake robin is not a bird but a wildflower). The book brought a letter from Elliott Coues: "Your book has been to me a green spot in the wilderness where I have lingered with rare pleasure. I can bear witness to the minute fidelity and vividness of your portraiture . . . pointing out new beauties I had missed before."

After he left Washington in 1873, Burroughs settled down to serious, continuous writing. He also worked part-time as a bank examiner in New York until the middle 1880s, when the Democrats won the election and threw Republicans out of federal jobs. In that position Burroughs said, "I was painstaking but was easily deceived," and in a report he wrote on corrupt financial practices, "Broken Banks and Lax Directors," he turned to nature to make his points. "Bees carry off honey from the hive and leave the comb all intact: and cashiers have been known to exhibit as clear and straight a set of books as need be when their accounts were little more than empty combs."

Immediately popular—"He takes you out into the open air," said Whitman, "where things are in an amiable mood"—Burroughs published a book every three or four years, writing in a comfortable declarative style, vivid in its directness. The downy woodpecker's "head is a trip hammer and he drives his beak into the wood with short sharp blows . . . while the nuthatch strikes more softly . . . delivers a kind of feathered blow." Yet he could descend into: "Do you hear the loud sonorous hammering . . . from the orchard or from the near woods. It is the downy but he is not rapping at the door of a grub; he is rapping at the door of spring." Or: "When nature made the bluebird, she wished to propitiate both the sky and the earth, so she gave him the color of the one on his back and the hue of the other on his breast, and ordained that his appearance in spring should denote that the strife and war between these two elements was at an end."

This, of course, is the kind of writing that drew a large audience, less interested in his businesslike prose about birds than in the poetry and romance that he found in them. "The song of the bobolink to me expresses hilarity; the song sparrow's, faith; the bluebird's, love; the cat-bird's pride; the white-eyed flycatcher's, self-consciousness; that of the hermit thrush, spiritual serenity: while there is something military in the call of the robin."

"Words are like lenses," he wrote. "They must be arranged in just such a way or they hinder rather than help the vision. When the adjustment is as it should be, then the lens itself is invisible." His precept led him to pithy observations that bring delighted recognition from birders—the whip-poor-will "whipping poor will until one pities him"; the winter wren's voice filling "those damp aeries as if aided by some marvelous sounding board"; and "in all the blackbirds we hear the voice of April not yet quite articulate; there is a suggestion of catarrh and influenza still in the air passages." When he remarks that a naturalist must, first of all, be able "to read the fine print of nature" or when he remarks that "Nature is all things to all men; she has whole truths, half truths and quarter truths, if not still smaller fractions," he discloses an urbane observer, skillful in manipulating the language.

Like so many of his generation, Burroughs went through the difficult transformation from collector to conserver. When he received a letter from S. W. Adams of Canaan, Connecticut, who asked whether a bird that had been sighted was a hermit or a wood thrush. Burroughs said to shoot it and make sure. When a reply revealed that the *S* in her signature stood for Sarah, he said that, of course, a lady couldn't carry a gun. Instead she should be patient and sharp-sighted. "As to shooting the bird," he said, "I think a real lover of nature will indulge in no sentimentalism on the subject. Shoot them, of course, and no toying about it." She might possibly, he added, think of getting an inconspicuous cane gun like his.

He himself shot birds as a help to science. Once, seeing a bird in the dim light, he was uncertain as to what it was. "It is for such emergencies, that I have brought my gun," he wrote. "A bird in the hand is worth half a dozen in the bush, and no sure and rapid progress can be made in the study without taking life, without procuring specimens." After writing his impassioned description of the hermit thrush's "holy" song and the "deep solemn joy" it aroused, he ended with a matter-of-fact: "Shot one." And, coming across another thrush, he shot that one too. "I open his beak," he went on, "and find the insides yellow as gold. I was prepared to find it inlaid with pearls and diamonds or to see an angel issue from it."

Like George Mackay and so many others, he eventually came to feel that the gun was used far too much. He changed into a determined, effective advocate for conservation—and was accused in *Auk,* after he had criticized collecting, of "slandrous intolerance begotten by ignorance." He had always been a propagandist for nature and through him, as much as anyone, Americans had come to understand and appreciate nature. So they were ready to protect it when he called on them to do so. With his friend John Muir, Burroughs came to personify the growing conservation movement.

He became, also, an advocate for female birders. "The new woman," he said, "is a great improvement on the old. She loves the open air like a man . . . seems to be more poetry in her soul than in man's." Women authors found him ready to advise, praise and introduce their books. His own wife, a hardheaded woman who, he grumbled, cared only about money and keeping house, tried to steer him away from birds and writing and even tried to get him to cut off his cherished beard. They lived, for some years, more or less separate lives. Burroughs found a kind of solace in young ladies—in groups. College girls were his delight and he was theirs. Smith students, made interested in birds by Florence Merriam, invited him to their campus and doted on him. "Never was wolf so overwhelmed by the lambs," he beamed after the visit. With unconvincing casualness, Burroughs remarked that "Vassar girls have got the notion of calling frequently" at his home near the Hudson. "One day I led them out to the little sassafras to see the chickadee's nest. The sitting bird kept her place as head after head appeared above the opening to her chamber and a pair of inquisitive eyes peered down upon her. Presently I heard a faint explosion at the bottom of the cavity when the peeping girl jerked her head quickly back with the exclamation: 'Why it spit at me!' " His home sometimes would be "awash with girls. They did not seem to care a fig for the birds," he said, sounding more pleased than put off, "only wanted to see me."

At a loftier level, Burroughs went birding with a fellow member of the Linnaean Society, Theodore Roosevelt, who sent him bulletins on White House birds—in 1908 he was pleased to report a white-crowned sparrow—and invited him to his camp at Pine Knot, where the two behaved like any competing birders, each trying to outdo the other. One weekend, Burroughs found two species the president had never seen—a swamp sparrow and pine warbler—and the president found two that were new to Burroughs—a Bewick's wren and a prairie warbler. "It was remarkable," said Burroughs of T.R., "how well he knew the birds and their notes." Roosevelt took Burroughs to a spot to see a little blue-gray gnatcatcher. "I've heard it here," he had told Burroughs, and there it was. At one White House lunch, Burroughs differed with the president on the chipping sparrow's song. It went *"t-wee twee,"* the president insisted. *"Twee twee t-wee,"* Burroughs argued. They apparently never came to an agreement and bird guides today side with neither version. "A simple *tsip,*" says one.

In December 1912, Burroughs wrote in his journal: "I had a surprising letter. Mr. Ford, of automobile fame, is a great admirer of my books—says there are few persons in the world who have given him the pleasure I have. He wants to do something for me—he wants to present me with a Ford automobile all complete. His sole motive is his admiration for me and my work. How can I accept such a gift from a stranger and keep my self-respect?" Ford explained that, to him, giving away a car "was no more than giving away a jackknife to most men." Burroughs accepted and, somewhat uncertainly, entered the machine age. After his first meeting with Ford, he wrote: "Mr. Ford is pleased with me and I with him. His interest in birds is keen and his knowledge considerable."

"The first thing I remember in my life," Ford once recalled, "was my father taking my brother and myself to see a bird's nest under a big oak. That must have been 1866 in June. I remember the nest with four eggs and also the bird and hearing it sing." It was, he guessed, a song sparrow. Ford's father was a stern man determined to overcome everything for his farm—he had to clear a forest to start it. But when he found a bird nesting in the field he was ploughing, he would swerve the plough to spare the nest.

Henry grew up learning about wildlife, about birds most of all, and when he had grown rich and his own farm at Dearborn encompassed thousands of acres, he still knew when the bobolinks came and where the nests were. "We have five hundred bird houses," he boasted. "We call them our bird hotels and one martin house has seventy-six apartments." The gardeners were instructed to leave some cherries unpicked in the orchard and strawberries in the garden so birds could get their natural fare—and so, said Ford, who was better able than other farmers to afford such largesse, "we have more different kinds of bird callers than anywhere else in the northern states."

"Birds are the best of companions," he mused, not just for their beauty but for "strictly economic reasons. The only time I ever used the Ford organization to influence legislation was on behalf of the birds and I think the ends justified the means." That was in 1914, when Congress was dawdling over the migratory bird treaty with Canada. "Birds do not vote," Ford observed, and decided to give them representation his own way. Hiring a public relations man to put pressure on Congress, he instructed every one of his six thousand auto dealers to tell their congressmen to support the bill. "It began to be apparent," Ford said dryly, "that birds might have votes." The bill went though and became the basis for all federal bird protection.

Ford's gift of the Model T gave Burroughs a somewhat dubious field advantage. Friends riding with him found the experience "a mingling of admiration, amusement and anxiety," as Burroughs bounced along, taking his hands off the wheel to point out an oriole and his eyes off the road to verify a yellow-breasted chat. He once drove the car through the side of his barn ("I am terribly humiliated and later scared," he said). Once, with a lady disciple at the wheel, the car turned over. Burroughs was only bruised. "If you are going to be wrecked in an automobile," he said, giving a questionable endorsement, "choose a Ford every time."

Ford took Burroughs, along with Edison and Firestone, on their famous camping trips and when Burroughs once mentioned that the Sea Island region of Georgia was particularly rich in wildlife, Ford began buying land along the Ogeechee River; by the time he had finished, he owned a hundred square miles of plantation, villages, rivers, island and beaches.

Twitting Burroughs, Ford argued that, contrary to his friend's belief, nature was often backward. "There has been no observable development in the method of making birds' nests," he pointed out, "since the beginning of recorded observations but that was hardly a reason why human beings should not prefer modern sanitary homes to cave dwellings." Burroughs had believed, Ford went on, that the automobile was going to kill the appreciation of nature. But the auto "completely changed his point of view. He made nearly all of his bird hunting expeditions from behind the steering wheel. When he had passed three score and ten he changed his view on industry. Perhaps I had something to do with that. He came to see," Ford concluded with some satisfaction, "that the whole world could not live by hunting bird's nests."

16

Revolution in the Bronx

In the early 1920s, an unexpected urban habitat began encroaching on the attentions of the birding community—the Bronx. This northern borough of New York City had never been widely known as a nature preserve. Half its area, a birder once concluded, is utterly inhospitable to birds and there is no spot in it that can be called an unspoiled natural area. Still, 227 species of birds (about half of all eastern U.S. species) have been sighted there, which shows how adaptable and enduring birds can be—and bird watchers as well.

Even today, in between the urban crowding and the often devastated streets are parks, botanical and zoological gardens and, on the borough's edges, huge dumps. There are tidewaters (industrialized and untidy) in the east, wetlands (littered) along the Bronx River in the middle, hills (built up) along the Hudson on the western boundary. From these areas in the 1920s a group of native schoolboys began sending their findings to the Linnaean Society and to *Bird-Lore*. Joseph Hickey found a little blue heron at the Hunts Point dump, then the first recorded double-crested cormorant for the area, along with a Florida gallinule (common moorhen) and a Wilson's phalarope.

Irving Kassoy saw a short-eared owl at Hunts Point and a barn owl in an abandoned mansion in the east Bronx—the caretaker had thought the place was haunted. John Kuerzi watched a three-toed Arctic woodpecker (now black-backed woodpecker) chiseling the bark off a dead hemlock tree at the Botanical Gardens. Kassoy and Hickey, out with John Matuszewski, recorded a red-headed woodpecker and bufflehead at Hunts Point, and Hickey and Kuerzi saw a black-bellied plover there. Hickey spotted a vesper sparrow at the Jerome Avenue Reservoir, where Allan Cruickshank saw a horned grebe. Cruickshank also saw a Wilson's snipe (common snipe) at Van Cortlandt Park and a mourning warbler in his backyard. Sitting together at a baseball game on University Heights, Hickey and Cruickshank spotted an American swallow-tailed kite, the first spring record of that southern bird for half a century. (Four ladies, unconnected to these young birders, reported three snowy egrets at the 242d Street subway station.)

In 1926, commenting on the annual Christmas bird census, the recorder of the Linnaean Society was moved to state that of all the reports, "the most remarkable" came from the Bronx—a total of eighty-three species, and 6,696 individuals, including rusty blackbirds, a sora, a king rail, an American bittern, a glaucous gull, a sharp-tailed sparrow, three oldsquaws, four snowy owls and an Iceland gull. Sizable counts had been coming in from the Bronx for several years: in 1924, seventeen species and 281 individuals, including a "very rare" pileated woodpecker; in 1925, twenty-one species and 481 individuals. One got the impression that the Bronx was filling up with birds. It was, of course, filling up with birders.

They were members of the Bronx County Bird Club, newly formed by high school boys living in the borough, doing their birding close to home. The Bronx at that time, though far from pastoral, had convenient stretches of open space and a long walk or a nickel for trolley or subway fare would take a watcher to a likely spot. Some members, like Allan Cruickshank, had started birding in a school club. The Kuerzi brothers had been taken on bird walks by their father. Joseph Hickey was birding on his own when he was twelve and, lacking glasses, climbed a high maple tree to see warblers close up. He was thirteen years ten months old—he remembers the big day exactly—when some gentleman he had met near the Bronx Zoo bird house gave him an old pair of opera glasses and moved him on into sophisticated watching.

Nine of the boys came together in the Kuerzi attic and organized themselves as the Bronx County Bird Club. As was the case with several other birding groups, its membership was exclusive: one had to live in the Bronx to belong. In 1924, Hickey, John Kuerzi, and John Matuszewski established a Bronx beachhead in organized birding by being elected to the Linnaean Society—"a fusty, awesome group," one young birder found it. The other Bronx boys followed and, in 1927, John Kuerzi was elected to the Linnaean Council—"after numerous ballots," the minutes state. The following year, he was elected secretary of the society.

Official membership of the Bronx club stayed at nine for years. After a while, a couple of outlanders were allowed to come along on the walks and join in their discussions—Roger Tory Peterson of Jamestown, New York, William Vogt of Long Island and, occasionally, Robert Porter Allen of Williamsport, Pennsylvania. With these intrusions, the Bronx—like Boston Harbor when the patriots dumped tea into it or the Finland Station when Lenin arrived there—became a starting point of a historic (for birders, at least) revolution, which was to turn bird watching from the pastime of a relative few into the pleasure of a great many.

As with so many revolutionary bands, the club's equipment was scanty and inadequate. The members had to share a couple of pairs of opera glasses. Their field references were pages torn from a New York bird book that had been retrieved from a rubbish can, and Chester Reed's *Guide to the Land Birds East of the Rockies.* This was their basic book—as it was for virtually every watcher of their generation everywhere in the country, the book on which they all got started.

It was a little book, only 3½ by 5½ inches, shaped like a checkbook to fit handily into a pocket, and it cost only two dollars. It was brief in text and clear in illustration. Each of Reed's two hundred illustrated pages (with a few exceptions) showed one bird and gave half a dozen sentences of description. His paintings showed the bird sitting on a branch, usually in half profile, drawn in attitudes that were both realistic and suggestive. Sometimes the identification clues were not entirely helpful. The adult kingbird "has a concealed orange patch," not of much use to a viewer seeing it from a distance. The pine siskin's call is "a slight nasal twang that will identify them from a distance after becoming accustomed to it." A birder using Reed needed considerable dexterity as he made his way back and forth from the generalized "Color Key" ("Birds with Red as Prominent Color" or "Birds with Blue as Prominent Color") to "Size" ("Near sparrow"; "Between robin and sparrow"; "Larger than robin"), thumbing the index to look up a page reference, going to another if that didn't seem right—all the time trying to remember exactly what the bird looked like when he saw it. And learning, by experience, the birder's maxim that you must look at the bird more than at the book: the bird will fly away, the book won't.

Reed's careful paintings made up for any lacks: they had an artful way of sticking in the visual memory, and so, with patience and familiarity, using the guide became a second-nature process. Reed gave his readers a compact course in how to be a proper birder: make notes on appearance, length, eye marks, "medium or superciliary line," bill shape, wing bars, food, nesting sites, etc.; memorize songs; keep tabs on the company it keeps. Do not shoot birds or rob their nests, he admonished, but since he was writing in an era of oology, he included descriptions of nests and eggs.

All this, of course, was aimed at getting the incipient bird watcher to take the all-important step from just looking at a bird and naming it to observing it and its way of life. Reed was puritanical in his rationale for bird watching. "It is the duty, and it should be the pleasure, of every citizen to do everything in his or her power to protect these valuable creatures. . . . Look at the little chickadee at the side of this page," he said, calling attention to the fact that she is shown carrying twenty-five plant lice to feed her seven young. "She and her mate carry 200 such loads a day." Making a conservative estimate that each insectivorous bird eats 100 insects a day, he calculated that the 25,600,000 birds in Massachusetts alone ate 2,560,000,000 insects, or 21,000 bushels per day every day from May to September, inclusive. The best way to protect such helpfully hungry creatures, he said, concluding his homely lecture on conservation, is "the creating of an interest in their habits and modes of life" and this is justification enough for the book.

Reed published his *Guide* in 1906 and died, six years later at thirty-six, before he could fully enjoy its huge success. It was, by far, the most widely used bird book of its time and, in relative terms, no guide has ever really outdone it. Bird-book counters have lost track of how many millions of copies have been printed since the first one. It is so convenient and its paintings so attractive that a revised edition is still being published today.

The Bronx club's first copy of Reed was a hand-me-down given one member by an older brother who used it to get a Boy Scout merit badge and had no further interest in it. They took it on trips along with pages cut from a volume of Elon Eaton's massive *Birds of New York,* which Joe Hickey had scavenged from a trash can. When the club members wanted to know more about a bird, they relied on Frank M. Chapman's *Handbook of Birds of Eastern North America.* Nobody in the club owned a copy but an agreeable member had memorized from it the dimensions of likely birds and he served in the field as a walking reference, quoting the dimensions of a species down to a hundredth of an inch. When they needed more data, they looked it up in the public library's copy.

From its first publication in 1895 to its last edition in 1940, the *Handbook* was the best advanced guide to American birds, distilling all the knowledge that had been amassed since the early naturalists and Baird and basing its identification on the keys first devised by Coues. It was not a book a Bronx birder could plunge into and gain quick knowledge even though the author, in a bit of playfulness, remarked: "If this book had been written in the last century it might have been entitled 'Ornithology Made Simple, or How to Identify Birds with Ease, Certainty, and Dispatch.'" Though he tried, he said, to write free of technicality in a book small enough to put in a pocket, he succeeded in neither. Users of the *Handbook* found that Ease came only with long use, that Certainty was achieved by mastering detail after detail and that Dispatch came slowly. And its five hundred 6-by-9-inch pages did not fit into any average pocket. The *Handbook* suggested the birder stow it in a fisherman's creel, which gives an indication of the social gap between Chapman's general audience and the Bronx boys.

A quick run through Chapman will show modern watchers how coddled they are by their present-day guides. The birder looking to identify a small brown bird with streaks and a dot on its breast would—like Mrs. Coues using her husband's *Key*—have to know a great deal more than that just to start the identification process. Aware—as the *Handbook* presumed he was—that the bird had four toes with the hind and middle of the same length, and twelve feathers in its tail, he would find in the Synopsis of Orders and Suborders, which he had been instructed to memorize, that it was in the order Passeres (Passeriformes), or perching birds. From its head, bill and feathers he would put it in the order Oscines; from the conical bill and apparent absence of rudimentary outer primary feathers it would go into the family Fringillidae. Then by a series of details and eliminations—narrow tail feathers, uncrossed mandibles, the absence of white or yellow tail patches—he would think it might be a song sparrow and, turning to the section on that bird he would read:

EASTERN SONG SPARROW. *Melospiza melodia melodia*
. . . Crown rufous-brown, with a grayish line through its center;
a grayish line over the eye; a rufous-brown line from behind the
eye to the nape; feathers of the back streaked with black and
margined with rufous-brown and grayish; greater wing-coverts
with black spots at their tips; no white wing-bars or yellow on
the wing; tail rufous grayish brown, the middle feathers darker
along their shafts; outer feathers shortest; sides of the throat
with black or blackish streaks; breast with wedge-shaped
streaks of black and rufous-brown which tend to form one *larger
blotch* on the center; sides washed with brownish and streaked
with black and rufous-brown; middle of the belly white. L.,
6.30; W., 2.52; T., 2.62; B, .49.

The text plainly was directed at the birder with the bird or notes
in hand. "Either you may shoot [birds]," Chapman said, "or study
them through a field- or opera-glass." If you would "name the birds
without a gun"—he added, quoting a remark by Emerson who
thought this was the proper way—you should visit a museum first to
make detailed notes. Take them with you along with a light opera
glass if you are going into the woods or with a higher-powered field
glass if you are going after water birds.

Complicated as the *Handbook* may seem now, it served admirably
for decades as an authoritative guide. A birder brought up on Reed
or the works of Miller or Wright or Blanchan or who was lucky enough
to have been imbued, could learn to make his way through Chapman
—and, of course, by the time he took up the book, he did not have
to be told what a song sparrow looked like. Chapman condensed a
great deal of information for ready reference yet was complete
enough to answer any reasonable question.

The *Handbook* also gave, in a hundred-page introduction, everything from a short course in the science and history of ornithology to
homely hints on how to be a more successful watcher. Go birding
alone, it instructed, keep the sun at your back and become part of the
background. "Go . . . in some inconspicuous garb and as quietly as
a cat," one of the few positive words for the cat to be found in all
birding literature. If you find yourself in an apparently deserted
thicket, forsaken by all birds, put your lips to the back of your hand
and kiss vigorously to produce a "squeak," like the call of a young or
wounded bird. In a few minutes, the *Handbook* promised, you will be
surrounded by curious or anxious birds.

And the birder was exhorted to a grander appreciation of his pastime. "Everyone," he declared, is born with a bird in his heart. "Birds add immeasureably to our enjoyment of life. Where in all animate nature shall we find so marvelous a combination of beauty of form and color, of grace and power of motion, of musical ability and intelligence, to delight our eyes, charm our ears and appeal to our imagination?"

In 1911, putting out a new edition, Chapman looked back to what had happened in the fourteen years since the first one: "Where one person knew common birds, now hundreds do. It is less as an exponent of natural laws than as a most attractive form of wild life that the bird has made its appeal. In the history of North American ornithology, therefore, this period may well stand as the Epoch of Popular Bird-Study." He himself had presided over this epoch and continued to for decades through his *Handbook,* through his post as curator and ornithological mentor at the American Museum of Natural History and his influence as editor and owner of *Bird-Lore.*

The son of a New York lawyer (who set out once to copy the Bible in his own hand and, working at it four hours a day, completed it in eleven months), Frank Chapman had been brought up in New Jersey farming country where he watched birds, collected them and their eggs and came to care deeply about them. When he went to work at a bank in New York, he spent his lunch hours at John Bell's famous taxidermy shop. In bird migration time, he got up at dawn to take a two-and-a-half-hour walk to the railroad, counting as he went and changing into city clothes at the Englewood station. Coues' *Key* was his favorite commuting reading—he memorized most of it—and he joined the Linnaean Society and the AOU. At the age of twenty-two, he was made head of his department at the bank and, assured of a prosperous future, weighed career against inclination. "It had become clear," he later said, "that there would soon be a serious conflict between the bank clerk and the bird man." So he applied to the American Museum of Natural History for a post as ornithologist, a profession that had few members, not much standing and offered a salary that was "but little above the vanishing point . . . facts to which no real bird student gives serious attention."

He got the job and on the side began publishing *Bird-Lore* magazine. When the Audubon movement firmed up, he persuaded the Audubon Society to make it its official organ, though he retained ownership. It was his idea, in 1900, to hold a Christmas census of birds, recruiting birders over the country to take it. The first one enlisted such eminent counters as Witmer Stone of the DVOC, Lynds Jones of the Wilson Club and Chapman himself, who, however, dropped out after the first year. The census became an integral part of the bird movement, adding to ornithological knowledge and birding techniques and to the moral and physical stamina of birders. It also stimulated the interest in competing lists which, for better or for worse, has also become an integral part of American birding.

The members of the Bronx County Bird Club used the Christmas census in their own way. Throughout December, they scouted likely spots, figured which birds were most likely to be where and had their foresight rewarded when counting day came. At the Linnaean Society, they knew Chapman himself only as a distant, Olympian figure. They were more drawn to a birder who, just as they were beginning to get a grasp on the Bronx, brought out a book that made their birding there much more efficient. The book, *Birds of the New York City Region,* became their scripture and its author, Ludlow Griscom, became their prophet. With high-handed self-assurance Griscom led the revolutionary generation out of the age that had been dominated by Brewster, Coues and Chapman—and the collectors.

He was, by birth and breeding, emphatically non-Bronx. One grandfather was a Union general, one uncle was an admiral, another an ambassador. Ludlow himself was a prodigy. At fifteen, he was accepted at Harvard but chose to stay at home studying music and languages. At seventeen, he thought seriously of becoming a concert pianist, although his parents wanted him to enter the foreign service —he could speak or read more than a dozen languages. But he chose birds, a subject that had interested him since he was six years old and found Central Park a wonderful place for them—and where he found inspiration and a companion in Miss Anne M. Crolius, who set a record for consistent urban watching by making observations 250 days a year from 1895 to 1915.

Griscom enrolled in Cornell University's Department of Ornithology, which had just been set up by Arthur Allen. A protean figure in American ornithology, Allen straddled the scientific and the popular aspects of ornithology. He initiated studies in conservation and ecology, helped establish the procedures of bird banding, made significant discoveries of bird diseases and, from his "Grad Lab," turned out the leading ornithologists of the future. As a patron of bird watching, he helped develop the field techniques of recording bird songs and of photographing birds, and, through his charming stories of bird life, drew thousands of young and adult Americans into the realms of bird watching.

Ludlow Griscom was the first of Allen's students to earn a graduate degree in ornithology and this led to a job at the American Museum of Natural History. He became a fearsomely exact birder, attributing this to a precocious blunder at a Linnaean Society meeting where, as a schoolboy, he reported a Bicknell's thrush (a variety of gray-cheeked thrush) solely on the basis of having heard its call note. "The resulting storm of criticism" at this departure from birding tenets "rendered me practically speechless," he said. "No event hurt more or was more beneficial." The young birders of the Bronx generation also benefited by his traumatic experience and by his stern advice, which is still a criterion for birders: [1] Learn by heart all the published data about birds in your locality. [2] Memorize the diagnostic characters, those that identify with certainty. [3] Get field knowledge of the birds of your locality. [4] Above all cultivate a scientific attitude and don't believe in your infallibility—but he didn't take that last instruction very seriously for himself.

Before having a sighting accepted, an observer would have to submit to questioning:

1   Is he thoroughly familiar with the birds of the locality and aware of the importance of his find?
2   Did he ever see the bird before?
3   Does he know the species it could be confused with?
4   Is his account of the circumstances of the observation thoroughly satisfactory?
5   Did he recognize the bird at once or did he have to look it up later?

Efforts to get answers to these questions, Griscom admitted, "frequently give offense" to the observer, in part because Griscom had developed what has been called "the retort discourteous." He was not very tolerant of inexactness or, for that matter, of most birders. But he was dedicated to birds and bird watchers and recognized in the Bronx boys a unique generation. He became their tutor, encourager, critic and role model. Some of them adopted, along with his birding precepts, his distinctive mannerisms, copying the way he parted his hair in the middle, the inflections he put into phrases like "common summer resident." His standard phrases became part of their birding jargon: "Let's stop here and flap our ears"; "That's just a weed bird"; "Please lower your voice to a howl"; "Put it down to sheer ignorance, incompetence and inexperience."

Less and less, as he went on, did Griscom believe in or rely on collecting. Once, he challenged an old-line Linnaean member to match gun against glasses. Griscom spotted a bird on the top of a sycamore tree and identified it as a female Cape May warbler, an uncommon bird with confusing field marks. The old boy then shot the bird and Griscom was right, which surprised none of the Bronx boys. Looking back at what he had done for them and eleven other birders, one of them said that Griscom symbolized the rise of the competent watcher. Demonstrating that birds could be accurately identified by seeing their field marks and not necessarily through shooting them, he bridged the gap between the collector and the binocular birders. Which is to say, between an old era of bird watching and a new one.

17

The Guide

The year the Bronx Christmas counters took their "remarkable" census, a more modest one was made in Jamestown, New York, by the watcher who would some years later be adopted by them and, pushing their revolution further, would lead American birders into the new era. In 1926, Roger Tory Peterson and a friend reported twenty-seven Jamestown species, and 2,844 individual birds, including two pileated woodpeckers, a prairie horned lark, 2,500 starlings and a Wilson's snipe (common snipe) that had been spending the last five winters in an open bit of water. The following year, among his thirty-two species were cardinals and titmice, two birds beginning to stay north for the winter but never before reported from the area.

By that time, Roger Peterson had taken part in five Christmas censuses and had been involved with birds for about half his nineteen years, ever since his seventh-grade teacher, Miss Blanche Hornbeck, got him to join the Junior Audubon Club and particularly since the day when he came upon a bird he knew by the name of the "heigh ho" sitting, immovable, on a low branch. Checking his copy of Reed, he learned that it was a flicker. "I thought it was dead," he remembers, and reached out to touch it. The bird burst into the air and

—here again that eventful moment—birds burst into the boy's life.

He went around the countryside with a copy of Reed always in his pocket and, because of Reed, confused the blue grosbeak with the indigo bunting. He pored over Chapman but was exasperated by the way the *Handbook* descriptions inevitably started with the beak and plodded systematically back to the tail—the text went more than half-way through the robin before it got to "underparts rufous." Spending his hard-earned dimes, he bought Junior Audubon pamphlets, getting in each a description, in rather adult terms, of a single bird. On his own, he painted birds, stiffly delineating the smallest pin feathers.

After high school, since there was not much family money, Roger took a job in a factory painting furniture under a boss who instructed him in the art of doing delicate, Chinese-style decoration. The oracles, meanwhile, were busy and prescient. The high school class prophet wrote of him: "Woods! Birds! Flowers! Here are the makings of a great naturalist." A few months after graduation, Roger went to an AOU convention with a couple of his bird paintings and there, striking up a conversation with an AOU member, asked him to sign his application for membership. Ludlow Griscom did his bit for the future of birding by signing. The bird artist Louis Agassiz Fuertes thought enough of the young man's painting to give him one of his paintbrushes, which Roger treasured until it fell through a crack in the floor and was lost. Encouraged, Roger sent his paintings west to a Cooper Ornithological Society exhibit and the catalog noted that "Roger Tory Peterson is but 17 years of age and has barely launched upon his artistic career which has the promise of being a notable one."

At nineteen, Roger moved to New York to study painting, first at the Art Students' League under John Sloan, the famous realist of the Ashcan School of painting, and then at the more traditional National Academy of Design. To pay his way, he went back to his old profession of painting furniture—some of the gaudier beds he decorated being destined, he understood, for the city's higher-class brothels. Moving in simultaneously on New York's birds and bird watchers, he made his debut at the Linnaean Society by reporting 130 Canada geese at Dyker Heights in Brooklyn and a ruddy duck at the 125th Street Ferry in Manhattan. The city was, for him, an astonishingly rich habitat and over the years he birded it devotedly, finding Bonaparte's gulls at the Ninety-second Street sewer outlet in Brooklyn, watching chickadees migrating down Seventh Avenue, counting curlews flying over Greenwich Village, spotting a woodcock on the ledge of the old General Motors Building and a peregrine falcon from a window in the Time and Life Building. On a very foggy morning, with Central Park full of confused fall migrants, he saw half a dozen scarlet tanagers in one tree and four rose-breasted grosbeaks in another, five species of thrushes, a Florida gallinule (common moorhen) and an Audubon's "bimaculated" duck—the one the artist had misnamed after Thomas Brewer. He listened to migrant warblers at night from the top of the RCA Building and tracked down a hermit thrush that had migrated into a florist shop at Sixty-third Street and Madison Avenue.

Most of his birding in the early New York days was done with members of the Bronx County Bird Club, whom he met at the Linnaean Society. "He was very shy at first," a member once recalled. "He didn't have the extrovert qualities some of us had." After a couple of outings, they came to respect his knowledge and especially his field instincts.

Bit by bit, birds drew Peterson away from art school, and a job as nature counselor in a summer camp pulled him away from decorating furniture. The camp job led, in 1931, to a position teaching art and natural history at a school near Boston. As a guest at the Nuttall Club he gave some informal reports on his sightings but was rebuffed when he applied for membership—"too cocky about his records," was the verdict. Made aware that what was expected behavior in the Bronx was unacceptable in Boston, he modified his manners and was admitted the next year. One evening the club played one of its favorite indoor games. About twenty bird specimens, all tricky to identify, were held up briefly and members had to name them. That night, Ludlow Griscom, generally looked on as the best field man in the country, was present and, of course, got all the birds right. So did Peterson, and the Nuttall members realized that their initiate had a right to be cocky.

At night, in his cubby-hole room at the school, Peterson had begun working out his dissatisfaction with existing bird guides by writing and drawing one of his own—a proper bird guide that, as he described it, would be "a boiling down of things so that any bird would be readily and surely told from all others at a glance or a distance"—and in nature, not in a museum. Almost all the books of the time conscientiously noted the minute differences between birds but "the really distinctive characteristics were overlooked." With too many confusing clues "the shadow of uncertainty" hung over all watching.

Peterson was sure he had a solution and in working it out he was given a push by a book he had known since childhood and by a friend, William Vogt, he had met through the Bronx County Bird Club. One

misty December day, the two were up along the Hudson River counting ducks for the Christmas census when, as Vogt wrote, "a barely
perceptible note fell from a flock of small birds overhead and my
companion said with unchallengable assurance, 'siskins.'" Vogt, a
first-class birder himself, felt "a bumbler by comparison" with Peterson. He began arguing earnestly with his companion. Peterson knew
more about identifying birds than almost anyone around and he also
could paint. Why didn't he put down what he saw and knew in a book,
a guide that would tell others how to look at birds the way he did? Not
too excited by the idea, Peterson asked who would buy the book. If
he did it, Vogt promised, he would guarantee to find a publisher. That
impressed Peterson.

The boyhood book that gave Peterson the other push was *Two
Little Savages* by Ernest Thompson Seton, a famous nature writer and
artist. Its hero was a boy who, Peterson remembered,

> discovered some mounted ducks in a dusty showcase and
> . . . painstakingly made sketches of their patterns.
>
> This lad had a book which showed him how to tell ducks
> when they were in the hand, but since he only saw the live
> ducks at a distance, he was usually at a loss for their names. He
> noticed that all the ducks in the showcase were different—all
> had blotches or streaks that were their labels or identification
> tags. He decided that if he could put their labels or "uniforms"
> down on paper, he would know these same ducks as soon as
> he saw them at a distance on the water.

Seton accompanied the text with little drawings, silhouettes that emphasized one or two characteristics of the ducks.

There was another work that reinforced the ideas Peterson already
had formed: *Guide to the Birds of New England and Eastern New York* by
Ralph Hoffmann, a prophetic but largely overlooked book that had
been published in 1904. As a boy in Stockbridge, Massachusetts,
Hoffmann was so expert a birder that when Matthew Arnold visited
the town and asked to be shown the native birds, thirteen-year-old
Ralph was called on to take the eminent English poet and schoolmaster out for a bird walk. He grew up to be a schoolteacher by profession
and a bird watcher by addiction—seeing a new bird, he wrote, "gives
one a peculiar thrill of exaltation and all the rest of the day one moves
in a kind of rapture, all one's thoughts suffused with an inward glow."

In his eastern guide and later in a companion guide to Pacific

Coast birds, Hoffmann had set out to "emphasize the aspect of birds as seen out of doors, to describe their general or most prominent colors rather than any mark difficult to see on the living birds and to call attention to the characteristic habits and haunts. There has been no attempt to give a complete description of the plumage, as it would look if the bird were held in the hand." The effectiveness of his method can be seen by going back to Chapman's lengthy description of the song sparrow. Hoffmann's far briefer, more selective description was interspersed with italics to call attention to the "most prominent or characteristic field marks that serve best to distinguish one species from others closely resembling it." The sparrow's head, he wrote, had "streaks of *gray* through centre and over each eye" and the breast streaks coalesce "to form a *large spot* in the *centre of the breast.*" The illustration, a closeup of the head, showed the line and, though not too clearly, the spot. In a recognizable way, this was what Peterson would do. And a clue to what he was seeking lies in Hoffmann's use of the expression "field marks." In the book Peterson finally produced, the operational word in the title was "field," a term rarely used before in bird book titles.

It took Peterson three years to finish his book, with its hundreds of illustrations, and Bill Vogt found it much harder to get someone to publish it than it had been to get Peterson to do it. Four or five publishers turned it down before Vogt showed it to the editor at Houghton Mifflin, Francis H. Allen. A member of the Nuttall Club, Allen knew Peterson's skills; he liked the book; and Houghton Mifflin had a tradition of publishing bird books, going back to the 1870s when it published John Burroughs and Olive Thorne Miller and, subsequently, Ralph Hoffmann and many of the country's best-known nature writers.

But this was 1933. The depression was getting worse and the book required expensive art work. Peterson's colleagues stepped in to convince the doubting publisher. Ludlow Griscom came over to test Peterson's drawings, the core of the book. They were set up at one end of a room and Griscom at the other end. Even at an unrealistic distance, he identified them all. When Allen said he was worried that the book would lose too much money, Richard Pough, whose own guide later became a competitor of Peterson's, said he was so sure the book would succeed that he would make up any money Houghton Mifflin might lose. Peterson himself agreed to forgo royalties on the first thousand copies—and then wondered whether it would ever sell more than that.

As soon as *A Field Guide to the Birds* came out in the spring of 1934, Dick Pough could forget about his guarantee and Peterson did not have to regret the royalties he had surrendered. The first printing of two thousand copies was virtually sold out in the first couple of weeks and, in the worst of economic times, the *Field Guide* went back to press again and again—and eventually it sold some three million copies. Peterson's elders, the men whose own books were from then on to seem archaic, were generous in their evaluations. The usually acerbic Griscom wrote that Peterson's "many qualities and talents . . . amounted to genius."

Like Baird's *History* and Coues' *Key,* the *Field Guide* changed everything for American bird watchers. What it did was give them an identification method to be used with the bird flitting through leaves and shadows, scurrying through reeds, flying off before the observers could get close enough to sort out all its markings and resembling other birds in tantalizing ways. It was geared to instant impression and quick judgment—and for people who wanted to know birds but had been discouraged by the difficulties of learning to tell one from the other.

To accomplish this, Peterson had eliminated all unnecessary marks from his drawings and all irrelevant facts from his text, singling out what was unique about a bird, what set it apart from all others. The drawings were spare and schematic, almost always in profile. They looked, some traditionalists sniffed, like wooden decoys. In each figure, little black lines jabbed at salient points of the bird, calling attention to its singular features. On one page, for example, four similar ducks were shown. A single line in each drawing gave the all-important clue, pointing to: the dark head of the greater scaup, the face crescent of Barrow's goldeneye, the round face spot of the male American goldeneye (common goldeneye), the white face mark of the female lesser scaup. The efficiency of this little line, which was Peterson's own invention, is amazing. In the latest edition of his *Field Guide,* one or two identifying lines are enough for ninety-five percent of the birds.

Everything in the *Guide* was pared down; nothing that wasn't essential was put in. This was something, it would seem, that should have been done before by somebody. But just anybody would not have been able to do it. Peterson had several interlocking skills. As a field observer, he had acute eyesight, able to register the smallest details and shadings, the significant differences in markings—and the ability to remember them so that he had an image of a bird fixed in his mind's eye before he sat down to draw it.

His ears were as useful as his eyes. Once, out with a birding expedition and unwilling to get out of bed on a rainy morning, he lay comfortably, half-awake, listening. When the rest of the party came back, soaked but satisfied with their count, Peterson gave them his list —forty-two species, more than any of the others. Except for his having to get up and check some passing curlews, they were all spotted by his ears.

He had a ferocious ability to concentrate; the bird was all and he could wipe everything else from his thoughts when he was after one. He had a childish disregard of wet, cold, dirt, danger and the stamina and will of other birders who found his zeal admirable but sometimes a little more than they wanted to match in the field. His training in art, both as a modern realist and as an old-fashioned academic, had taught him how to draw with finicky accuracy, to match colors, to use shadings for small or broad effect. His mental discipline enabled him to ignore unneeded detail, and a stubborn confidence in his own system—he had, ornithologically, very few doubts about himself— enabled him to eliminate what other guides had always put in. He was not concerned with being complete, just comprehensible, and he had developed, with no tutoring, a laconic writing style that matched his spare drawings. There was little room for discursion in his *Guide,* which allowed only a few lines of text for each bird, rarely more than twenty in which to give the bird's popular and scientific names, the field marks of male and female, tick off similar species and how they differed, give the calls and songs, the habitat and range.

Peterson raised the use of the word "only" to high art—few prose writers have gotten so much mileage out of it—so that the bird watcher could dismiss all irrelevant differences from his mind, For example, the oldsquaw is the "only sea duck combining much *white on the body and unpatterned dark wings.*" The common screech owl is "our only *small* eastern owl with ear tufts." The barn swallow is the "only native Swallow that is truly 'swallow-tailed.' " His classic description was that of the male goldfinch. Chapman, more briefly than was usual with him, described it: "Bright canary-yellow; crown, wings and tail black; wing-bars and inner vanes of tail-feathers white; longer upper tail-coverts gray; *lesser wing: coverts yellow.*" Hoffmann wrote: "Crown black; body bright yellow; wings and tail black, spotted with white." Peterson just said: *"The only small yellow bird with black wings."*

In the most recent edition of the *Field Guide,* technicalities and
demands of space have truncated and even deleted some of the descriptions, to the dismay of admirers who enjoyed reading Peterson
just for his style. There was an impatient authority in some passages,
as on the yellow-headed blackbird: "the name identifies it," or on the
kingbird: "the white band at the tip of its fanlike tail leaves no doubt
as to its identity." And there was an aphoristic imagery in many
descriptions. The spotted sandpiper "teeters . . . as if it were too
delicately balanced on its slim legs," while the solitary sandpiper
"teeters more than it nods." Grebes "normally hold their necks quite
erect; Loons and Ducks do so mostly when alarmed." The whip-poor-
will "flits away like a large brown moth," the ovenbird is "a voice in
the woods."

The description of bird songs could be both evocative and irrever-
ent. The nighthawk's boom: "a sudden deep whir that sounds like the
well-known Bronx cheer." The catbird's song: "a disjointed succession of notes and phrases, some musical." The American (water)
pipit's note: "a thin *jee-eet* or, by a stretch of the imagination, *pi-pit.*"
And Henslow's sparrow "utters one of the poorest vocal efforts of any
bird . . . it ejects a hiccoughing *tsi-lick.* As if to practice this 'song' so
that it might not always remain at the bottom of the list, it often
hiccoughs all night long."

While he was working on his *Guide,* Peterson had changed careers.
The Junior Audubon clubs, built up under Mabel Wright, were now
moribund and the whole membership, in fact, had fallen away. In a
kind of palace revolution, a new regime took over. Bill Vogt was made
editor of *Bird-Lore* and Peterson was taken on as staff artist, to redraw
the pamphlets, rewrite their text, go out to give lectures and, in
between, take care of the Audubon Society's supply room, which went
in heavily for bird feeders. Peterson's drawing gave a new realism and
liveliness to the magazine, while his experience as teacher made the
revised pamphlets intelligible and attractive to young birders. His
lectures, full of fact and enthusiasm, were hugely popular. The new
leadership had invigorated the Audubon Society, and membership in
Junior Audubon, which was one of Peterson's prime concerns, eventually went up to the millions.

The generation he and the Bronx County Bird Club represented
was now at the center of the American birding movement. The Linnaean Society had become their base and the source of their influence.
They and the club circle had become a loose confederation whose
members succeeded each other as officers of the Linnaean Society,

and were goads at the Audubon Society. Joe Hickey, taking over where Griscom had stopped, became a mentor to a far greater number of watchers than Griscom ever taught. In 1943, he published *A Guide to Bird Watching,* which was so full of sensible and witty advice that it has remained in print for decades. It started off with an unforgettable definition of bird watching: "a mild paralysis of the central nervous system which can be cured only by rising at dawn and sitting in a bog." Going on to tell readers how birds behave and how birders should, it encouraged watchers to study habits and living places, urged them into banding birds and protecting them—not just what to do but also why to do it. Hickey himself, in what was to become an almost standard procedure for birders, became a tremendously influential conservationist, going out to the University of Wisconsin to work with and then succeed Aldo Leopold, the pioneer in methods of managing wildlife and the environment. Hundreds of Hickey's students have moved into and built up the structures of modern conservation and environmental study.

William Vogt, as editor of *Bird-Lore,* promoted the new techniques of identification and helped revive the old Audubon Society crusading spirit. Leaving Audubon after an abortive attempt to make himself head of the society, he explored larger concepts of conservation. His book, *The Road to Survival,* was one of the first to show the linkage between conservation and birth control. Attacked—as so many radical conservation statements have been—as wild-eyed and blasphemous, it proved correct and prophetic.

Robert Porter Allen, a latecomer to Bronx-Linnaean birding circles, took a field job at the Audubon Society assigned to make the first study of the plight of the whooping crane. His work, more than any single project at the time, dramatized the crisis of endangered species, injecting a note of desperation into the often pious but uncommitted acceptance of conservation. A raffish Pennsylvanian with a seaman's vocabulary and a frontiersman's bravado, Allen wound up at the Audubon Society with the most seraphic of titles: Director of Sanctuaries.

Allan Cruickshank became a superb photographer, perhaps the best at combining a beauty and clarity that made black-and-white photographs a new tool for bird identifiers. Following a practice begun by William Finley of Oregon, who was a pioneer both as bird photographer and missionary for bird protection, Cruickshank spread his teaching in Audubon classes and camps and in his standard *Birds Around New York City*.

Roger Peterson had become established as the preeminent birder of his time. Because his *Field Guide* included only birds found east of the Rockies, he prepared a companion guide to western birds. He did bird paintings for the fledgling *Life* magazine, which increased both his and the magazine's circulations, and wrote voluminously. The war interrupted his birding, though not altogether. Listing himself as an artist, he was assigned to the signal corps to do training manuals and also, using his field guide method, to advise on airplane-identification manuals for civilian spotters. Sent to Florida as a naturalist to investigate the effects on the environment of the new pesticide, DDT, he warned that it was lethal to birds—but had no evidence, so early, of its appalling residual effects. After the war he settled in near Washington, D.C., no longer with the Audubon Society, busy on a major revision of the *Guide,* editing a long series of nature guides and starting to paint large portraits of birds.

Birds and he had served each other very usefully. And bird watching had become well known to many who had once looked on it as the crotchet of people with, perhaps, not much else to do. Americans were thus able to understand what was going on when, in the late 1940s, they were caught up in a historic case of alleged treason in which a bird with an odd name played an important role. Peterson himself had a tangential relationship to the case.

One day an FBI agent called on him in Washington and showed him a photograph of a man. Did Peterson know him? He looked familiar, Peterson said, someone he used to meet in Rock Creek Park while out watching. They would exchange good mornings. Did he ever have any letters from him—typewritten? No, he didn't know his name. The agent said the name was Alger Hiss but left without explaining why he had called. Peterson found out, of course, when the Hiss-Chambers hearings began, and he realized what the agent had been fishing for.

When Whittaker Chambers accused Hiss of having been involved with him in a Communist conspiracy, the investigators had difficulty verifying Chambers' statements that he knew Hiss intimately. Pressed, Chambers remembered that Hiss and his wife were ardent bird watchers and recalled particularly the time that Hiss was very excited over having seen a prothonotary warbler, a not too common bird. Later, when Hiss testified before the congressional subcommittee, the questions by design moved around to his hobbies. He was, he said, an ornithologist but "maybe I am using too big a word to say ornithologist because I am pretty amateur."

Congressman John McDowell, a birder himself, had been particularly struck by the mention of the warbler and asked Hiss a question about it. The hearing transcript goes:

> Mr. McDowell: Did you ever see a prothonotary warbler?
> Mr. Hiss: I have, right here on the Potomac.
> Mr. McDowell [showing off his own knowledge]: I saw one in Arlington.
> Mr. Hiss [matching this bit of gamesmanship]: They come back and nest in these swamps. Beautiful yellow head, a gorgeous bird.

Growing wary of this innocent interest in his birding, Hiss insisted that anybody who wanted to could find out that he was a bird watcher. "The fact that [it] is one of my hobbies appears in *Who's Who,*" he said. But, came the response, the fact that he saw a prothonotary warbler wasn't in *Who's Who.* "I have told many many people that I have seen a prothonotary warbler," said Hiss, "and I am very very proud. If Mr. McDowell has seen it," he added pointedly, "he has told very very many people about it. Bird watchers boast." And his own boast was one of the convincing pieces of evidence that Chambers had really known Hiss well.

The Hiss case is, of course, only a parenthesis in the history of birding (which is full of interesting detours). But it does have a bearing. A century earlier, this testimony would have been arcane to most Americans. Peterson—along with his generation—had made it intelligible even to those who could not tell a warbler from a wigeon. And this fact has a larger relevance. Peterson had done more than any single man to push birds into the American consciousness. Through him they had come to understand not just which bird was which but how all birds fitted into the whole scheme of nature and, in turn, how crucial each part of the scheme was to the whole ecology and to their daily lives.

All this, meanwhile, had made Peterson the best known of living naturalists, recipient of endless honors, an almost legendary figure who, obsessively revising his own work, moved between the drudgery of his drawing board and the gratifying world of fame and influence. He has sometimes been amused by what has happened to him.

Once, thinking back, he told a friend how grateful he was for what birds had done for him. They had taken a shy, rather lonely boy and given him the friendship and support of people who recognized his special genius and cast him for a role he had never dreamed of for himself. Others, long ago, had dreamed it for him—that high school prophet, for example, who had read the future in his oddball classmate's addiction to such things as flowers and woods and birds.

18

Listers and Savers

Speaking very broadly, a history of American bird watching could be divided into three recognizable time periods: the period begun by Baird, during which Brewster and his colleagues organized watching, and Coues, through his *Key*, made it more efficient; the period in which the Audubon Society popularized bird watching and spread the gospel of bird protection; and the era of the bird guide, initiated by Roger Tory Peterson, which moved the number of watchers up into the millions. His *Field Guide* found a wider and wider public, in good part of its own making. For years it stood alone, the one guide everyone used, the unchallenged best seller. In the prosperity that came after the war, bird watchers multiplied like house sparrows in a new habitat, and other guides were published, all adopting the Peterson philosophy of emphasizing recognizable field marks, though not copying his technique.

Richard Pough, Peterson's early supporter, came out with a very good guide of his own, *Audubon Land Bird Guide.* Its text was longer than Peterson's, its paintings by Don Eckelberry were more portraits than schematic drawings and it has served in many ways as a supplement to Peterson. The first direct challenge to Peterson came, thirty years after the publication of his first guide, with Golden Press's *Birds*

of North America with paintings by Arthur Singer and text by Chandler
S. Robbins, Bertel Brunn and Herbert S. Zim. Complete, more con-
veniently arranged than Peterson and brilliantly condensed, it outsold
Peterson but did not displace it. In fact, the competition seemed to
help all the guides and they began to proliferate. The *Audubon Society
Field Guide,* which had considerable text by John Bull and John Farrand, Jr., departed from convention by using photographs instead of
paintings—and thereby opened up a whole new area for birding argument: whether a photograph was as good a tool for identification as
a painting. The *Audubon Society Master Guide to Birding,* edited by Farrand, employed some four dozen contributors for its three volumes
and reversed the trend towards simplifying and compacting bird data
by amplifying both text and illustration. The National Geographic
Society used a company of artists, writers and consultants to produce
its *Field Guide to the Birds of North America.* Like the *Master Guide* it was
directed at a somewhat more sophisticated layer of birders, interested
in the finer points of identification and bird behavior—as an increasing number of bird watchers are. Peterson meanwhile undertook an
exhaustive revision of his works. Where the other guides were col-
laborations of writers and artists, Peterson still worked in the tradition
of Wilson and Audubon, doing the observing and the painting and the
text himself, although he did enlist his wife, Virginia, to do the maps
of bird ranges.

The proliferation of guides did not glut the market. Birders may
have a favorite work but, like cooks with cookbooks, they are omnivo-
rous, comforted by having more than one guide to lead them. No
matter how many guides they may already own, they are always ready
to buy another. Probably some three-quarters of a million general
bird guides are sold in the United States every year and in addition
there are auxiliary guides—guides to birds of a specific region, or of
a state, or a city; or guides to the best places to find birds; or guides
to the best equipment with which to observe or photograph them;
guides to bird songs; even a guide to bird clubs which tells the best
places to find bird watchers.

The advent of field guides, the development of better and less
expensive binoculars, a greater interest in nature and deeper concern
for the environment (which bird watching itself impelled), all contributed to the expansion of bird watching. But just as bird watchers
often do not accept each other's sightings of birds, they also do not
necessarily accept each other's statistics on bird watchers. Depending
on what is defined as a birder—the expert, the committed, the casual

—the birders' self-census gets as high as ten or even fifteen million watchers. Some objective statistics have been developed through studies made for the U.S. Fish and Wildlife Service under the direction of Dr. Stephen Kellert of Yale. One out of four Americans questioned in a survey said they did some bird watching over a two-year period. That would project to an improbable sixty million watchers. However, only about half of them could identify ten species of birds, which eliminates them as real watchers. Only one out of four knew as many as twenty birds, which eliminates them too. Three in a hundred knew at least forty species and one in a hundred knew a hundred or more. Classifying the last two categories as qualified bird watchers would bring the number of American birders to some seven million. If only those who know a hundred or more were taken in, some two million Americans would qualify as committed birders—those who watch with some regularity, use a field guide and keep some kind of list.

This count, while more suggestive than exact, seems reasonable. The numbers themselves, however, are not all that important; the scale is. Among outdoor activities connected with nature, only fishing stands ahead of bird watching, and hunting is about on a par with it. Fishing and hunting are labeled "utilitarian" activities since one object, though often secondary, is to get food. Birding is decidedly non-utilitarian. The reason for watching birds, given by most of those surveyed, was aesthetics: they were attracted by the beauty of the birds. Committed birders more often cited a personal fascination with birds. A number in both categories said they went birding to be close to nature.

This last lies at the heart of all watching. On the surface, birders find watching a wholesome pastime which gets them out into the fresh air, alerts them to stimulating sights and sounds, provides the fun of being both competitive and companionable. On a deeper level, it becomes a peculiarly intense personal experience, conscious or subliminal—the astonished awareness that comes in some unguarded moment when the watcher is left oddly vulnerable to feelings that only nature can provoke.

The Kellert studies gave some clues to the sociology of bird watching. Among interested birders, i.e., those who knew forty or more birds, the average age was forty-two. More than seventy percent of them were male. They were above average in education and income. A third of them had professional occupations and more than ten percent were executives or managers. Only fourteen percent were

employed in what the report called "untrained sales, service or la-
borer occupations." Still, this last figure indicates that birding, which
was once almost exclusively an upper- or upper-middle-class activity,
has been somewhat democratized. A recent president of the Delaware
Valley Ornithological Club, for example, was head of a Philadelphia
labor union. Bird watchers today may represent a cross-section of
American society but it is still an unbalanced cross-section.

A corollary survey, conducted by Kellert with Miriam O. Westervelt, confirmed the fact that birders get their best start as children,
particularly between the ages of nine and eleven, when their curiosity
about nature is most readily aroused. Among schoolchildren, three
times as many girls as boys said they were interested in birds, which
reverses the adult ratio, but this statistic must be qualified since boys
turned out to know more about birds than girls. Three times as many
boys as girls could identify thirty or more species.

The hardest core of American bird watching is made up of birders
—some ten thousand of them—who subscribe to and contribute to
American Birds, the insiders' magazine, published by the National
Audubon Society. They are the kind who read their field guides from
cover to cover; do some watching several days a week and keep up a
week-by-week watch on birds in their localities; and check against past
records. On the basis of reports from this group, and from professional ornithologists, *American Birds* reports and records changes in
bird population—distribution, migration and habitats and general
health of birds. A prime source for this data is the Christmas Bird
Count, inherited from *Bird-Lore,* in which forty-one thousand counters take part every year.

In this core, there is a more specialized group, represented by the
four thousand members of the American Birding Association, which,
among its other activities, follows watchers with long life lists. In 1984
there were five U.S. members who reported life lists of over 700 (out
of some 800 species known in the United States). The interest in—
or, some say, the obsession with—life lists has intensified in the past
quarter century. Ludlow Griscom, the nonpareil watcher, had a life
list of 318 for Massachusetts but did not want to tell too many people
about it because he thought it was immodestly large—and considera-
tions of modesty were rare in Griscom. Today he would rank only
fifteenth in the state.

Birders have found special ways to add to their lists. Going to
Rockport, Texas, is one. For years, this was the special province of a
lady named Connie Hagar, who wore neatly ironed dresses on her

birding treks through woods and marshes and introduced the country's most famous birders to what may be the most efficient year-round listing spot in the country. It offers more birds in less time than anyplace else: three-quarters of the species found in the United States can be seen there—seabirds, migrating birds, strays that come over from Mexico. Birders anxious to add three or four special species to their lists go to the island of Attu in the Aleutians, which offers birds that wander over from Siberia. California and Florida have the greatest number of species—in fact, Joseph Grinnell once remarked that if a birder stayed in California long enough, he would see almost every migrant species in North America.

There are subclassifications in lists. One is called the Big Year List and consists of all the U.S. species that can be spotted in a single year. James Vardeman of Jackson, Mississippi, set out in 1981 to compile a 700-species list between January 1 and December 31. Organizing a network of local observers to telephone news of what species was where, he dashed around by plane and helicopter and swamp buggy and, spending some fifty thousand dollars, just missed. His total was 699. Two years later, in 1983, Benton Basham, an Arkansas anesthetist, set out to beat Vardeman. Scurrying from Florida to the Aleutians, he had great luck in catching accidentals, strays and vagrants, i.e., birds that wandered from their accustomed habitats. One morning, when he was about to leave for the Salton Sea in California to catch a spotted redshank, phone calls came telling him that there was a black noddy in the Dry Tortugas off Florida and a Ross' gull in Colorado. He flew to the Salton Sea for the redshank, then, choosing noddy over gull, he flew to the Tortugas and got it. A frantic car ride took him to Hypoluxo Island, Florida, barely in time to see a stripe-headed tanager, which waited until he stepped out of his auto, then went off to its accustomed home in the Bahamas and has not been seen again. Basham, succeeding where Vardeman failed, wound up with 711 species—and a few second thoughts. "I hope," he remarked rather wistfully, "that no negative feelings about birders or birding result from the endeavor."

This defensive attitude shows frequently among the high-list birders. "It was a shattering discovery for me to learn," said one high-lister, "that some of the competitive birders enjoyed birding for the ego-satisfaction that the competition itself can bring rather than for the joys of seeing and appreciating birds." These comments may seem ingenuous for, on most occasions, such birders glorify competition. Every year on a "Big Day" the country's highest listers get

together as teams to see how many species they can see within fourteen hours. One year, a Texas team claimed a record 235 species but
the claim was later disqualified: a groove-billed ani that had been
included turned out to have been sighted across the Rio Grande in
Mexico, and hence was an ineligible alien. California was declared the
winner that year.

Neither state came up to Big Day records set in Africa: 288 from
Zambia and 264 from Kenya. These two countries have become prime
birding spots for watchers who keep world lists of birds, a relatively
new facet made easier by plane travel and organized birding tours.
The tours attract clients by guaranteeing to swell their life lists. One
tour, calculating closely, declared that on its Panama trip it could offer
birds at the bargain rate of $2.93 per species. A rich area is the upper
Amazon rain forest of Peru, where a prehistoric drought and the
configurations of the Andes have created dozens of separated habitats
in which numberless species and subspecies have evolved. In a single
day, one birder saw 330 of them. Some birders, in a sense looking
through the wrong end of their binoculars, count birds in a restricted
space. Noble Proctor, watching over a fifty-by-fifty-yard piece of Connecticut, counted 166 species there in a single year.

The compulsion to add to life lists has engendered some appall-
ingly bad manners among watchers, inconsiderate of both bird and
man. In the Berkshires, where a great gray owl that had strayed from
the northwest was reported in a tree nursery, birders knocked down
fences, cut barbed wire and trampled on seedlings until the owner in
self-defense was going to shoot the owl, which, happily, flew off before
he carried out his threat. In the town of Patagonia, Arizona, where a
resident had attracted a rare plain-capped starthroat to a feeder,
watchers swarmed over the lawn, made life unbearable for the family,
and when they desperately took down the feeder, the watchers simply
put up another one. A boreal owl in Massachusetts was rudely taken
from its roost and had some of its feathers plucked out as proof of the
sighting. Some twenty-five thousand birders upset a whole habitat onc
spring by cramming into the canyons of southwest Arizona to see a
flock of eared trogons, Mexican residents that fly over the border and
hence are eligible for U.S. life lists. The trogons all left. Such inva-
sions have driven common black-hawks and gray hawks from south-
western breeding places. Some birders play tape recordings of bird
songs, luring males out to chase imaginary rivals from their territory
and upsetting the whole nesting cycle.

Bird alerts, a system by which birders can, by phoning, learn about unusual birds anywhere, once brought some ten thousand birders to Massachusetts to see the first Ross' gull sighted in the contiguous United States for dozens of years. Alerted birders from Florida have rushed to Chicago to see an Arctic tern. An African western reef heron, which somehow landed in New England, drew a binoculared audience of several thousand who were set back a little by the warning that it might possibly have escaped from a cage, not flown the ocean, in which case it could not be legitimately listed.

Listers have felt increasingly confused and aggrieved by fussy ornithologists who, by changing names and classifications of birds, affect their lists. Sometimes the taxonomists take several different species and lump them into one; other times they take one species and split it into several. A species, by definition, is made up of a population of birds which breed freely with each other. When four species of juncoes—the "slate-colored," the "Oregon," the "white winged," the "gray-headed"—were found to interbreed they were put together as one species, the dark-eyed junco. When species are lumped this way, birders have to subtract names from their list. When they are split— as when the screech-owl was divided into eastern and western species or the red-breasted sapsucker was declared different from the yellow-bellied sapsucker or when one species of Pacific shearwater was split into five—they can add names.

All changes are distressing and the distress was acute in the case of the oriole. The AOU Committee on Taxonomy and Nomenclature decreed that two separate species of U.S. orioles, the Baltimore oriole and the Bullock's oriole, were one. The two had not been known to interbreed, because they lived in widely separated regions: the Baltimore east of the Great Plains and the Bullock's west of them. No trees grew on the Plains and the orioles, being tree nesters, did not inhabit the area. During the 1930s, huge belts of trees were planted on the Plains to stop wind erosion. As the trees grew, orioles moved in from east and west. And, being together, they interbred. So the ornithologists had to lump them as one species: the northern oriole. Birders, particularly those who cherished the Baltimore oriole as one of the loveliest of birds, railed at the new name as "dull, uncomely" for so bright a bird, and die-hards accused the renamers of being "interested only in exercising their power" and of flaunting "the latest elegance" in their discipline. The die-hards may still prevail: though the Baltimore and Bullock's can interbreed, they seem to have little interest in doing so and man's science may have to bow to birds' sexual preference.

A couple of years later when the muttering over the "infamous case of the oriole" was still heard, the committee aroused new complaints. It changed the whistling swan to tundra swan and the green heron to green-backed heron. Nit-picking, birders said, wearily, and the nature writer Frank Graham, Jr., expressed the views of some of his constituency: "Green-backed heron? Locally it's still a shite-poke and the AOU can go soak its head." When the Florida gallinule became the common moorhen there was widespread outrage: moorhen, many birders pointed out, is a British name and the gallinule is an American bird. Moreover, there are no moors in Florida. Why give it so misleading a name? The committee primly answered that moorhen was the name the bird bore in international nomenclature and the United States should not let chauvinism contradict science.

Birders point to all the discrepancies that have been perpetuated: the Cape May warbler is a rarity on Cape May, the Connecticut warbler in Connecticut and the Acadian flycatcher is never found in Acadia, or Nova Scotia. The names became so embedded in nomenclature that taxonomists have not dared face the confusion that change would produce. They have an unsettling precedent in the case of the robin. Even that irreproachable bird has had a number of ornithological aliases. The early settlers, confusing it with their homeland redbreast, called it robin. But it is more closely related to the European blackbird, so the great classifier, Carolus Linnaeus, called it *Turdus migratorius.* One technicality after another beset the bird, whose name was changed to *Merula migratoria,* and, when structural changes made that inaccurate, to *Planesticus,* which was not suitable. So the nomenclaturists went back to *Turdus migratorius,* which Linnaeus had named it in the first place.

Of course, the change of name, which means so much to the birder, rarely means anything to the bird. Some years ago, however, English ornithologists decided that St. Kilda's Wren, a rare bird prized by collectors, was not a separate species so they demoted it to a subspecies. Having lost status, the bird was no longer sought by collectors and lived more securely from then on. The British have, incidentally, added vividly to the nomenclature of birders themselves. Where Americans still split hairs over terms like "birder" and "bird watcher," the British have gone on to introduce new classifications of watchers. One of them is "twitcher," a watcher who gets his greatest pleasure by putting check marks, or "twitches," on his list. A superior species is one who is blessed with the ability to recognize a bird's "jizz," or "giss," a character or attitude in a bird not related to any field mark—its *je ne sais quoi* or "quintessence," which is defined, not too helpfully, as a birder's gestalt, or intuition, or ESP. The term may have derived from a World War II acronym used in identifying planes: "general impression, size and shape." For example, the way a hermit thrush cocks its tail is part of its "jizz."

All this is esoterica to most birders today, who are much more relaxed about their watching. They go out whenever they can on weekends, enjoy their bird club walks and movies and gossip sessions. Where there were a handful of small birding societies a century ago, there are now hundreds of clubs, loosely linked through state federations and the National Audubon Society, which now has 450,000 members enrolled in its affiliates. New York has been challenged as the center of birding. Watchers in California and Texas seem to be especially vigorous and assertive. Massachusetts Audubon has, perhaps, the most engaged and peripatetic roster of members. Philadelphia, the seedbed of American natural history, is leading the way into the study of the finest details of identification and the style of watching: what a birder sees in a bird is not quite so important as how he looks at it. The Wilson Society, which has lost some of its populist flavor, is widely respected for its penetrating ornithological studies. In general, bird watchers today know far more about their subject than their predecessors did. Because of the accumulation of knowledge, says Christopher Leahy in his *Birdwatcher's Companion*, "a 'serious' birdwatcher today could easily instruct an 'ornithologist' of 150 years ago."

The old-line birding societies, though the members are more sophisticated than they used to be, still draw the average birder to their meetings but their journals are given over to ornithological science with little direct reference to watching. Birders find themselves in limbo insofar as reading material is concerned. *American Birds* and *Birding* are of special interest to a relative few. *Bird-Lore* has been replaced by *Audubon* magazine, which deals with all aspects of nature, rather than with birds alone, and has become the handsomest and perhaps the finest nature magazine ever published in America. Birders turn to their clubs' mimeographed newsletters for local news and, for the personal stories and helpful hints the journals used to publish, as well as sophisticated ornithological news, they have *Bird Watcher's Digest.*

In all of the publications there is an ever-present emphasis on the traditional preoccupation of watchers: conservation. Birders today are the largest, most insistent and often the most vociferous group of conservationists. Aside from tradition, this is inherent in what they do. Constantly outdoors, disciplined to make specific and repeated observations and records, they are immediately sensitive to changes in environment and through their network are able to confirm any wide harm that man may be doing to it. The National Audubon Society has become as much involved with environmental issues as a whole as with birds in themselves. Someone checking up a few years ago found that nine of ten people holding office in environmental and conservation groups had been bird watchers to begin with.

Birds themselves are a highly sensitive gauge of changes. Pollution may kill them off or drive them away from their nesting places—and thereby calls attention to the situation. Deforestation cuts back nesting places for woodland birds and a drop in their population sounds an alarm: an absence of wood warblers in the eastern United States in recent years has revealed severe overcutting of forests in Central America where the birds winter. The devastating residual effects of pesticides were convincingly documented when ornithologists found that DDT was causing egg shells to become so fragile that eggs could not survive to hatch, notably in the case of birds of prey.

The prime mover in this last area was a life-long bird watcher. Rachel Carson, who more than any other person was responsible for making the dimension of the pesticide disaster plain to America, was a biologist by training but her perceptions of nature came from the sea creatures she studied and the birds she enjoyed. With a quiet grimness she used bird imagery to conjure up a nightmare planet poisoned by uncontrolled use of chemicals. "There was a strange stillness," she wrote. . . . "On the mornings that had once throbbed with the dawn chorus of robins, catbirds, doves, jays, wrens . . . there was now no sound; only silence lay over the fields and woods and marsh." Nothing could stab more sharply at the consciences of people who ordinarily gave only a passing thought to nature than the now famous title she gave to her historic book. *Silent Spring* presented them with the bleak vision of a world they could hardly believe and could not bear—a world without birds.

Epilogue

The six-hundred life-lister, the vagrant watchers who hurry between Attu and the Amazon, the twitchers who are off at the first alert to see an alien bird, all lend an exhilaration to today's birding, conferring not just status but also knowledge of different habitats and wisdom about the ways of other birds. More modest watchers, though they may envy these superstars, are inclined to scold them a little for changing a generally cooperative occupation into a competition. They are dubious about the life list as a criterion, leaning perhaps towards the one set in the beginning by the Nuttall founders, who inquired more into a man's "qualities of heart and mind."

These bird watchers follow an older tradition of birding, keeping pretty much to home grounds, more content to welcome back the phoebe and the oriole which came last year than to hunt exotic strangers. They hold to the classic tenet that there is more to be found and understood by watching steadily over one place than in giving frantic attention to many—to reach, as Paul Brooks puts it in his illuminating book *Speaking for Nature,* an "intimate acquaintance with one cherished spot."

Such a spot can become to birders what a remembered poem, or a piece of music, or a painted scene is to others—something to be sought out again and again: some marsh where the bitterns always settle in by May; some ridge the red-tailed hawks always glide over in the fall; some mud flat that the yellowlegs never miss in August. A few historic habitats have become, not shrines really, but places a birder visits and revisits to find, along with the familiar birds, the reassurance that nature gives in always bringing them back there. This feeling pervades Concord, Massachusetts, which has been birded and documented longer and more diligently than any other place in America. In its uncut woods and unploughed meadows, William Wood, three and a half centuries ago, saw the birds he rhymed in his "New England's Prospect." Much later, Ralph Waldo Emerson made its village birds into metaphors. "A bargain in blue jays and bobolinks," he called the house he had just bought.

Today's watchers at Concord are haunted by yesterday's. A contemporary keeper of Concord's traditions, Richard K. Walton, feels the past almost tangibly. "I stand in line to count the snipe," he writes, because already there "in front of me are Thoreau, Brewster, Griscom." Walton is a schoolteacher, a watcher who has made in his *Birds of the Sudbury River Valley* the latest of the many rediscoveries of the place. Ludlow Griscom, having moved from New York to Cambridge, had gone out to Concord and, studying its history and making his own impeccable observations, memorialized the spot in *The Birds of Concord.* William Brewster, who liked to take his friend Forbush on his birding expeditions, had stood there blinking at doves and, lying in bed in the autumn nights of his own autumn years, had listened to the warblers flying over his October Farm.

And going back even further in Concord, either to its site or to its spirit, a birder comes upon a solitary watcher, Henry David Thoreau, who, on Walden Pond back in 1845, had "suddenly found myself neighbor to the birds" and had gone on to make one of the most complete studies up to that time of an American birding habitat. His anthologist, Helen Cruickshank, used Thoreau's words to describe his process: "He squeezed the marrow" from his observations. At his shack or on what he called his saunterings, he watched "a tantivy of wild pigeons," set down the schedules by which the interminable whip-poor-wills "chanted their vespers," and exchanged stares with a drowsing owl until it flew off "feeling his twilight way" through the branches.

Thoreau could spot field marks with the best of them—a bird new to him was "slate-colored above and dirty beneath . . . bright orange crown along the middle of the head . . . bounded on each side by a black segment," therefore a golden-crowned kinglet. Bird watchers today can get this, however, from any life history. What they get from Thoreau is a transcendent reality: "the warm pine woods are all alive with the jingle of the pine warblers . . . as if it were calling the trees to life," he writes. It "rings through the woods like an electric shock." Watching hawks, he thinks "the heavens are full of eyes." And he gives an odd clue to what impels a bird watcher into watching: he speaks of having "caged myself" to be near the birds.

This clue can be followed by going back across the centuries and an ocean to the English village of Selborne and a remarkable clergyman named Gilbert White, who is acknowledged by devoted birders to be the father of them all, past and present. Thoreau himself was a disciple of White: if he would only put aside his idling, Emerson once said, Thoreau might be "a worthy successor" to White. But everybody who appears in this book—William Brewster and Arthur Bloomfield, Althea Sherman and Elizabeth Dickens, Charles Pennock and Roger Peterson—are his descendants and it is time, perhaps, that this history got around to paying attention to him.

Between 1740 and 1790, White was watching birds in a way that other men were not: out in the field, day after day, believing what his eyes told him rather than what his books did, making notes and lists. And then, with a charm and wit that few nature writers have matched, he put down what he saw, what he knew and what he didn't know in a book that has had a more enduring popularity than any other bird book ever written: *The Natural History of Selborne.* For most of the last century and all of this, in edition after edition, *Selborne* has never been out of print.

White writes of many things in his history and journals—forests and farmland, determined sows and somnolent tortoises—but birds are his true delight and concern. Ornithologists today pay homage to him as a pioneer in station observation (studying one area closely over a long period of time), and for his astute discoveries and classifications. Bird watchers, getting to know him on a more subjective level, feel a quite unscientific kinship as they go along with him on his birding triumphs and frustrations, his braggings and his bemoanings. Like the sincerest of them, he finds modest excuses for his failings. "It has been my misfortune," he says, "never to have had any neighbors whose studies have led them towards the pursuit of natural knowledge," so that, he sighs, "for want of a companion to quicken my industry and sharpen my attention, I have made but slender progress."

He began carrying "a list in my pocket of the birds that were to be remarked as I rode or walked about my business," which was to serve as curate to a rather small parish in Hampshire. He is admirably terse and disciplined in recording his observations: "the stone curlew lays its eggs, usually two, never more than three, on the bare ground . . . the young run immediately from the egg and . . . skulk among the stones which are their best security, for their colors are so exactly the color of our gray spotted flints. . . ." But he cannot contain himself —what birder can?—when he has the chance to show off his knowledge, pouring out fact after fact: fern owls (nightjars) feed themselves on the wing; nightingales "when their young first come abroad, make a plaintive and jarring sound." Redstarts shake their tails horizontally "as dogs do when they fawn," while a wagtail's tail "bobs up and down like that of a jaded horse."

He lays down the law to his birding heirs as sternly as Ludlow Griscom would. "The investigation of the life and conversation of animals," he declares, "is not to be attained but by the active and inquisitive mind." And his inquisitive mind prods him into pausing for questions rather than rushing into answers. What keeps prodigious flocks of birds together in winter time? Love? he wonders. (No, because birds do not mate in winter and in "amorous seasons" are belligerently jealous of each other.) "Hunger?" (No, food is too scarce in cold weather.) To keep warm? Or to be safe? Or is it the feeling of "helplessness . . . as men crowd together when under great calamities though they know not why?" The questions hang in midair, unanswered.

He anticipates the jargon of birding, and no one has defined the modern term "jizz," for example, as elegantly as he did. A watcher "should be able to distinguish birds by their air as well as by their colors and shapes," he remarks. "There is somewhat in most genera that at first sight discriminate them." For example: "kites and buzzards sail around in circles with wings expanded and motionless"; "the kestrel has a peculiar mode of hanging in the air in one place, his wings all the while being briskly agitated"; owls "move in a buoyant manner . . . they seem to want ballast," while "herons seem encumbered by too much sail for their light bodies."

White clearly thought of Selborne as being what today's watchers call "a hot spot." His district, he said proudly, has "near half the species that were ever known in England" and more than half as many, in fact, as all of Sweden (120 species versus 221). He does not give Selborne all the credit. As is expected of a birder, he takes some of it for himself since he had added several species to his parish's list —a sandpiper, a shrike, a ring ousel and the lesser whitethroat. It was not all that easy, since even his parish has shortcomings. He refers wistfully, for example, to the deprived jackdaws of Selborne which have to build their nests in rabbit burrows because the region is "meanly furnished with churches." In wealthier parishes, jackdaws had their choice of steeples.

As they go along, readers more and more realize that this long-ago bird watcher, going out without guides or glasses, was a complete birder. He identifies not just by seeing but also by by hearing. His most admired taxonomic feat, classifying the "three species of willow wrens," was accomplished by analyzing their songs—the "harsh loud chirp" of one, "the joyous easy laughing note of another," the "sibilous noise" of the third. He worked, as only recent generations have been disciplined to do, at analyzing the songs the way a musicologist might. The owls of Selborne, he concluded, after they had been matched to a tuning fork, hoot in A-flat and B-flat and G-flat, while cuckoos sing in D and D-sharp.

In a great many birders there is an unhatched poet, pecking to get out. White's prose was specific, straightforward, full of plain details. Yet, by some transmutation, it ends up not as a series of facts but as a procession of images: "Jan. 1 [goes his 1785 journal]. Much snow on the ground. Ponds frozen up & almost dry. Moles work: cocks crow. No fieldfares seen; no wagtails." White did resort to verse, once, to explain the revealing contradiction that nature embeds in "the curious mind"—"a melancholy joy . . . a pleasing kind of pain."

In his studies, he was as likely to go back to poets as to scientists. When he needed an authority on the nighttime habitat of the nightingale, he cited Milton's "in shadiest covert hidden." When he wanted a description of the wood pigeon's flight he went to Virgil: *"Dat tecto ingentem—mox aere lapsa quieto, Radit iter liquidum, celeres neque commovet alas,"* and then, for his readers' convenience, translates it: "At first she flutters:—but at length she springs / To smoother flight, and shoots upon her wings."

And he would go back to Geoffrey Chaucer, who observed birds as astutely, perhaps, as he observed people. Historians of ornithology are impressed by the fact that in a single poem, "Parlement of Foules," Chaucer noted thirty-seven birds and that must have been only a portion of his life list. White was too true a birder to have fallen into the modern fallacy that numbers are the thing. What is really important are the perceptions, and Gilbert White must have quivered with recognition, knowing just how Chaucer felt when he wrote

> *whan that the month of May*
> *Is comen,*
> *and that I here the foules synge . . .*
> *Farewel my boke, and my devocioun!*

This discursion into the past has been, like so much of this book, an effort to understand birders, who are generally not all that good at telling themselves, or anyone else, just what it is that got them into the world of watchers and irrevocably holds them there. Here is Henry Thoreau, who "caged myself" to be near the birds, and Gilbert White delighting in his "melancholy joy," and Geoffrey Chaucer guiltily abandoning books and duties and all else when he hears the springtime birds begin to sing. And to their company come James Russell Lowell with that bird always singing in his brain and even Charlie Pennock trying to get away from his life but helpless to do it because he cannot get away from birds. Somehow one winds up with the feeling that true bird watchers—whatever else they may be—are really the captives of the airy creatures they pursue.

Acknowledgments

My first acknowledgment—although it is after the fact—must go to the men who edited the birding journals and compiled the primary sources for any history of American bird watching: Lynds Jones, Joseph Grinnell, Witmer Stone, Joel Asaph Allen, Frank M. Chapman and the others. Many people and institutions have been helpful. I thank the Department of Ornithology of the American Museum of Natural History, particularly Helen Hays and Mary Lecroy, for the use of its superb library. I have used the resources of the Academy of Natural Sciences in Philadelphia, The National Audubon Society in New York, the Museum of Comparative Zoology at Harvard University, the New York Public Library, the Nyack Library at Nyack, New York, the Finkelstein Library in Spring Valley, New York. Linda Hill provided perceptive research for the chapter on the poets. Mary Grace read and improved the manuscript. I am grateful to John Farrand, Jr., for his astute comments on the manuscript and to others who read and commented on all or parts of it: Dean Amadon, Roland C. Clement, Howard L. Cogswell, Roxane Coombs, Helen Cruickshank, Dr. William E. Davis, Jr., Susan Drennan, Peter Dunne, Maitland Edey, Joseph Hickey, Dr. Stephen R. Kellert, Lloyd F. Kiff, Robert M. Peck, Phillips B. Street, Richard K. Walton. The final responsibility for the facts and judgments is, of course, mine. Joseph Miao patiently guided me through the intricacies of word processing. Sharon Zimmerman and the copy readers at Alfred A. Knopf were invaluable. And I am indebted, once again, to Charles Elliott for his thoughtful editing.

Bibliography

The constant sources for this book are the journals and records of the bird-watching and ornithological societies: the *Auk* of the American Ornithologists' Association (1884 et seq.); *Bird-Lore* of the National Association of Audubon Societies (1899–1940); *Audubon* of the National Audubon Society (1940 et seq.); *Bulletin of the Nuttall Ornithological Club* (1876–83); *Cassinia* of the Delaware Valley Ornithological Club (1901 et seq.); *The Condor* of the Cooper Ornithological [Club] Society (1899 et seq.); *Archives, Memoirs, Minutes, Proceedings and Transactions of the Linnaean Society of New York* (1878 et seq.); *The Wilson Bulletin* of the Wilson Ornithological [Club] Society (1894 et seq.). Also consulted were the twenty-one volumes of *Life Histories*, all but the last volume written, compiled and edited by Arthur Cleveland Bent (Washington, 1919–68); *Biographies of Members of the American Ornithologists' Union*, by T. S. Palmer and others (Washington, 1954); *Ornithology from Aristotle to the Present*, by Erwin Stresemann, with a foreword and epilogue on American ornithology by Ernst Mayr (Cambridge, 1975); *The Audubon Encyclopedia of North American Birds*, by John K. Terres (New York, 1980); *The Bird Watcher's Companion*, by Christopher Leahy (New York, 1982); *Birds and Men*, by Robert Henry Welker (Cambridge, 1955; New York, 1966); *Speaking for Nature*, by Paul Brooks (Boston, 1980); *Bird Watching* (London, 1901) and *Realities of Bird Life* (London, 1923), by Edmund Selous; and *The Art of Bird Watching*, by E. M. Nicholson (London, 1931).

PROLOGUE
The incidents reported come from works cited elsewhere in this bibliography by Elliott, Cassin, and Cutright and Brodhead, as well as biographies.

CHAPTER 1 *The Forerunners*
The data on Indians is from "Milicete [sic] Indian Natural History," by Tappan Adney (*Transactions of the Linnaean Society of New York*, Feb. 1, 1893); "Material Aspect of Pmo Culture," by S. A. Barrett (*Bulletin of the Public Museum, City of Milwaukee*, March, August 1952); "Birdlore of the Eastern Cherokees," by John Witthoft (*Journal of the Washington Academy of Science*, Jan. 18, 1946). This period is dealt with authoritatively in "The History of American Ornithology Before Audubon," by Elsa Guerdrum Allen (*Transactions of the American Philosophical Society*, N.S., vol. 41, 1951). Primary sources are: *A New Voyage to Carolina*, by John Lawson, edited by Hugh Talmage Lefler (London, 1709; Chapel Hill, 1967); *The Natural History of Carolina, Florida and the Bahama Islands*, by Mark Catesby (London, 1731–43); "Sir Charles Blagden, Earliest of Rhode Island Ornithologists," by Reginald

Heber Howe, Jr. (*The American Naturalist,* June 1905); "Letters of Sir Charles Blagden to Sir Joseph Banks 1776–1779" (*Bulletin of the New York Public Library,* November 1903); *American Ornithology, or the Natural History of Birds of the United States,* by Alexander Wilson (Philadelphia, 1808–14); *Ornithological Biography,* by John James Audubon (Edinburgh, 1831–39); *The Birds of America,* by John James Audubon (New York and Philadelphia, 1840–44; New York, ˜1967); *Manual of the Ornithology of the United States and Canada,* by Thomas Nuttall (Boston, 1832–34); *A Report on the Ornithology of Massachusetts,* by William B. O. Peabody (Boston, 1839); *Birds of Long Island,* by Jacob P[ost] Giraud Jr. (New York, 1844); *Illustrations of the Birds of California, Texas, Oregon, British and Russian America . . . 1853 to 1855,* by John Cassin (1865). Also, *Alexander Wilson, Naturalist and Pioneer,* by Robert Cantwell (Philadelphia, 1961); *Audubon the Naturalist,* by Francis Hobart Herrick (New York, 1938); *John James Audubon,* by Alice Ford (Normal, 1964); "John Cassin," by Witmer Stone (*Cassinia,* vol. 5, 1901); also, Stone's essay in *Dictionary of American Biography.* Material in this chapter was drawn from a previous book by this author, *A Species of Eternity* (New York, 1977).

CHAPTER 2 *The Recruiter*
The main source for this chapter is *Spencer Fullerton Baird,* by William Healey Dall (Philadelphia, 1918), an interesting but inadequate work that points up the astonishing lack of a proper biography of this most important scientist. Also, "Spencer Fullerton Baird," by Robert Ridgway (*Auk,* January 1888); *Biographical Memoir of Spencer Fullerton Baird,* by John S[haw] Billings (Washington, 1895). Works by Baird: *Birds of North America,* by Spencer F[ullerton] Baird, John Cassin and George N[ewbold] Lawrence (Philadelphia, 1860); *A History of North American Birds,* by Spencer F[ullerton] Baird, T[homas] M. Brewer and R[obert] Ridgway (1874, 1884). *Ornithologists of the United States Army Medical Corps,* by Edgar Erskine Hume (Baltimore, 1942), is the main source on Baird's medical recruits. Also, *Reports of Explorations and Surveys . . . from the Mississippi River to the Pacific Ocean,* vol. 12, ch. 1, "Land Birds," by J[ames] G[raham] Cooper, and ch. 2, "Water Birds," by G[eorge] Suckley, edited by S. F. Baird (Washington, 1860); *Ornithology of California,* by James G. Cooper, edited by S. F. Baird (Cambridge, 1870); *Life Histories of North American Birds, with Special Reference to Their Breeding Habits and Eggs,* by Charles E[mil] Bendire (Washington, 1895).

CHAPTER 3 *The Model Watcher*
This chapter relies on William Brewster's own writings: *Birds of the Cambridge Region of Massachusetts* (Memoirs of the Nuttall Ornithological Club, no. 4, Cambridge, 1906); *The Birds of the Lake Umbagog Region of Maine* (Cambridge, 1924); *Concord River Selections from the Journals of William Brewster,* edited by Smith O. Dexter (Cambridge, 1933); "October Farm," from the *Concord Journals and Diaries of William Brewster,* with an introduction by Daniel Chester French (Cambridge, 1936). Also, letters in the library archives of the Museum of Comparative Zoology, Harvard University. The account of the Nuttall Club draws on *Bulletin of the Nuttall Ornithological Club* (Cambridge, 1876–83); *An Account of the Nuttall Ornithological Club, 1873 to 1919,* by Charles F. Batchelder (Memoirs of the Nuttall Ornithological Club, no. 8, 1937). Also, *The Land-Birds and Game-Birds of New England,* by H[enry] D[avis] Minot, edited by William Brewster, 3d ed. (Boston, 1903); *Queen of the Woods* (Hartford, Mich., 1899) and "Kegon Penay-Segant Win-ge-see" (*Osprey,* vol. 1, no. 4), by Simon Pokagon; *The Passenger Pigeon,* by W. B. Hershon (New York, 1907); *Fifty Years Progress of American Ornithology* (Lancaster, Pa., 1933).

CHAPTER 4 *The Great Sparrow War*
The English Sparrow in North America, by Walter B. Barrows (Washington, 1889), is the historic survey. Also, "The European House Sparrow," by Thomas M. Brewer (*Atlantic Monthly,* May 1868); "English Sparrows," by Elliott Coues (*American Naturalist,* October 1874); *Birds of the Boston Public Garden,* by Horace Winslow Wright (Boston, 1909); [*Ornithological*] *Papers of George Newbold Lawrence (1846–1899).* Modern sources include *Wildness Is All Around Us,* by Eugene Kinkead (New York, 1978); *The House Sparrow,* by D. Summers-Smith (London,

1963); "Elliott Coues and the Sparrow War," by Michael J. Brodhead (*New England Quarterly*, September 1971).

CHAPTER 5 *The Prodigious Troublemaker*
Elliott Coues, Naturalist and Frontier Historian, by Paul Russell Cutright and Michael J. Brodhead (Urbana, 1981), is an essential source for this chapter—as it must be for any work on Coues. Also, Hume (1942). Works by Coues: *Key to North American Birds* (Salem, Mass., 1872; Boston, 1874, 1881, 1884, 1887, 1903); *A Check List of North American Birds* (Salem, 1873, 1874; Boston, 1882); *Birds of the Northwest: A Handbook of the Ornithology of the Region Drained by the Missouri River and Its Tributaries* (Washington, 1874); *Field Ornithology, Comprising a Manual of Instruction for Procuring, Preparing and Preserving Birds, and a Check List of North American Birds* (Salem, 1874); *Birds of the Northwest* (Washington, 1874; Salem, 1877); *Birds of the Colorado Valley* (Washington, 1878); *New England Bird Life*, revised and edited from the manuscript of Winfrid A. Stearns by Dr. Elliott Coues (Boston, 1881); *Biogen: A Speculation on the Origin and Nature of Life* (Washington, 1882; Boston, 1884, 1885); *Citizen Bird*, by Mabel Osgood Wright and Elliott Coues (New York, 1897). The obituary note is from the *Journal of the Maine Ornithological Society* (January 1900).

CHAPTER 6 *Men of Standing*
Much material comes from the *Archives, Memoirs, Minutes, Proceedings and Transactions of the Linnaean Society of New York* (1878 et seq.). Other sources: *Theodore Roosevelt, the Naturalist*, by Paul Russell Cutright (New York, 1956); *Mornings on Horseback*, by David McCullough (New York, 1982); *The Charm of Birding*, by Viscount [Edward] Gray of Fallodon (London, 1927); *Birds of Washington and Vicinity*, by Lucy Maynard (Washington, 1908); "The President Goes Birding" (*The Conservationist*, May 1977); *Franklin D. Roosevelt: The Apprenticeship*, by Frank Friedel (Boston, 1952); *Franklin Roosevelt at Hyde Park*, by Olin Dows (New York, 1949); *Before the Trumpet: Young Franklin Roosevelt*, by Geoffrey Ward (New York, 1985); "The Birds of Dutchess County New York from records compiled by Maunsell S[chiefflin] Crosby by Ludlow Griscom" (*Transactions of the Linnean Society of New York*, December 1933).

CHAPTER 7 *The Protectors*
Much of this, of course, comes from the Audubon Society publications: *Audubon* (1887–88) and *Bird-Lore* (1899–1940). Also, *Adventures in Bird Protection*, by Thomas Gilbert Pearson (New York, 1937); *Birds of Massachusetts*, by Edward Howe Forbush (Boston, 1925); *The Domestic Cat*, by Edward Howe Forbush (State Board of Agriculture Economic Biology Bulletin 2, Boston, 1916); *John Muir and His Legacy*, by Stephen Fox (Boston, 1981); *Last of the Naturalists. The Career of C. Hart Merriam*, by Keir B. Sterling (New York, 1977); *Life Histories of North American Marsh Birds*, by Arthur Cleveland Bent (Washington, 1926); "From Outrage to Action," by Frank Graham, Jr., and Carl Buchheister (*Audubon*, January 1973); *Wildlife and America*, edited by Howard P. Brokaw (Washington, D.C., 1978); *Wildlife in America*, by Peter Mathiessen (New York, 1959).

CHAPTER 8 *The Good Fellows*
This chapter draws on Witmer Stone's classic *Bird Studies at Old Cape May* (Philadelphia, 1937; New York, 1965); *Proceedings of the Delaware Valley Ornithological Club* (1890–91); and *Cassinia* (1891 et seq.). The "good-fellow" quotation is from *Cassinia* (1909). The career of Charles J. Pennock was followed through several decades of ornithological journals: *Cassinia, The Wilson Bulletin, The Condor, The Oologist, Bird-Lore, Auk*, as well as Bent's *Life Histories* and the archives of the library of the Academy of Natural Sciences in Philadelphia.

CHAPTER 9 *The Collectors*
The Condor over the years is a main source of this chapter. Others include *Bird Killing as a Method in Ornithology*, by Reginald C. Robbins (Cambridge, 1902); *Audubon and His Journals*, by Maria R. Audubon (New York, 1897, 1960); Coues (1877); Brewster (1906, 1933); Forbush (1925 et seq.); Hume (1942); Bent (*Birds of Prey, Marsh Birds, Shore Birds, Wildfowl*).

Shooting Journal of George Henry Mackay, 1865–1922, edited by John C. Phillips (Cambridge, 1929), is used by courtesy of the library of the Museum of Comparative Zoology, Harvard University. "Conserve the Collector," by Joseph Grinnell (*Science,* February 1915), is also in Joseph Grinnell's *Philosophy of Nature* (Berkeley, 1943). The section on field glasses draws on *The Journal of Henry David Thoreau* as excerpted by Helen Cruickshank in *Thoreau on Birds* (New York, 1964); *Birds Through an Opera Glass,* by Florence Merriam Bailey (Boston, 1900); *50th Anniversary of the Nuttall Ornithological Club,* by Witmer Stone (Cambridge, 1913).

CHAPTER 10 *A Pastime for Chums*
Oology journals on which much of this chapter is based are *Ornithologist and Oologist* (originally the *Oologist,*), which was published from 1881 to 1882; *The Young Oologist,* which started in 1884, became *The Oologist* in 1886, and continued publication until 1946. The anecdotes are from *The Young Oologist* (September–November 1880, June–September 1887). Oology field guides include *Nests and Eggs of North American Birds,* by Oliver Davie (Philadelphia, 1889); *North American Birds' Eggs,* by Chester A. Reed (New York, 1904); *A Field Guide to Western Birds' Nests,* by Hal N. Harrison (Boston, 1975); *Birds' Nests: A Complete Field Guide to Nests in the United States,* by Richard Headstron (New York, 1970). Also, *Egg-Shells,* by Michael Prynne (London, 1963), and *The American Oologist Exchange Price Lists of North American Eggs* (Lacon, Ill., 1922).

CHAPTER 11 *A Friend of Bird and Birder*
Edward Howe Forbush's magnum opus, *Birds of Massachusetts and Other New England States,* is in three volumes (Boston, 1925, 1927, 1929). It contains some of Louis Agassiz Fuertes' finest paintings and a Forbush biography (in vol. 3) by John Richard May, who completed the editing of that volume. Another biography is "Edward Howe Forbush," by T. Gilbert Pearson (*Auk,* April 1930). Also consulted was correspondence in the archives of the Department of Agriculture, Boston; and *Useful Birds and Their Protection,* by Edward Howe Forbush (Boston, 1907).

CHAPTER 12 *The Independent Midwest*
The history of the Wilson Society (originally the Wilson Ornithological Club) is traced through various publications with which it was associated: *The Curlew* (1889); *Ornithologist and Ooologist Semi-Annual* (1890–91); *The Semi-Annual* (1891); *The Taxidermist* (1891–92); [*The Wilson*] *Quarterly* (1892); *The Journal* (1893); *Bulletin* (1894–98); *The Wilson Bulletin* (1898 et seq.). Two brief histories are "History of the Wilson Ornithological Club," by Lynds Jones (*The Wilson Bulletin,* March 1914), and "A History of the Wilson Ornithological Club," by R. M. Strong (*The Wilson Bulletin,* March 1939). The Gabrielson material is in *The Wilson Bulletin* (June 1912, September 1914) and *Auk* (September 1914). Jones' trip is in *The Wilson Bulletin* (October 1900) and *The Condor* (August 1901). The Nathan Leopold story is traced through *The Wilson Bulletin* (March 1921), *Bird-Lore* (March 1922, December 1923), *New York Times* (1924 et seq.) and the autobiographical *Life Plus 99 Years,* by Nathan J. Leopold (New York, 1958). Also, "The Kirtland's Warbler in Its Summer Home," by N[athan] F. Leopold (*Auk,* January 1924); *Checklist of Birds of Puerto Rico and the Virgin Islands,* by N[athan] F. Leopold (Rio Piedras, 1963). The biographical material on Althea Sherman comes from the introduction to *Birds of an Iowa Dooryard,* by Althea R. Sherman, edited by Fred Pierce (Boston, 1952). Various quotations by Sherman are found in that book and in *Auk* (July 1913), *The Wilson Bulletin* (December 1913) and *The Condor* (1923). The house wren to-do is taken from *The Wilson Bulletin* (March 1925, September 1925), *Bird-Lore* (1925, pp. 30, 97, 168, 197, 234, 242, 243, 245, 263); also Bent's *Life Histories.*

CHAPTER 13 *The Scientist and Her Singer*
This chapter comes largely from *Studies in the Life History of the Song Sparrow,* by Margaret Morse Nice (*Transactions of the Linnaean Society of New York,* 1937, 1943; published also New

York, 1964). Also, *The Watcher at the Nest,* by Margaret Morse Nice (New York, 1939, 1967); *Research Is a Passion with Me,* by Margaret Morse Nice (Toronto, 1979).

CHAPTER 14 *The Imbuers*
All the birding journals yielded material for this chapter; also *Biographies,* Forbush (1925); *Journal of the Maine Ornithological Society* (March 1906, March 1907); *The Warblers of North America,* by Frank M. Chapman (New York, 1907). The material on Elizabeth Dickens comes from her unpublished journals (courtesy William Lewis), her unpublished bird records (courtesy Audubon Society of Rhode Island) and the affectionate memoir *Elizabeth Dickens,* by Harold S. Whitman, and interviews with her former pupils. Other references come from *Bird-Lore* (1916, 1919, 1926, 1927), *Auk* (April 1930, 1932). Also, *The First Book of Birds* (1899), *Little Brothers of the Air* (Boston, 1892) and *Bird-Ways* (Boston, 1885), by Olive Thorne Miller; *Birdcraft,* by Mabel Osgood Wright (New York, 1895); *Bird Neighbors,* by Neltje Blanchan (New York, 1897); *A-Birding on a Bronco* (Boston, 1896), *Birds of Village and Field* (Boston, 1898), *My Summer in a Mormon Village* (Boston, 1899) and *Birds Through an Opera Glass* (Boston, 1900), by Florence A. Merriam. By the same author under her married name of Florence Merriam Bailey: *Handbook of Birds of the Western United States* (Boston, 1902) and *Birds of New Mexico* (Washington, 1928). Also, *Birds of the Connecticut Valley in Massachusetts,* by Aaron Clark Bagg and Samuel Atkins Eliot, Jr. (Northampton, 1932).

CHAPTER 15 *The Great Connector*
The quotations from John Burroughs come from several of his books: *Birds and Poets* (Boston, 1895); *Wake Robin* (Boston, 1871); *Field and Study* (Boston, 1919); *Far and Near* (Boston, 1904). Many of the quotations are found in *The Birds of John Burroughs,* edited by Jack Kligerman (New York, 1976). Also, *Camping and Tramping with Roosevelt,* by John Burroughs (Boston, 1907); "Bird Study," by John Burroughs (*Auk,* January 1886); *John Burroughs Talks* (Boston, 1922); *Notes on Walt Whitman as Poet and Person,* by John Burroughs (New York, 1867); *Whitman, A Study,* by John Burroughs (Cambridge, 1896). Two books by Clara Barrus are basic: *The Life and Letters of John Burroughs* (Boston, 1925) and *The Heart of Burroughs' Journals* (Boston, 1928). Also, *The Real John Burroughs,* by William Sloane Kennedy (New York, 1924); Robert Henry Welker's admirable *Birds and Men,* previously cited, discusses all the poets in this chapter, as does Norman Foersters' *Nature in American Literature* (New York, 1958). The poem extracts are from: Walt Whitman, *Complete Poetry and Selected Prose,* edited by James E. Miller, Jr. (Boston, 1959); *Poems of William Cullen Bryant* (New York, 1914); James Russell Lowell, *Complete Poetical Work,* edited by Horace E. Scudder (Cambridge, 1925); *The Works of Henry Wadsworth Longfellow* (New York, 1966). Among the biographies consulted were *The Solitary Singer,* by Gay Wilson Allen (New York, 1955); *Walt Whitman: A Life,* by Justin Kaplan (New York, 1980); *William Cullen Bryant,* by Albert F. McLean, Jr. (New York, 1964); *James Russell Lowell: His Life and Work,* by Ferris Greenslet (Boston, 1905). Roosevelt sources are cited in Chapter 6. Also, *Henry Ford: Expansion and Challenge,* by Allan Nevins and Frank Ernest Hill (New York, 1959); *My Life and Work,* by Henry Ford in collaboration with Samuel Crowther (New York, 1926).

CHAPTER 16 *Revolution in the Bronx*
The records of the Linnaean Society of New York and the Christmas censuses in *Bird-Lore* are sources, along with interviews and correspondence with the subjects of the chapter. *Guide to the Land Birds East of the Rockies,* by Chester Reed (New York, 1906, 1909, 1951); *Handbook of Birds of Eastern North America,* by Frank M. Chapman (New York, 1895, 1912, 1932, 1939); *What Bird Is That,* by Frank M. Chapman (New York, 1920); *Bird Life,* by Frank M. Chapman (New York, 1897); *Autobiography of a Bird Lover,* by Frank M. Chapman; "Problems of Field Identification," by Ludlow Griscom (*Auk,* January 1922); *Birds of the New York City Region,* by Ludlow Griscom (New York, 1923); *The Birds of Concord,* by Ludlow Griscom

(Cambridge, 1949); *The Birds of Nantucket,* by Ludlow Griscom (Cambridge, 1948); obituary of Griscom by Roger Tory Peterson (*Auk,* October 1965).

CHAPTER 17 *The Guide*
The sources for this chapter are Peterson's own books, *A Field Guide to the Birds of the Eastern United States* (Boston, 1934, 1939, 1947, 1980; the words "of the Eastern United States" do not appear in the revised editions) and *A Field Guide to Western Birds* (Boston 1941, 1961); *Birds Over America* (New York, 1948). Also, *The World of Roger Tory Peterson,* by James C. Devlin and Grace Naismith (New York, 1977); "The Battle of the Bird Books," by Joseph Kastner (*New York Times,* Apr. 15, 1979). Also, *Guide to the Birds of New England and Eastern New York* (Boston, 1904) and *A Guide to the Birds of the Pacific States* (Boston, 1927), by Ralph Hoffman; *A Guide to Bird Watching,* by Joseph Hickey (New York, 1943); *Birds Around New York City,* by Allan Cruickshank (New York, 1942); *On the Trail of the Vanishing Birds,* by Robert Porter Allen (New York, 1957). Also, *Alger Hiss: The True Story,* by John Chabot Smith (New York, 1975); *In the Court of Public Opinion,* by Alger Hiss (New York, 1957).

CHAPTER 18 *Listers and Savers*
The field guides mentioned are *Audubon Land Bird Guide* (New York, 1946) and *Audubon Water Bird Guide* (New York, 1951), by Richard H. Pough; *Birds of North America,* by Arthur Singer, Chandler S. Robbins, Bertel Brunn and Herbert S. Zim (New York, 1966); *Audubon Society Field Guide to North American Birds, Eastern Region,* by John Bull, John Farrand, Jr., and Susan Rayfield (New York, 1977); *The Audubon Society Guide to North American Birds, Western Region,* by Milpo D. F. Udvardy and Susan Rayfield (New York, 1977); *Audubon Society Master Guide to Birding,* edited by John Farrand, Jr. (New York, 1983); *National Geographic Society Field Guide to the Birds of North America* (Washington, 1983); *Public Attitudes Towards Critical Wildlife and Natural Habitat Issues* and other papers prepared for the U.S. Fish and Wildlife Service by Stephen R. Kellert with Joyce K. Berry and Miriam O. Westervelt (Washington, 1979). Periodicals used include *American Birds,* published by the National Audubon Society (New York), *Birding,* the publication of the American Birding Association (Austin) and *Bird Watcher's Digest* (Marietta). Also, *Checklist of North American Birds,* published by the American Ornithologists' Union (Lancaster, Pa., 1931).

EPILOGUE
Speaking for Nature, by Paul Brooks (New York, 1980); Cruickshank (1964); *Birds of the Sudbury River Valley,* by Richard K. Walton (Lincoln, Mass., 1984); *A Natural History of Selborne,* by Gilbert White (London, 1792 et seq.)—an edition of particular interest was edited by the ornithologist James Fisher (London, 1941); *Gilbert White's Year, Passages from the Garden Kalendar and the Naturalist's Journal,* selected by John Commander (London, 1979). The Chaucer quotation is from the prologue to *The Legend of Good Women,* Globe Edition (London, 1907).

Index

Abbott, Charles Conrad, 63
Abbott, Clinton G., 63
Abbott, Harriet, 157
Adams, S. W., 180
Agassiz, Louis, 20, 132
Agassiz Association, 132
Agriculture, U.S. Department of,
    42–5
Aldano, Frank, 80
Alfred, Lord Tennyson, 64
Allen, A. A., 63
Allen, Arthur, 192–3
Allen, Elsa Guerdon, 9
Allen, Francis H., 199
Allen, Joel Asaph, 38, 56, 105, 119
Allen, Robert Porter, 187, 203
American Bird Banding Association,
    91
American Birding Association, 210
American Birds, 210, 215
American Indians, 6–8, 10, 35–6, 65
American Museum of Natural History,
    64, 67, 191, 193
American Ornithologists' Union
    (AOU), 51, 58, 91, 134, 179, 191
  Committee on Bird Protection of,
    105
  Committee on Taxonomy and
    Nomenclature of, 213–14
  formation of, 38, 56, 61, 135

journal of, 38, 63, 95, 97, 102,
    105, 111–12, 119, 134, 160
  membership rules of, 104–5
  protection and, 73
  Roosevelt family in, 65–8
  women in, 168
American Ornithology (Wilson), 10–12,
    18
American Society for the Prevention
    of Cruelty to Animals, 42
American Society of Bird Restorers,
    42
Anderson, Charles J., 122
Anderson, William Wallace, 23–4
Apaches, 6, 49
Army, U.S.
  medical corps of, 48–54, 104
  naturalists in, 22–7
Arnold, Matthew, 198
Audubon, John James, 11–14, 52, 58,
    60, 64, 110, 179
  Baird and, 18–20
  journals of, 70
  killing of birds by, 98
Audubon, Lucy, 70
Audubon, Maria, 37–8, 58
Audubon (magazine), 71
Audubon Land Bird Guide (Pough), 207
Audubon Society, 202, 207
  average birders as target of, 72

Audubon Society (*continued*)
　cat controversy and, 80–2
　formation of, 60, 70–1
　journals of, 71, 72, 74, 77–80,
　　82–4, 191
　motto of, 70
　national character of, 74
　protectionist purposes of, 70–2,
　　74–82
　worries of, 82–3
Audubon Society Field Guide (Bull and
　Farrand, Jr.), 208
Audubon Society Master Guide to Birding,
　208
Auk (birding journal), 38, 63, 95,
　97, 102, 105, 111–12, 119, 134,
　160

Bailey, Vernon, 168
Baily, William, 90
Baird, Lucy, 21, 29
Baird, Mrs. Spencer Fuller, 22
Baird, Spencer Fullerton, 17–30, 37,
　60, 137, 207
　as administrator, 20–1
　Audubon and, 18–20
　background of, 17–18
　collections of, 19, 20
　Coues and, 48–51, 53–4, 56
　death of, 29
　eccentricities of, 18
　"missionaries" of, 21, 28
　other scientific interests of, 21–9
　personality of, 28–9
　philosophy of power of, 29
　at Smithsonian, 20–1
Bairdian School of American
　Ornithology, 17, 28
Baldwin, Dorothy A., 124–5
Banks, Joseph, 9
Barlow, Chester, 106
Barnes, R. Magoon, 119
Barrows, Walter B., 42–4
Barton, Benjamin Smith, 10
Bartram, John, 10
Bartram, William, 10
Basham, Benton, 211
Bath, Mrs. L. H., 79
Battell, Harriet Chapman, 143
Beach, Grace, 64

Beecher, Henry Ward, 41–2
Bell, John G., 19, 65, 108, 191
Belliat, Letson, 118
Bendire, Maj. Charles Emil, 25–7, 91,
　107
Bent, Arthur C., 92, 96, 99–100,
　117
Bergh, Henry, 42
Berlepsch, Baron, 83
Bermuda, conservation edict in, 72
Berthollet, Claude, 9
Bewick, Thomas, 14–15
Bicknell, Eugene Pintard, 38, 61, 62
Biddle, Lydia Spencer, 17–18
"Big Day," 211–12
Big Year List, 211
Biological Survey, U.S., 94
bird alerts, 212–13
bird calls, 33, 36, 90, 92, 95, 121,
　193
Birdcraft (Wright), 166
birders
　use of term, 4
　see also bird watching
birding, 215
"Bird Killing as a Method in
　Ornithology" (Robbins), 97–8
Bird-Lore (magazine), 72, 74, 77–80,
　82–4, 106, 138, 144, 185, 191,
　202, 203, 210, 215
Bird Neighbors (Blanchan), 167
birds
　courting behavior of, 26
　European vs. American, 9
　identification of, 189–90
　Indian names for, 6–7, 10, 35, 65
　killing of, 97–112, 194
　lists of, 37, 46
　loyalty of, 122–3
　merits vs. defects of, 122–5
　name changes of, 213
　in poetry, 171–8
　resourcefulness of, 123
　self-reliance of, 123
　territory of, 148–9, 151
　thriftiness of, 123–4
　see also specific birds and topics
Birds and Men (Welker), 170
Birds Around New York City
　(Cruickshank), 203

Birds of America, The (Audubon), 12, 18, 179

Birds of California (Dawson), 117

Birds of Concord, The (Griscom), 218

Birds of Dutchess County, The (Griscom), 68

Birds of Eastern Pennsylvania and New Jersey, The (Stone), 89

Birds of Kansas, The (Goss and Goss), 26–7

Birds of Long Island, The (Giraud), 12–13, 172

Birds of Massachusetts and Other New England States (Forbush), 120–2, 157

Birds of Minnesota, The (Roberts), 135

Birds of New England (Brewer), 37

Birds of New Mexico (Merriam), 168

Birds of New York (Eaton), 188

Birds of North America (Baird), 20, 25, 50

Birds of North America (Singer, Robbins, Brunn and Zim), 207–8

Birds of the Colorado Valley (Coues), 52

Birds of the New York City Region (Griscom), 192

Birds of the Northwest (Coues), 52

Birds of the Sudbury River Valley (Walton), 218

Birds of Washington and Vicinity (Maynard), 66

Birds Through an Opera Glass (Merriam), 168

Bird Studies at Old Cape May (Stone), 86–9

Birdwatcher's Companion (Leahy), 215

Bird Watcher's Digest, 215

bird watching (bird watchers), 33
  American Indian names for, 35
  bad manners among, 212
  forerunners in, 6–16
  life list of, 7–11, 37, 46, 105, 134, 210–13, 217
  love and, 5
  national, 42–5
  nomenclature of, 214–15
  as non-utilitarian, 209
  observation criterion for, 193
  scale of, 209
  sensitivity of, 63
  sociology of, 209–10
  solitary vs. group, 60
  statistics on, 208–9
  time periods, 207
  use of term, 4

Bird-Ways (Miller), 165

blackbird
  Brewer's, 14
  red-winged, 32
  yellow-headed, 202

Blagden, Sir Charles, 9–10

Blake, Eli, 44

Blanchan, Neltje, 167

Blavatsky, Helena, 57

Bloomfield, Arthur, 69, 219

bluebird, 33, 62

blue jay, 32, 33, 121–2, 139

bobolink, 159, 174

bobwhite, 116

Bradley, Guy, 78

Braislin, William C., 63

brant, 8, 10

Bremer, Jacob, 133–4

Brewer, Thomas, 13–14, 28, 37, 60
  in Great Sparrow War, 41, 42, 46–8

Brewster, William, 30–8, 54, 68, 71, 99, 111, 218, 219
  ailing birders befriended by, 35–6
  as curator, 31, 34
  journals of, 31, 36–7
  Mackay's correspondence with, 101–2
  as Nuttall Club president, 30–1, 34, 37–8

Briefe and True Report of the New Found Land of Virginia, A (Hariot), 7–8

Britwell, Francis J., 117

Brodhead, Michael J., 55

Bronx County Bird Club, 185–95
  equipment of, 187–91
  formation of, 186–7
  Griscom and, 192–4
  Peterson and, 195, 197

Brooks, Alan, 82

Brooks, Paul, 217

Brown, Wilmot, 108

Brunn, Bertel, 208

Bryant, William Cullen, 174–5

Bryers, O. M., 144

Bull, John, 208
bunting, 11
Burgess, Thornton W., 125
Burnett, Frances Hodgson, 29
Burroughs, John, 111, 169–84, 199
  as advocate of female birders, 181–2
  Bryant and, 174–5
  as collector vs. conserver, 180–1
  Ford and, 182–4
  Longfellow and, 177–8
  Lowell and, 175–7
  Whitman and, 170–4, 179
  writing style of, 179–80
buzzard, 79
Byrd, Mary Elizabeth, 5

Cabot, Samuel, Jr., 137
Caraway, Mr., 75–6
calls, 33, 36, 90, 92, 95, 121, 193
cardinal, 8
  Texas (*Pyrrhuloxia*), 15–16
Carpenter, Capt. William L., 27
Carson, Alma, 72
Carson, Rachel, 216
Carter, Isabel Paddock, 157
"Case of the People of North
    America versus the House
    Wren" (Sherman), 138–9
Cassin, John, 14–17, 20, 29, 85, 89
Cassinia (journal), 89, 96, 89, 91
Catalog of North American Birds (Baird),
    17, 20
Catalogue of Birds of North America
    (Bartram), 10
catbird, 33, 82, 134, 202
Catesby, Mark, 9
cats, control of, 34–5, 80–2, 122
Cavendish, Henry, 9
Century Dictionary, The, 54
Chambers, Whittaker, 204–5
Champlain, Samuel de, 8
Chapman, Bertha, 157
Chapman, Frank M., 55, 62, 63, 65,
    71–2, 74, 106, 112, 157, 189–92,
    196, 199, 201
Chase, Agnes, 133
Chase, Sydney, 123–4
Chaucer, Geoffrey, 221–2
Check-list of North American Birds (AOU
    list), 46, 134

Check List of North American Birds
    (Coues), 50–1, 54–5
*Checklist of the Birds of Puerto Rico and
    the Virgin Islands* (Leopold), 138
Cherokees, 7
Chippewas, 7
Chuck-will's widow, eggs of, 26
Churchill, Sylvester, 22, 23
Churchman, Mordecai, 11
Citizen Bird (Wright, Coues, Fuertes),
    58, 166–7
Clapp, Charles, 43
Clayton, John, 9
Cochise (Indian chief), 25
collecting, 97–112, 126, 180–1
  commercial, 108
  of eggs and nests, 113–19
  field glasses and, 110–12
  regulation of, 103–10
  as self-limiting, 110
  shooting vs., 98–9
Concord River (Brewster), 31, 36–7
condor, 7, 104
Condor, The, 104–11, 135
Congress, U.S., 28, 75–7, 183
conservation (conservation
    movement), 4, 183, 215–16
  collecting vs., 97–112, 180–1
  history of, 72–3
  oology and, 119
  songbirds not protected by, 40
  see also Audubon Society
"Conserve the Collector" (Grinnell),
    109
Cooper, James Graham, 24, 37, 104
Cooper, Susan Fenimore, 21–2
Cooper, William, 24, 104
Cooper Ornithological Club (now
    called Society), 61, 104, 132, 196
cormorant, 103, 116
Coues, Elliott, 28, 37, 38, 41, 46–59,
    69, 166–7, 179, 189, 191, 207
  in army medical corps, 48–54
  background of, 48–9
  Baird and, 48–51, 53–4, 56
  death of, 58–9
  editorial work of, 54
  in Great Sparrow War, 41, 46–8
  shotgun school of ornithology and,
    99

spiritualist thinking of, 56–9
  wives of, 48, 49, 53–4, 57, 189
counting birds, 91, 140, 186, 191–2,
  195, 210
cowbird, 13
Craigmile, Esther, 133
crane, sandhill, 8
Crawford, Samuel Wylie, 24
Crispin, William C., 117
Crolius, Anne M., 192
Crosby, Maunsell, 68–9, 96, 133
crow, 82, 122–3, 126–7
Cruickshank, Allan, 186, 203
Cruickshank, Helen, 218
cuckoo, black-billed, 88
Currier, Freeman B., 122–3
Cutright, Paul Russell, 55, 65

Daggett, Frank S., 104–5
Dall, William Healy, 27
Darrow, Clarence, 138
Davis, Jefferson, 22
Dawson, William Leon, 45, 117, 118,
  135
"Day with a Young Collector, A"
  (Leigh), 113–14
de la Vega, Garcilaso, 7
Delaware Valley Ornithological Club
  (DVOC), 60, 89–96, 210
Denys, Nicolas, 8
*Description and Natural History of the
  Coasts of North America* (Denys), 8
Dickens, Elizabeth, 156, 158–64,
  219
Dickens, Lovell, 161
Doolittle, E. A., 83–4
Doubleday, Nelson, 167
Dred Scott decision, 73
duck, 80, 116, 133–4
  "Brewer," 13–14
  goldeneye, 122
  oldsquaw, 9
  sea, 201
  wood, 129
du Pont de Nemours, E. I., &
  Company, 82
Dutcher, William, 61, 65, 71, 105

eagle, 36, 79
  bald, 88, 129

Early, E. H., 82
Eastman, Sarah Chandler, 158
Eaton, Elon, 188
Eckelberry, Don, 207
Edwards, John F. T., 43
Egg Act of 1902, 76
eggs, 32, 34, 91, 98, 149
  collecting of, 105–6, 113–19
  description of, 26, 116, 122
  fakes and, 118
  of owls, 26
  prices of, 117–18
egret, American, 88–9
Elliot, Daniel Giraud, 64
Emerson, Ralph Waldo, 171, 190,
  218, 219
English sparrow, *see* sparrow: house
Enlightenment, Age of, 10
Everett, Edward Addison, 136

falcon, 33
Farrand, John, Jr., 208
feathers, bird, Audubon campaign
  against use of, 74–8
feeding behavior, 31–2, 36, 80, 103,
  123–4, 134, 144, 166
  of English sparrow, 40, 41, 43, 44
  feeders and, 82–3
Ferris, John C., 44
field glasses, 110–12, 194
field guides, 11–12, 207–8; *see also
  specific guides*
Field Guide to the Birds, A (Peterson),
  200–2, 204, 207–8
Field Guide to the Birds of North America
  (National Geographic Society),
  208
finch
  Bachman's (sparrow), 33
  California purple, 37
  house, 46
Finley, William, 203
First Book of Birds (Miller), 165
Fish and Wildlife Service, U.S.,
  209
flamingo, 8
flicker, 32
flycatcher, 214
  Coues', 23
  crested, 116

flycatcher (*continued*)
  Hammond's, 23
  yellow-bellied, 18
Foard, Andrew Jackson, 24
Forbush, Edward Howe, 81, 102,
    103, 120–31, 157, 161, 218
Ford, Henry, 182–4
Forest and Stream, 70, 76
Forester, Frank, 100
Foster, Mrs. E. G., 64
Franks, Robert, 136
French, Daniel Chester, 34
Friedmann, Herbert, 123
Fuertes, Louis Agassiz, 58, 166, 196

Gabrielson, Ira, 134
game wardens, 77–9, 81–2
Gardiner, John L., 11
Gault, Benjamin T., 133
Gifford, Harold, 107
Giraud, Jacob Post, 12–13, 19, 64,
    172
goldfinch, 46, 63, 201
Goss, Capt. Benjamin F., 26–7
Goss, Col. Nathaniel S., 26–7
Graham, Frank, Jr., 214
Grant, Gen. Ulysses S., 36
Gray, Asa, 20
Great English Sparrow War, 39–47
  national bird watching and, 42–5
grebe, 9, 80, 202
  Holboell's (red-necked grebe),
    105–6
Grey, Lord, 66
Grinnell, George Bird, 70, 168
Grinnell, Joseph, 106–9, 211
Griscom, Ludlow, 68–9, 94, 96, 196,
    210, 218, 220
  background of, 192–3
  Bronx County Bird Club and,
    192–4
  Peterson and, 196, 197, 199, 200
grosbeak, 32
grouse, 8
  spruce, 6
Guide to Bird Watching, A (Hickey),
    203
*Guide to the Birds of New England and
    Eastern New York* (Hoffmann),
    198–9

*Guide to the Land Birds East of the
    Rockies* (Reed), 187–8, 195–6
gull
  Franklin's, 136
  Heermann's, 108
  laughing, 102

Hagar, Connie, 210–11
Hamilton, Caroline, 125
Hammond, William Alexander, 23–5
*Handbook of Birds of Eastern North
    America* (Chapman), 71–2,
    189–91, 196
*Handbook of Birds of the Western United
    States* (Merriam), 168
Harding, Warren G., 84
Hariot, Thomas, 7–8
Harrison, Arthur, 123
Harrison, Whitfield, 136
Harvard Museum of Comparative
    Zoology, 31, 34
hawk, 33
  Cooper's, 127
  red-tailed, 7
  sparrow (American kestrel), 78–9,
    141
Hennier, W. F., 134
Henry, Joseph, 20, 28, 29
Henshaw, Henry Weatherbee, 6,
    30
Herbel, M. H., 83
heron, 8, 80, 93, 115, 129–30, 160–1,
    214
Hickey, Joseph, 185–8, 203
Hill, T. W., 44
Hiss, Alger, 204–5
History of North American Birds, A
    (Brewer, Ridgway and Baird), 28
Hoffmann, Ralph, 198–9, 201
Holleneck, F. B., 133
Holmes, Oliver Wendell, 76–7
Hoover, Theodore Jesse, 110
Hornbeck, Blanche, 156–7, 195
Houghton Mifflin, 199
Howe, Inez Addie, 157
Huff, H. C., 43
hummingbird, 8, 11
  Anna's, 14
Huxley, Julian, 154
Hvoslek, Johann, 136

Illustrations of the Birds of California,
   Texas, Oregon, British and Russian
   America . . . 1853 to 1855
   (Cassin), 14
imbuers, 156–68
   teachers as, 156–64
   writers as, 164–8

jay, blue, 32, 33, 121–2, 139
Jefferson, Thomas, 11, 22, 65
Jenks, F. T., 44
"jizz," 214–15, 220
Johnson, Frank, 64
Johnson, Samuel, 9
Jones, Lynds, 133–5, 192
Jordan, Jake, 78
journals, 37–8, 111, 215; *see also*
   specific journals
junco, 34, 213
Junior Audubon Club, 195–6, 202

Kassoy, Irving, 186
Kellert, Stephen, 209–10
Kendall, Joe, 101
Kennicott, Robert, 28
Key to North American Birds (Coues),
   49–50, 54, 55, 189, 191, 207
killdeer, 115–16
killing of birds, 97–112, 194
kingbird, 166
   gray (*Tyrannus dominicensis*), 94
kingfisher, 115
Kinsey, Rolla Warren, 83
Kirtland, Jared P., 137
kite, 26–7
Kouwenhoven, Mary, 44
Krider, John, 108
Kuerzi, John, 186–7

Lacey Act, 75
Lahontan, Armand Louis de, 8
Land-Birds and Game-Birds of New
   England, The (Minot), 35
Langdon, F. W., 75
lark, horned, 116
Latham, Mrs. F. E. B., 64
Lawrence, George Newbold, 14, 17, 19
Lawson, John, 9
League for Extermination of Amateur
   Ornithologists, 107

Leahy, Christopher, 215
Leigh, Benjamin, 113–14
Leopold, Aldo, 203
Leopold, Nathan J., 136–8
Lewis, Billy, 164
Lewis, Meriwether, 11
Lewis and Clark expedition, 22, 58
Life Histories of North American Birds,
   with Special References to their
   Breeding Habits and Eggs
   (Bendire), 27
Life History of Marsh Birds (Bent), 96
Lilford, Lord, 41
Lincoln, Abraham, 36
Linnaean Society, 60–9, 91, 179, 182,
   191, 192, 193
   Bronx County Bird Club and,
      185–7, 197, 202–3
   formation of, 60–1
   Peterson and, 196, 197
   Proceedings of, 63, 65
   women in, 64
Linnaeus, Carolus, 214
Lintner, J. A., 44
Loeb, Richard, 136, 137
lollipop hoax, 76
Longfellow, Henry Wadsworth, 177–8
Long Island Bird Club, 68
loon, 21, 123–4
Lorenz, Konrad, 154
Lowell, James Russell, 175–7, 222

McAtee, Waldo Lee, 144
McCall, Col. George A., 15
McClellan, Capt. George B., 22–4
McCown, Capt., J. P., 15–16, 93
McDowell, John, 205
Mackay, George H., 100–3, 111, 181
McLean, George P., 76
McLoad, Columbus G., 78
McNeil, Charles A., 83
Madison, James, 11
Maine Ornithological Journal, 58–9
Malecite Indians, 6, 8, 65
mallard, 128
Manual of the Ornithology of the United
   States and Canada (Nuttall), 12
martin, purple, 94
Massachusetts Audubon Society, 71,
   215

Massena, Victor, 14
Matuszewski, John, 186, 187
Maynard, Lucy W., 66
meadowlark, 14, 159
Merriam, Clinton Hart, 56, 61–2, 168
Merriam, Florence, 58, 64, 111,
    167–8, 181
migrations, 6–7, 89, 91, 148
Migratory Bird Act of 1913, 76
Migratory Bird Protection Treaty
    (1916), 76, 183
Miller, I. E., 118
Miller, Luther, 78
Miller, Olive Thorne, 57–8, 64,
    165–6, 199
Miller, Tom, 136
Minot, Henry Davis, 35, 61, 65
Mitchill, Samuel Latham, 11
Mitchum, Jackson, 78
mockingbird, 7, 9, 62, 64, 133, 172–3
Moore, William H., 122
Morris, Robert, 17
Mosher, Frank, 123
Muir, John, 181
Munsterber, Hugo, 83
murrelet, Craveri's, 108
mynah, crested, 46

National Association of Audubon
    Societies for the Protection of
    Wild Birds and Animals
    (National Audubon Society),
    71–2, 210, 215, 216; *see also*
    Audubon Society
National Crow Shoot, 82
National Geographic Society, 208
National Museum (of Natural
    History), 28
natural history, romantic vs. modern
    era of, 16
*Natural History of Carolina, Florida and
    the Bahama Islands* (Catesby), 9
Natural History of Selborne, The
    (White), 219–22
Naturalist's Ramble About Home, A
    (Abbot), 63
nature, Americans' ambivalence
    toward, 98
nests, 31, 32, 34
    building of, 115–16, 123, 149

collecting of, 113–19
    of house sparrows, 44
    of owls, 26
New England Bird Life (Stearns), 54
New England's Prospect (Wood), 8–9
Newkirk, Garret, 106
New Voyage to Carolina, A (Lawson),
    9
New York Sun, 57
Nice, Margaret Morse, 145–55
nighthawk, 7, 128
nightingale, 7
Notes on Virginia (Jefferson), 11
*Notes on Walt Whitman as Poet and
    Person* (Burroughs), 171
Nuttall, Thomas, 12, 14, 60
Nuttall Bulletin, 37–8
Nuttall Ornithological Club, 30, 34,
    37–8, 42, 197
    formation and membership
    requirements of, 30–1
    as model for other clubs, 60–1
    protection and, 73
    woman in, 90

October Farm (Brewster), 31, 36
"October Farm," 36
"Old World Sparrow, The" (Bryant),
    175
Oldys, Henry, 83
Oologist, The (journal), 81, 113, 115,
    119
oology
    method in, 114–15
    see also eggs; nests
oriole, 21–2, 31–2, 116, 213–14
Ornithological Biography (Audubon),
    12, 34
ornithological clubs
    early, 4, 30–1, 37–8
    see also specific clubs
*Ornithologists of the United States Army
    Medical Corps* (Hume), 23
ornithology
    amateur vs. professional in, 4
    Bairdian Era, 17–30
    classifications in, 213–14
    nomenclature in, 39–40
    see also bird watching
Ornithology (Wilson), 73

Ornithology of California (Cooper), 24, 104
Osborne, S. D., 61
osprey, 35–6, 115
"Out of the Cradle Endlessly Rocking" (Whitman), 172
owl, 92, 95
  Arctic, 131
  boreal, 212
  great gray, 212
  great horned, 26, 31, 127, 136
  saw-whet, 66
  screech, 31, 35, 139, 201, 213

Parson, Katherine, 81
partridge, 15
  Massena (Montezuma quail), 14
passerines, 116
"Pauperizing the Birds" (Oldys), 83
Peabody, William B. O., 12
Pearson, T. Gilbert, 74
Peary, Adm. Robert, 117
Pease, Charles, 137
pelican, 7, 80
Penn, William, 90
Pennock, Charles J., 91–6, 219
Pennock, Herb, 91
Pennsylvania Audubon Society, 90
Penrose, Boris, 18
Penrose, Charles, 18, 20
pesticides, 119, 204, 216
Peterson, Roger Tory, 157, 187, 195–208
  background of, 195–7
  Griscom and, 196, 197, 199, 200
  influences on work of, 198–9
Peterson, Virginia, 208
pheasant, 46
Philadelphia Academy of Sciences, 89, 91, 92, 95
phoebe, 135–6
Pickering, Charles, 41
pigeon, 33
  passenger, 14, 34, 36, 66, 117–18
Pike, Gen. Zebulon Montgomery, 58
pipit, American (water), 202
plover, 7, 10
poetry, birds in, 171–8
Pokagon, Simon, 35–6
Pomos, 7

Pough, Richard, 199–200, 207
Proctor, Noble, 212
ptarmigan, 23–4
Purdie, H. A., 37
pyrrholoxia, Texas cardinal, 15–16

quail, 128

Rafinesque, Samuel Constantine, 22
rail, 11
"Rare Birds on Block Island" (Dickens), 160
raven, 24
Reardom, R. R., 114
redstart, 32
Reed, Chester, 118, 187–8, 195–6
Reed, James A., 77
Reeves, L. P., 78
Reno, Maj. Marcus, 51
Report on the Ornithology of Massachusetts, A (Peabody), 12
Richard, John H., 28
Ridgway, Robert, 28, 56, 83, 143
Road to Survival, The (Vogt), 203
Robbins, Chandler S., 208
Robbins, Reginald, 97–8
"Robert of Lincoln" (Bryant), 174–5, 178
Roberts, Thomas S., 135–6
robin, 32, 34, 37–8, 115, 165
  American, 9
  conservation measures and, 80, 81
  redbreast, 9, 214
Rogers, Col. Archibald, 69
Roosevelt, Corinne, 66
Roosevelt, Eleanor, 67
Roosevelt, Franklin D., 65–9, 75
Roosevelt, Robert B., 44, 61
Roosevelt, Sarah, 67–8
Roosevelt, Theodore, 42, 44, 68, 182
  Linnaean Society and, 61, 65–7

sanderling, 87–8
sandpiper, 202
  spotted, 6
sapsucker, 213
Schiefflin, Eugene, 44
Schooler, Dean, 118
Scott, Gen. Winfield, 22
Seldon, Col. J., 43

Seton, Ernest Thompson, 55, 107, 198

sexual behavior in birds, 26, 45, 142, 148–50, 213

Sharples, R. P., 119

Sherman, Althea, 138–44, 219

Sherman, Amelia, 140–1

Sherman, Roger, 139

Shooting Journal of George Henry Mackay 1865–1922 (Mackay), 100–1

Shorebirds of North America, The (Elliot), 64

shrike
  loggerhead, 35
  northern, 37

Silent Spring (Carson), 216

Silloway, P. M., 105–6

Singer, Arthur, 208

skimmer, black, 8, 10

Skinner, Gen. F. E., 71

skunk, 127–8

Skylarks, Missouri, 52

Slaughter, C. H., 90–1

Sloan, John, 196

Smith, Alfred E., 75

Smith, John, 8

Smith, Wilbur B., 124

Smithsonian Institution, 20–9, 56
  arranging and storing specimens at, 21, 29
  funds of, 20, 28
  Henry and, 20, 21, 28, 29

Smithwick, Richard P., 117

snipe, 7

"Some Florida Herons" (Pennock), 92–3

Song of Hiawatha, The (Longfellow), 177–8

"Song of Myself" (Whitman), 172

songs, 6, 32, 33, 52, 64–6, 137, 202
  of sparrows, 147, 149, 151–4, 182
  of swans, 3, 64–5
  of thrushes, 165–6
  of yellowthroats, 88–9

Sparks, Marion E., 133

sparrow
  Brewer's, 14
  classification of, 40
  fox, 32, 34
  grasshopper, 161

Harris', 117

Henslow's, 202

house or English (*Passer domesticus*), 39, 61, 63, 140, 142, 143, 175

Le Conte's, 139

song, 115, 145–55

Speaking for Nature (Brooks), 217

Spencer Fullerton Baird Club, 90

spiritualism, 56–9

starling, European, 46

Stebbins, Fannie, 156, 157

Stephens, John L., 137

Stephenson, Louise, 75–6

Stokton, J. B., 43

Stone, Witmer, 91–3, 95, 112, 192

storm-petrel, Leach's, 6

Studies in the Life History of the Song Sparrow (Nice), 145–55

Suckley, George, 24

Supreme Court, U. S., 73, 76–7

Sutton, George M., 117

swallow
  cliff, 115
  tree, 124–5

swan, 214
  mute, 16
  song of, 64–5

Swarth, H. S., 107

swift, 32
  chimney, 11

Swope, Eugene, 83

Taft, William Howard, 76

Tales of a Wayside Inn (Longfellow), 177

tanager, scarlet, 123

Taylor, H. R., 111

tern, 128–9

Thatcher, Arthur, 44

Thaxter, Celia, 71

Thayer, A. H., 83

Theodore Roosevelt, the Naturalist (Cutright), 65

Theosophical Society of America, 57

theosophy, 57

Thomson, Maurice, 117

Thoreau, Henry David, 36, 110, 218–19, 222

Thorne, Capt. P. M., 27

thrasher, brown, 9, 82, 134
thrush, 108
  hermit, 33, 165, 171
  wood, 11
Tillisch, Mary Agnes, 156, 157, 164
titmouse, 63, 136
Toregson, Almira, 136
"twitcher," 214
Two Little Savages (Seton), 198

"Universal Bibliography of
  Ornithology" (Coues), 53
Useful Birds and Their Protection
  (Forbush), 126

Vanburgh, P., 43
Vardeman, James, 211
Victoria, Queen of England, 74
vireo, 31
  nests and eggs of, 114, 116–17
  red-eyed, 114
  warbling, 114
Vogt, William, 187, 197–9, 202,
  203
Voorhees, David C., 43
vulture, 94
  California (condor), 117

Wake Robin (Burroughs), 179
Walton, Richard K., 218
warbler, 7, 63, 214
  black-and-white, 52
  chestnut-sided, 123
  Kirtland's, 137–8
  prairie, 52
  prothonotary, 204–5
  Verivorma virginiae, 23
  yellow, 13
  yellow-rumped, 62
Warblers of North America (Chapman),
  157
Ward, Jake, 78
War Department, U.S., 22
Warner, Willis H., 143
Warren, Herbert M., 124
waxwing, cedar, 7, 124
Weigle, Mrs. Charles F., 143
Welch, George O., 124
Welch, George T., 43
Welker, Robert Henry, 170, 172

Western Foundation for Vertebrate
  Zoology, 119
Westervelt, Miriam O., 210
"When Lilacs Last in the Dooryard
  Bloom'd" (Whitman), 171–2
whip-poor-will, 9, 26, 34, 36, 202
White, Gilbert, 219–22
White, John, 8
Whitman, Walt, 170–4, 179
Widman, Otto, 143
Wildfowl of North America, The (Elliot),
  64
Wilkinson, James, 11
Williams, John, *see* Pennock, Charles J.
Willison, John, 124
Wilson, Alexander, 10–12, 18, 60,
  73, 88, 110
Wilson Bulletin, The, 92–6, 132–4,
  138–9
Wilson Ornithological Club, 60,
  132–8
Wilson Society, 215
Wirt, W. J., 118
women's rights, 57–8, 90
Wood, A. J., 44
Wood, William, 8–9, 218
woodcock, 31
woodpecker, 32, 116
  downy, 50–1
  hairy, 7
  ivory-billed, 117–18
  Lewis', 24
  red-headed, 10
World War I, 80
wren
  canyon, 52
  Carolina, 63
  house, 7, 138, 142–4
  nests and eggs of, 115, 116
  St. Kilda's, 214
Wright, Mabel Osgood, 58, 64,
  166–7, 202

Xántus, János, 24–5

yellowthroat (common), 88–9
Young Oologist, The (later *The Oologist*),
  81, 113, 115, 119

Zim, Herbert S., 208

A Note About the Author

Joseph Kastner is a former editor of *Life* magazine. He is the author of *A Species of Eternity,* which was nominated for a National Book Award in history in 1978, and of many articles and reviews in the fields of natural history and horticulture. A bird watcher himself, Kastner lives in Grandview, New York, and has a summer home on Block Island.

A Note on the Type

This book was composed in a computer version of Baskerville, a modern recutting of a type originally designed by John Baskerville (1706–1775). Baskerville, a writing master in Birmingham, England, began experimenting in about 1750 with type design and punch cutting. His first book, published in 1757 and set throughout in his new types, was a Virgil in royal quarto. It was followed by other famous editions from his press. Baskerville's types, which are distinctive and elegant in design, were a forerunner of what we know today as the "modern" group of type faces.

Composed by ComCom, a division of Haddon Craftsmen, Allentown, Pennsylvania.
Printed and bound by Fairfield Press, Fairfield, Pennsylvania.